Management Ethics

DIMENSIONS
OF
INTERNATIONAL BUSINESS

MANAGEMENT ETHICS

An Intercultural Perspective

WILLIAM A. EVANS

Professor of International Business Administration
American College in Paris

KLUWER · NIJHOFF PUBLISHING
BOSTON/THE HAGUE/DORDRECHT/LANCASTER

DISTRIBUTORS FOR NORTH AMERICA:
Kluwer Academic Publishers
190 Old Derby Street
Hingham, Massachusetts 02043, U.S.A.

DISTRIBUTORS OUTSIDE NORTH AMERICA:
Kluwer Academic Publishers Group
Distribution Centre
P.O. Box 322
3300 AH Dordrecht, The Netherlands

Library of Congress Cataloging in Publication Data

Evans, William A
  Management ethics.
  (Dimensions of international business; 1)
  Bibliography: p.
  Includes indexes.
  1. Industry — Social aspects. 2. Business
ethics. I. Title. II. Series.
HD60.E9   658.4'08   80-24649

ISBN 0-89838-055-3

CONTENTS

Business responsibility is defined as the responsibility of individuals within the corporation. A conflict intimately connected with this responsibility stems from ethical duality, the distinction between the social-political-economic universe and personal-religious-moral perspectives. The language of business responsibility is explained. The nature and historical development of the modern business enterprise is discussed, and current thought in business responsibility analyzed, specific attention being paid to the problems facing multinational corporations. Practical examples of problems in business ethics are reviewed.

Ethical problems that stem from the contrast of cultures are examined against the background of increasing speed in communications. Conflicts that are the products of political-economic and social-ethical differences are analyzed, and a survey of different religious codes and the ethics of socialism is presented. The balance between West and East and the Third World is also examined.

3 PHILOSOPHICAL ANTECEDENTS TO MODERN THOUGHT   57

Four perspectives of the individual — self, state, law, and church — are examined. Historical, social, and philosophical thought is surveyed; the past is related to the present. The continuum of ethical thinking is stressed, as is the pervading theme of the duality of personal morality.

4 ETHICAL MANAGEMENT: PROBLEMS IN DECISION MAKING   87

We return to the present. A comprehensive analysis of different categories of ethical problems is offered. The categories are distinguished in two groups, extraorganizational and intraorganizational issues. Situational examples in each category are used to illustrate the difficulties facing modern business decision makers.

The relationship between authority and power as the basis for business responsibility is reviewed. The following questions are considered: How can managers be held accountable for their ethical behavior? What are the merits and disadvantages of social auditing? How are ethical objectives built into the corporate plan?

Some of the more common theories of ethics are studied, and an attempt is made to establish a structure for the novice to use in seeking a method of analysis and ethical justification for management decisions. No individual conceptual framework of business behavior is possible without a conceptual framework of life. Practical help for managers trying to find points of reference in confused ethical situations is offered, with situational ethics as a guide. The importance of education in business and the need for social marketing are both emphasized.

7   INDIVIDUAL BEHAVIOR IN BUSINESS   187

The role of the individual in business is reintroduced and is supplemented by the results of recent research by the author into the comparative ethical values of senior North American and British executives. The nature of management motivation and some behavioral experiments into the nature and consequences of stress are examined, as is the conflict between intellectual reasoning and the business instinct. Behavior as a product of culture and history and its place in modern business life are discussed.

ACKNOWLEDGMENTS

The idea for this book was a seed sown several years ago when a colleague and I spent many evenings talking together into a tape recorder and many daytime hours reading the rather garbled transcript. We experimented with the results in the classroom, and we were encouraged by the reception. To Richard Bruce, therefore, I owe my first thanks, because it was with him that I began to see the light through the darkness and the shape the book might take.

Since then, there have been others whose opinions have to some extent influenced what is written here: colleagues in different places and at different times, students at all levels, and friends too numerous to mention who, professional and layman alike, have found in the subject a focus for rich discussion. I offer my gratitude to Phil Jones, my editor, for his guidance and help; at times I have felt that he should have written the book himself. Also to Sarah Evans, production controller, I must express my thanks for the meticulous care that she applied to the improvement of my manuscript. As it is, whatever faults and shortcomings the book contains are entirely due to me.

I appreciate the time and efforts of typists in three countries, and I am grateful to the many authors whose thoughts and writings I have drawn upon in the development of my ideas. I hope that those ideas stimulate readers to think hard about what I believe to be a fascinating and important topic.

PREFACE

Society is a nexus of individual perceptions. The world is as we each see it, no more and no less. To hope that we shall all agree on what is good or bad is to hope in vain. This is not solipsism transferred to moral philosophy; it is realism born of observation.

This book tries to remind its readers that you can be responsible only if you understand the basis of your responsibility; that you can exercise responsibility only if you have the power to do so; that you cannot lay down a conceptual framework of behavior in business if you have no framework of life; that every facet of your conduct as a manager and employee involves a delicate balance between rebellion and absolute conformity. Indeed, it may be that the hardest lesson is that of learning that compliance and silence and obedience are frequently more desirable than protest when all stands to be lost. To gamble on a poor card hand is the act of either an excessively foolish or a supremely clever man; since the proper judgment of risk is an uncommon facility, poor hands are normally lost.

There is no such thing as a corporate attitude, just as there is no such thing as the will of the people. If a government is elected on the strength of 51 percent of the electorate, what happens to the will of the other 49 percent? Similarly, the policies of corporations are decided either by a majority of boardroom opinion or through the personal values of the chief executive.

The nonexistence of a corporate attitude is central and essential to the theme of this book. We frequently read and hear of new and strange terminology in the language of management. As an example of the more bizarre, the term *corporate social responsibility* is preeminent; it has even appeared as the title of a book. We are told that General Foods or Chrysler Corporation or Shell has a corporate responsibility policy, but what is really meant is either that most members of the General Foods, Chrysler, or Shell managements have agreed on such a policy or that the chief executives of these companies think it is a good thing to do. We are not told how many employees do *not* think it is a good thing to do. The same is true also of companies that apparently have *no* so-called corporate social responsibility program.

The individual is not necessarily classifiable. Thus, we cannot lay down rules of behavior for one type of person or another. One may be similar to others in education, in social background, in financial status, but one may have totally different views from theirs about the proper course of action in a particular situation. This suggests that there is something other than our common demographic type that prompts our ethical decision, and this something can be only our personality, which, by definition, varies with people.

The following chapters look at management behavior from the standpoint of the individual, and in doing so, they allow for an infinite attitudinal range in the decisions each manager may make in the face of a variety of situations. In this, the book differs from every other book written about social responsibility. Certainly, it ignores and disallows "corporate" responsibility. It does not take the correlation between value category and individual values for granted. If that were proved, there would be no need for this book.

Questions about social responsibility can never be satisfactorily answered; for every view put forward in a classroom discussion of a case that deals with the social aspects of business — whether it be community involvement, the environment, consumerism, or minority groups — an opposing view will be offered. There are rarely any "right" answers. However, since this book is intended as a text to be used in courses dealing with problems of ethical and moral behavior in management, readers will no doubt want to discover in its pages some guidelines that will help to define that behavior in such a way as to satisfy their own personal standards and that, in some cases, will help to establish the standards themselves. Therefore, what the book tries to do is to help its readers (many of whom, it is likely, have had no practical experience of the problems a manager must face) to understand the constraints and stimuli of the business environment insofar as they affect decisions about what is right and what is wrong. The book's overriding purpose is to explore the practical possibilities of the individual social conscience.

The book makes extensive use of situational examples. It is not intended as a particularly North American or European text, although the survey of management attitudes in Chapter 7 does indicate some fundamental differences between the personal values of executives on opposite sides of the Atlantic; instead, it aims to avoid time and geography by concentrating its attention on the basic problem posed by the relationship that exists in all Western societies between the genuine (i.e., inherited and self-cultivated) ethical framework of the individual manager and the sometimes artificial and imposed standards one is required to observe as a member of an organizational hierarchy. In the process, the social and moral contrasts, discords, and meeting points created by an increasingly polarizing international environment (particularly the discussions between East and West, developed and developing nations, and socialism and capitalism) are studied at some length. Having examined the bibliography of social responsibility, I think such a study is timely, for the dilemmas are frequently ignored.

This book is published in the United States, but it would be wrong to think of it as only an American book. It is written by an Englishman who knows Europe, Canada, and the United States well; in the context of this book's subject matter, I would like to think I am as qualified as most to comment on the differences, not only between these areas, but also between the industrialized West and the emerging nations of Africa and the Far East. American culture is very mixed as a result of its multiple heritage; it is a great culture, but despite its greatness and its vitality, it tends to an unhappy parochialism. Most American news bulletins prove the point — the news is often local, state, and national, in that order. Of students polled in the Midwest, 95 percent have never seen the sea; this may be an accident of geography, but it has significant sociological implications.

I hope, therefore, that the international and intercultural flavor of this book will contribute something to the opening of the reader's eyes to life and problems elsewhere. We live in a world in which we can no longer be islands unto ourselves. Business ethics, social responsibility — call it what you will — is a personal affair, and people the world over have to learn these days to live more closely together.

Finally, I make no apology for the excursion into moral and social thought in the third chapter. This is not the perverse indulgence of my own interest, but a real attempt to put the modern manager's attitudes into focus. Indeed, I think many managers would benefit from the realization that their ethical values owe almost as much to Aristotle and Kant as to the Ten Commandments and the Sermon on the Mount. Whatever you believe, your belief is likely to be stronger if you know why you believe it.

1 THE PROBLEM OF SOCIAL RESPONSIBILITY

When legislators are wise, they avoid, as far as possible, framing laws in such a way as to compel conscientious men to choose between sin and what is legally a crime.

— Bertrand Russell[1]

THE INDIVIDUAL AND THE CORPORATE ENTERPRISE

If you enter any well-stocked university library and make for the shelves containing all those rather intimidating and sometimes incomprehensible business textbooks, and if you look at the section marked "Business and Society" or some such thing, you will almost certainly find several titles having one word, or a variation of it, in common.

The word is *corporate*.

Now there is nothing wrong with this word; it is a perfectly respectable word. It has an impeccable Latin pedigree and is useful for describing things that form part of a body. In modern business terminology, it is the adjectival counterpart of the corporation, company, or firm. We talk of corporate strategy, corporate affairs, or a corporate image, and these terms are completely intelligible.

1

It is not the use of the word that offends; it is its misuse. In those many book titles that employ it, it is misused to describe the concept of social responsibility; this book has to begin by trying to show that *corporate social responsibility* is a term that at best is misleading and at worst is meaningless.

Let us examine the title of this book: *Management Ethics. Management* is a term used every day, but what many of us forget is that it depends on people (managers), sometimes hundreds or thousands of them, to implement it, and that without individuals a business cannot exist. This is an important, though obvious, point, which it will be wise to remember as we progress through the following chapters.

The second important word in the title is *ethics*. Ethics postulates responsibility. The *Oxford Dictionary's* definition of "responsible" is "liable to be called to account, answerable, morally accountable for actions," and its definition of "responsibility" is "charge for which one is responsible." It stands to reason that one must be answerable or accountable or responsible to *somebody*; in the context of this book, that "somebody" is *society,* a term we shall have to enlarge upon and explain later. For the moment, we can expand and fill out the book's title to mean "a study of those activities of individuals in business organizations for which the individuals can be held to be responsible to society."

It may be clear by now why we have taken such exception to the use of the word *corporate* to describe social responsibility. Since we have defined a business, or corporation, as consisting of individuals, it is individuals, and individuals only, who can be called to account. A corporation's activities are the activities of its individual members; the members of the corporation are its life and its being; it is they who have the responsibility for its performance; and it is they who make the decision about what is right and what is wrong. Without these decisions, there is no activity and no corporation. Thus, *corporate social responsibility,* that term so universally favored in the literature, is either misleading because it suggests that there is an impersonal collective focus for the accountability of industrial or commercial behavior or meaningless because it allows for decision making without people. Either way, it is a term that is unsatisfactory and one that we shall avoid.

This book will therefore deal essentially with the responsibility of the individual as an executive, manager, and employee, in contrast with most of the rest of the literature, which concentrates on the corporateness of business responsibility. The method that will be followed in the approach to the subject is outlined in the following section.

MANAGEMENT ETHICS: THE SCOPE OF THE BOOK

The remainder of this first chapter will examine further the relationship between the individual and the corporate enterprise, taking into particular account the contrast between the role of citizen and that of business manager. It will also define the terminology that will be employed throughout the book, including the all-important concept of "society." Finally, it will discuss the nature of the business enterprise, its origins and present problems, paying specific attention to the issues that face multinational corporations, which operate in a cross-cultural environment and upon which lie the twin responsbilities of proper behavior as required by both ethical norms and international political-economic priorities.

Chapter 2 analyzes in greater detail the ethical problems that emerge from this contrast of cultures. This is by way of a preamble to the survey of historical social and philosophical writings and thought contained in Chapter 3. Wherever possible, this survey relates the past to the present, both to explain and to provide a contrast with modern ethical perspectives. It must be emphasized that modern man is not a different species from his ancient progenitors, but a similar being who accepts or rejects their experience in the continuation of life. While the analysis examines the development of such thought through particular and conveniently labeled periods of history, the pervading theme is the duality of personal morality, of which, as Russell[2] states, "any adequate ethical theory must take account."

In Chapter 4, we return to the present. Different categories of ethical problems are postulated, and their essential characteristics are discussed. Situational examples in each of these categories are analyzed to illustrate the difficulties that modern business decision makers face. This whole discussion is set against the background of the earlier chapters.

Chapter 5 reviews the relationship between authority and power. Chapter 6 questions the value of the social audit and suggests that some of the techniques and models used to measure responsible management are dangerously fallible. It studies some of the more common modern theories of ethics and tries to establish a structure for the manager to use in seeking a method of analysis and ethical justification for management decisions. Since ethical attitudes are largely subjective, no individual conceptual framework of business behavior is possible without a conceptual framework of life. In this regard, Chapter 6 echoes the theme of the third chapter; it also attempts to offer some practical help to those managers who perhaps have no points of reference except their own confusion of conscience when they are confronted with ethical issues and when a decision, whose possible consequences are not always clear, has to be made.

The final chapter reintroduces the role of the individual in business, using as background recent research conducted by the author into the comparative ethical values of senior North American and European executives.[3] It examines the nature of management motivation, as well as the problem of the consequences of human stress as it has been observed by behavioral scientists. This discussion is intended to give the reader food for thought about the stress created when intellectual reasoning and the competitive business instinct pull in opposite directions. Lest this finale should seem depressing, the book ends with some recapitulation of Chapters 1 and 6, striking a more encouraging note for practicing managers.

ETHICAL DUALITY

A recurring topic in the discussion of social responsibility is the often-suggested conflict between the law and individual conscience, or, in the more specific context of business, between company policy and the ethical values of the employee. Everyone needs some framework of values to guide personal behavior, since one is, to a degree at least, a free agent. The degree to which one is not a free agent is controlled by the law, and since the law exists for one's own protection and that of one's fellow citizens, one must think very hard before disobeying it; and if one does disobey it, there must be strong, conscientious reasons for doing so. Such was the case in England in 1688 and America in 1776.

This dual source of ethical standards — social-political, on the one hand, and personal-religious-moral, on the other — is both natural and necessary, but it has undoubtedly created difficulties for those commentators who wish to suggest a neat formula for the observance of social obligations in business. One factor that is not present in decisions about personal social behavior, but that is important in management situations, is the need for the continuing healthy and profitable existence of the company that employs the decision maker. This is an economic and utilitarian consideration that cannot lightly be discarded; consequently, management decisions, unlike personal or domestic decisions, cannot be made on criteria that are totally independent of material benefits. If a manager has to decide, for instance, on whether or not to make a product twice as safe as the minimum legal standard, that person is not merely considering a question of right or wrong; he or she must also take into account the cost to the company, the effects on profits, and the resulting reaction of shareholders. At home, on the other hand, an individual may double a contribution to a worthy charity without necessarily having to compute the effect on the domestic budget.

However, as we shall see in Chapter 4, a very real conflict *can* exist between personal and managerial ethics, between the individual as a citizen and the individual as an employee. As was indicated at the beginning of this chapter, the firm is an abstraction; it has no feeling except those of the people who run it, and it has no reason for existence apart from the reasons that its executives feel are proper and desirable. Thus, when we refer to such an abstraction, we are really referring to the physical beings who control the firm. In many cases, these beings are few in number, perhaps only one, and in these few or one is vested considerable power. The policy of the firm — or, more accurately, of its members — reflects the values of the few or of the one, and the voice of the many is often unheard. This is where the ethical conflict may occur, and it is a problem to which we shall continually return, for it is central to any discussion of individual business behavior.

THE LANGUAGE OF BUSINESS RESPONSIBILITY

We have already seen that imprecision pervades the literature of business responsibility, and it is thus necessary and desirable to establish an agreeable terminology for our study. Some of the language that will be employed is both unequivocal and universally acceptable, but some needs to be defined as to its specific use and meaning in order to avoid confusion and misunderstanding.

Business

The term *business* is used to describe any type of industrial or commercial enterprise; this includes both manufacturing and service activities, privately and publicly owned companies, nationalized or government-subsidized utilities and industries, profit-making and nonprofit organizations (other than government departments), and international and multinational firms. Though the activities of governments themselves are excluded from this definition, the relationship between business and government will be studied in detail later in this chapter.

Society

A common error in the discussion of business responsibility is the over-compartmentalization of interests. It is an easy mistake to imagine that consumers, shareholders, and employees are discrete, nonoverlapping groups; yet there are times when the same person belongs to all three groups. Business is not separate from society; it is an integral part of it, as are government, the media, suppliers, customers, and so forth. Society is not an element in the system; it *is* the system. We therefore define society as the total of all those individuals, irrespective of their membership in particular interest or reference subgroups, who are bound together through their membership in a common political and economic unit; they are protected by its laws, are subject to its sovereignty, and contribute to its output. The inclusion of business in this definition of society is important, since it avoids the danger of assuming some natural conflict of interests between business and society and at the same time emphasizes the possibility and frequent reality of multiple and interrelated social roles.

Thus, according to our definition, if business does harm to society, it can conceivably do harm to itself. Put another way, if individuals in business do not maintain acceptable standards of behavior, it is possible that they themselves, being members of a total society, will suffer the consequences.

Responsibility

As we have seen, responsibility requires a focus. You cannot be responsible if there is nobody who holds you to account; responsibility does not exist in a vacuum. Earlier, we described the focus of responsibility as society, which we have just defined as the sum total of individuals in the political-economic system. Thus, since business consists of individuals who are responsible to society, of which they themselves are members, it can be claimed that they are in part responsible to themselves.

This is not a meaningless juggling of words. It is a step toward a basic truth, realized over the centuries by philosophers and social thinkers:

Ethical standards are the product of conscience, and if a man offends his own conscience, he is the first to know his own guilt.

Ethics and Morals

Though many people have attempted to distinguish between the terms *ethics* and *morals*, the distinction has never been entirely satisfactory. Both describe rules of conduct, and both are concerned with differentiating between right and wrong. Perhaps we sometimes do intend to convey another meaning if we say that an action is *immoral* rather than *unethical*; perhaps the former description connotes some contravention of religious law, some imperative that never changes, while the latter merely indicates a departure from traditional or customary behavior. But the difference can only be subjective, since the two words, the one Latin (from *moralis,* the adjective of *mos* — custom — and *mores*, morals) and the other Greek (from *ethikos,* the adjective of *ethos* — moral behavior), are linguistically interdependent and historically synonymous.

We shall therefore regard these terms — *ethics* and *morals, ethical* and *moral* — as indistinguishable, since, as we shall see in the next chapter, the foundations of individual behavioral criteria are complex, varied, and rooted in both political and religious sources; the Law and the Prophets of the Old Testament are a prime example of the separation between politics and religion, as is the distinction between the official hierarchical morality of the Middle Ages and the personal moral teaching of the mystics of the same period. Today, the sources are less easy to isolate, as are many nuances of different terminological usage.

Individual

We have already adequately established that no social entity, particularly a business organization, can exist purely as an abstraction and that society derives life only from the individuals who comprise it. While it is possible to divide society into demographic, behavioral, and attitudinal categories for the convenience of market research or sociological experiment, it has to be remembered that such classifications are very general; there is no such thing as the "average" person, John or Jane Doe, the "man in the street." These generalizations hide billions of ever-so-slightly different ethical frameworks, cognitive maps, attitude patterns, and behavioral experiences, and it is these differences that distinguish the individual from the rest of the group and make the individual the all-important focus in a proper examination of the problem of business responsibility.

Authority

Without authority, there is anarchy, and without individual freedom of conscience, there is tyranny. The proper balance between the two has exercised the minds of philosophers and political theorists for centuries. In the business world, particularly in Britain, the authority of management has been qualified (some might say nullified) by the countervailing growth of the trade unions and the universally accepted right of workers to withdraw their labor, as well as by an increasing weight of government legislation designed to protect the interests of the employee.

Unlike power in the armed forces, where authority derives from the state, power in business is vested in individuals through ownership or the financial interest of shareholders. Also unlike military authority, business authority can in certain circumstances be disobeyed without penalty; there is no crime of mutiny in business.

It is not, however, quite as simple as that. Authority in business means more than the power to decide product policy or sales targets or plant investment; such decisions are taken in the interests of the organization's future prosperity and progress, and subordinates must act (and usually do act) upon them. Few industrial disputes result from such decisions; rather, they stem from questions of remuneration, working hours, or layoffs (redundancy). The conflicts in business are largely material conflicts, conflicts about matters that have relatively little to do with marketing strategy or product design. The problems begin when those in authority make decisions that actually create conflict between a subordinate individual and his conscience — for example, when superiors, in the interests of higher productivity, require a plant manager to empty more than a reasonable amount of polluting effluent into a river. The plant manager is torn between observance of company policy, duty to family (better company performance may mean more income), and ethical distaste at what is being asked. It is the authority vested in a worker's superiors that causes the trouble; two different ethical standards face each other, one supported by the power of authority, the other not. This is a less uncommon dilemma than might be supposed; the whole question of authority and responsibility is reviewed in Chapter 5.

THE NATURE OF THE BUSINESS ENTERPRISE: A
HISTORICAL OVERVIEW

The modern business institution has its roots in three fundamental concepts: freedom of association, ownership, and governance (i.e., authority tempered by responsibility). Of these, the most important is freedom of association, but it has been the subject of much debate.

The fact that the corporation possesses the legal standing of a person and can be sued, convicted, and punished has been the source of one of the most popular misconceptions in current business literature. Since "the institution can endure beyond the natural lives of the members of the association,"[4] commentators have been tempted to conclude that any responsibilities or obligations that companies may have toward the societies in which they exist are corporate and should be observed through an institutionalized corporate conscience. According to the *concession theory* of business, corporations exist through a mandate conferred upon them by the state (or society), and if they are "guilty" of not fulfilling their obligations, they are liable to public regulation.

In the modern world, at least in North America and Britain, where the debate on social responsibility is most vociferous, the concession theory (born of English common law, bred by the early American colonists, and confirmed by what has now become known as Jacksonianism) has apparently for the time being won out over the Germanic *inherence theory* eloquently postulated by Otto von Gierke, who maintained that the corporation exists as a free association of individuals requiring no prescriptions from society.[5] Certainly, the concept of a corporate soul is more in keeping with the former theory than the latter.

The central thrust of this book is toward the thesis that corporate social responsibility is basically a meaningless term. Although this is by no means a new view, it does have implications that have not yet been fully explored. The corporation may be a legal "person," but if a criminal charge is brought against it and it is convicted, some individual member must be named, as the notorious Great Electrical Conspiracy showed. You cannot "incarcerate the Pennsylvania Railroad or Standard Oil (N.J.) complete with all its works."[6] Thus, the corporation is in reality "an artificial being, invisible, intangible and existing only in contemplation of law."[7] How, then, can a corporation be responsible, unless it is through the responsibility of its members who have the authority to implement their ethical values? N. H. Jacoby's standpoint is that the touchstone of business responsibility is the degree to which it has fostered progress toward consensual goals.[8] These goals are the goals of the "system," and Jacoby thus appears to be suggesting a total "merger" of government and business. This view is a thoughtful extension of the trends in attitudes toward business over the last four hundred years. These trends are excellently summarized by James W. McKie, who identifies three evolutionary stages of business philosophy.[9]

First, according to McKie, was the classical view of economic behavior as separate and distinct from other types of behavior and of business organizations as separate and distinct from other organizations, even though the same individuals might be involved in business and nonbusiness affairs. This raises questions very germane to the problem of ethical duality raised earlier in this chapter. The classical view, enduring from about 1600 to about 1875, was further characterized by its contention that the primary criteria of business performance are economic efficiency and growth in the production of goods and services, including improvements in technology and innovation in goods and services. This attitude was reinforced by Adam Smith's belief that such criteria lead to the enhancement of public welfare; the primary goal and motivating force for business organizations is profit, and profits are kept to reasonable or appropriate levels by market competition:

> Every individual necessarily labours to render the annual revenue of the society as great as he can. He generally, indeed, neither intends to promote the public interest, nor knows how much he is promoting it. . . . By directing that industry in such a manner as its produce may be of the greatest value, he intends only his own gain, and he is in this, as in many other cases, *led by an invisible hand* to promote an end which was no part of his own intention. Nor is it always worse for the society that it was no part of it. By pursuing his own interest he frequently promotes that of the society more effectually than when he really intends to promote it. *I have never known much good done by those who affected to trade for the public good.* It is an affectation, indeed, not very common among merchants and very few words need be employed in dissuading them from it.[10]

The italics are added, and the parts of this famous passage so emphasized clearly show the wide gulf between the classical and the modern views. Jacoby would no doubt contend that the "invisible hand" consists entirely of thumbs if it is to be judged on results. The point is well made in the following poem by Stephen Leacock:

> Adam, Adam, Adam Smith
> Listen what I charged you with!
> Didn't you say
> In the class one day

That selfishness was bound to pay?
Of all your Doctrine, that was the Pith
Wasn't it, wasn't it, wasn't it, Smith?

Don't you remember your book begins
With a Panegyric on making Pins?
Didn't you say that the more we made
The bigger would be External Trade
We sold the pins and the Foreigners had 'em
That was the big thought, wasn't it, Adam?

And didn't you say — don't think it funny —
That the greatest thing in the world was money,
And didn't you say — now please don't shirk —
That the basis of value was human work,
And the Worker must be content with his lot
Being worth precisely just what he got?
Come, don't evade it,
Long-winded Scot,
Just, whether you said it
Or whether not?
And if you said it, you must confess
You have brought the World to a terrible Mess
For a hundred Years since your Grave was made
We've been making Pins and Machines and Trade,
All selfish as Hogs, whether rich as Sin
Or as poor as Rats — Ah! why begin
To teach us about that fatal Pin?

How can you venture to look in the Face
Of an honest fellow like Stuart Chase?
How can you dare to be blocking the way
Of an Enterprise such as the NRA!

Smith, come up from under the sod,
Tell me what did you do with God?
You never named him, I understand
You called him (Book IV) an invisible hand;
You gave him the system all geared and speeded
With none of his Interference needed.
It wasn't worthy a man of your size,
Smith, — come up and apologize.[11]

Note that the philosophy of the classical economists concentrates on
the demands on the corporation; the demands on the economic system,
such as equity in income distribution and stability in employment and

prices, are different. To place these responsibilities on a corporation is to deny the central argument of classical theory. A business cannot pay less than competitive prices for particular factors of production and should not pay more. To do so would distort the efficient allocation of resources. It is up to the management of the system — the government — to change the distribution of income.

From 1875 to 1935, according to McKie's scheme, there was a transitional period of change, due to significant developments in social, economic, and political thought. This period witnessed the growth of the big corporations, which had two kinds of effects. First, economic power became increasingly concentrated in a few large units and resulted in a high degree of monopoly in certain important markets. Second, the legal structure of the corporation changed into a complex framework of ownership, with large constituencies of nonowners dependent on it in various ways and with professional managers who were not identical with the owners.

This concentration stemmed from two major merger movements. The first, at the turn of the century, resulted in horizontal combinations that grew out of pooling practices or trust arrangements, such as those of U.S. Steel, Standard Oil of New Jersey, and Eastman Kodak. The second, in the 1920s, resulted in large public utility mergers and, in manufacturing and mining, in both horizontal and vertical mergers. The horizontal mergers involved those companies in the tier just below the top (i.e., third, fourth, and fifth largest) and resulted in a broader operational base. The vertical mergers involved the acquisition of medium-size firms producing parts and components. Chrysler Corporation (1925) became Chrysler-Dodge in 1928, and National Dairy Products, incorporated in 1823, acquired 331 dairies between 1923 and 1932 and now controls the Kraft Cheese Company.

The stock market crash of 1929 and the depression ended this period, which had seen economic activity organized across a wide spectrum of business organizations of different sizes and strengths instead of being centered, as it had been previously, on small, powerless, "atomistic" firms. A few large firms were well protected against the depression and possessed a number of alternative policy options. Others were large enough to have some discretionary power but were constrained by rivalry with other large companies. The smaller firms, however, were powerless. Thus, questions of business responsibility centered increasingly on the large corporations, which are now the focal points of interest for commentators and case writers.

McKie's third stage of evolutionary business philosophy represents the managerial view, which is concerned with the actual organization and behavior of corporations within society. The concept of "trusteeship" became more important, and the large corporation was thought of as a *permanent* institution, not merely as an extension of its owners. A classic example of this view is the case of Rolls-Royce; in this instance, the institution was felt to be of such importance that after the debacle of the Lockheed 1011 aero engine contract, the British government rescued it and reformed it into Rolls-Royce (1972) Ltd. Such corporations are assumed to have a life and purpose of their own, involving both their internal constituencies and the groups with which they must deal.

This is a view that has evolved over time. In the 1920s, although managers of large firms had taken on a much more positive outlook in that they no longer thought the market would take care of most problems while government would solve the rest, the definition of their sphere of responsibility was still relatively limited — consumerism, minority rights, and the environment were still unknown issues. However, despite the limitation of responsibility, managers *were* inclined to work more positively to help other elements in the economic system. McKie identifies four causes for this more responsive attitude: The economic collapse encouraged a business-government partnership; there was a loss of public confidence in private enterprise as a means of achieving economic stability, which resulted in increased government involvement; corporations were given the legal right to make charitable donations a business expense; and groups other than business interests, such as the unions, farmers, and consumers, all of them sanctioned by the government, began to form power blocs. Thus, management more frequently found itself confronted by some other power or faced with government intervention on behalf of some affected group.

This third stage seems to welcome a partnership between business and government to attack social problems, making use of the particular strengths of each and recognizing the limitations of both, but in reality the limits of such a partnership still remain to be determined. Jacoby's "consensual goals," which are the goals of the "system," and his business-government "merger" concept, already alluded to, would appear to suggest a limit much further away than most of us would admit; it suggests the growth of totally new types of institutions in the future.

BUSINESS AND ETHICS

At ground level, the concept of the social responsibility of business is a question of personal ethics, as has already been suggested. This topic is extensively discussed in Chapter 6. For the moment, we shall restrict ourselves to an examination of business responsibility in its very broadest sense — that is, the role of business in the modern social system and its interrelationships with other elements of that system, including the business-government partnership suggested by Jacoby.

Put in its simplest form, the doctrine of the social responsibility of business is that business is not an entity in itself, independent of the social system; rather, it depends on the system for its continuing existence. Thus, business decisions must not only further the interests of the corporations that employ the decision makers; they must also improve the quality of life for the whole of society. The focal areas of such responsible action are community needs, the environment, consumerism, the needs of minority and disadvantaged groups, and other causes worthy of corporate support. In addition, such action must include consideration of the traditional need for good relations with employees and the proper guardianship of shareholders' investments. As may be imagined, this concept of social responsibility has prompted a lengthy, and sometimes acrimonious, debate.

There is a growing bibliography in the field of business responsibility, the product mostly of the revolution of the late 1960s "against measuring progress predominantly in economic and technical terms." [12] The poles of opinion are extreme. At the one end, the militantly antagonistic view is championed by Milton Friedman, who labels the concept of social responsibility a "betrayal of capitalism" and a "fundamentally subversive doctrine." [13] At the other, a whole host of consumerists wants the quality of a Cadillac for the price of a Mini. In between lie the moderates, whose attitude is perhaps best summarized by R. Townsend: "Money, like prestige, if sought directly, is almost never gained. It must come as a by-product of some worthwhile objective or result which is sought and achieved for its own sake." [14]

Perhaps the most cogent argument in favor of business responsibility is that society supplies the mandate for business's existence and that business must therefore react and respond to changes in society. Unless it satisfies society's needs, it has no mandate. No longer is it enough merely to satisfy society in an economic sense; since society has grown more affluent, it is now seeking less tangible satisfactions, such as a clean environment, respect for human dignity, and a community that benefits from business help. In other words, profit is not the only objective against which performance is measured; business may keep its mandate only if it satisfies its social obligations at the same time as it realizes profits.

One of the powerful voices raised against this view is that of Theodore Levitt, who suggests that top business managers may be in danger of being taken in by pretty words: "Business will have a much better chance of surviving if there is no nonsense about its goals — that is, if long-run profit maximization is the one dominant objective in practice as well as in theory. . . . In the end business has only two responsibilities — to obey the elementary canons of everyday face-to-face civility (honesty, good faith, and so on) and to seek material gain." [15] Levitt maintains that the idea of social responsibility may have started as a defense against public criticism, but that it has now become an end in itself; moreover, he contends there is a danger that the preoccupation with considerations other than profit will turn the corporation "into a twentieth-century equivalent of the medieval Church."

A frequently expressed argument in favor of business responsibility is that it improves the environment in which business has to operate. Response to the demand to improve the quality of life will result in a better community in which to do business; this will be manifested in a labor force of better quality, a reduction in crime, and the expenditure of less money for the protection of property. Consequently, funds allocated to social activity will eventually improve profits. This view is perhaps best presented by Arjay Miller, a former president of Ford Motor Company: "Under current conditions, management cannot effectively discharge its long-run responsibilities to shareholders unless it also behaves responsibly toward employees, customers, government, education and the public at large. The ability of a corporation to protect and enhance the stockholders' equity depends crucially upon the prosperity, goodwill and confidence of the larger community. Acceptance of a large measure of responsibility toward the community is therefore good business as well as good citizenship." [16]

It is further claimed that social responsibility improves the public image of business. In other words, social responsibility helps to gain more customers and to enhance a firm's financial standing with the banks that lend it money and the investors who buy its shares. Viewed in this light, the concept is merely an extension of traditional business practice.

Perhaps one of the most common reasons for interest in social responsibility is the feeling prevalent in many industries that if business avoids the issues, the government will step in with increasingly restrictive regulations that could eventually cramp the firm's freedom of action. For many business managers, government intervention is a move toward destruction of the free enterprise that is central to the capitalist system. Thus, it is essential, they say, for business itself to participate in setting the rules for its conduct: "There can be no greater danger than to permit the new rules to be formulated by either the small group of critics armed only with malevolence toward the existing system or the much larger group sincerely motivated by concern for ameliorating social ills but grossly handicapped by their ignorance of the techniques and dynamism of private enterprises.''

Extending this argument, D. B. McCall contends that business possesses the greatest incentive of all groups in the system to tackle social problems: It is guided by the profit motive. He claims that social problems are getting worse, not better, and that governments at all levels sometimes behave in such a way as to make people believe that they would prefer to live with the problems rather than have someone solve them at a profit. He concludes, ''We clearly have two choices. Either we change the form of economic society which we have had for two centuries by eliminating the profit sector and attacking those social problems as they are attacked in Russia and in other socialist countries, or we retain the system we have and use it truly for the public good, not as a cover-up for inaction, delay, and nonperformance. I prefer the second choice.'' [17]

J. B. Quinn applies this view in specific terms to the problem of pollution. [18] If business responsibility is here to stay, he suggests, there is money in it. Instead of the task of pollution control and improvements being a drain on the GNP, it could become a dynamic, profitable market for industry itself. Business is the one sector of the social system having the skills and the resources to capitalize on the opportunities offered by such a demand; it can accomplish the work more quickly, more efficiently, and more cheaply than government, and it can do so at a profit. This is an interesting view, but one that unfortunately cannot be satisfactorily extended to other areas of social action.

Another argument for business's being socially responsible is that power entails responsibility, which should be measured in terms of power. Business wields an enormous amount of power, with the big corporation obviously having more than the small firm; thus, the responsibilities incumbent on the former are greater than those facing the latter. ''If each institution is to perform its social role in an orderly relationship with other institutions, then responsibility must be accepted wherever there is power. Any other arrangement invites irresponsible behavior.'' [19] This argument is based on the thesis that modern society is an interdependent system and that almost any internal business action has an influence on the world outside. Thus, because they have the power to affect the quality of life, business organizations must assume responsibility for that quality.

Protagonists on the other side of the debate, including Friedman and

Levitt, advance the classical doctrine of profit maximization. In their view, business's top priority is its economic function, not its social one, and business decisions should be made with protection of shareholders' interests as the criterion, within the constraints of the law. Friedman goes so far as to say that "any businessman who boasts to the public that he has been using corporate funds to exercise a social responsibility should be regarded as asking for an investigation by the Antitrust Division of the Justice Department."[20] Also, according to Friedman:

> In a free enterprise, private property system, a corporate executive is an employee of the owners of the business. He has direct responsibility to his employers. That responsibility is to conduct the business in accordance with their desires, which generally will be to make as much money as possible while conforming to the basic rules of the society. . . . Insofar as his actions in accord with his "social responsibility" reduce returns to stockholders, he is spending their money. Insofar as his actions raise the price to customers, he is spending the customers' money. Insofar as his actions lower the wages of some employees, he is spending their money.[21]

Friedman clearly believes that the only constraint on business action is the extent of legal sanctions and that any expenditure not directed at increasing profits and shareholders' wealth is intolerable. It is not entirely clear where he stands on those social issues in which no expenditure is involved; presumably, he would argue that there is a time cost on all activity, even though it may not appear specifically in a budget statement.

Opposition to the responsibility concept also focuses on the cost to society. Pollution control is a good example. Arguments surrounding this problem are whether it should be the government or the polluting firm that provides the funds for pollution control equipment and its operation, and whether such programs should be initiated through government legislation or through some rules that the firm imposes on itself on either an individual or a collective, industrywide basis. Whatever the course of action chosen, it is argued that the cost will eventually have to be borne by society itself, either in the form of increased taxes to finance a government policy of pollution control or in the form of higher prices imposed by the firms to pay for the extra internal costs involved. In a sense, this argument begs the question. Of course, there is a difference between paying taxes and paying higher prices; the one is mandatory and the other discretionary in that we have the option of not buying the products involved, academic though this proposition may be. Yet the truth is that firms exist at society's pleasure, as do government and other elements in the system; if they provided no benefits, they would cease to exist, but since they do exist, the benefits they provide are a cost to society as a whole.

Arguments against business responsibility are not restricted to members of the business and academic communities. Labor leaders also base their arguments largely on economic issues when they campaign for their members. G. Brooks observes that to act on any other basis "violates the ethics of . . . a trade union leader . . . no matter how worthy the purpose."[22] Increasing personal income for the labor force, like the maximization of corporate profits in Friedman's argument against business's social responsibility, is thus held to be the first, and perhaps the only, objective.

So the debate continues. In many ways it is futile, largely because social issues and economic theory are uncomfortable bedfellows. Perhaps this is an appropriate note upon which to move to another area, for, in the words of Andrew Schonfield:

It is arguable that the disappointment with our current performance in the management of the economy is the result of expecting economics to do on its own a job that requires a joint, and massive, effort by the whole range of social sciences. It is as if one had turned to the surgeons during the early days of the development of modern medicine, and commanded them on their own to take over responsibility for curing all bodily ailments: no doubt a few more people would have lived; but a lot more would have had their limbs chopped off.[23]

BUSINESS IN A MULTINATIONAL ENVIRONMENT

It has been estimated that in 1973 some 15 percent of the gross world product derived from multinational corporations and that by 1980 this share grew to about 30 percent. Multinational enterprises are a phenomenon of the mid-twentieth century; they have evolved as a result of several factors, the most important being the increasingly global perceptions of trade, the rapid improvement in world communications, and the emergence of the so-called Third World with its need for both a better standard of living and a share of the economic benefits of an industrialized society.

One of the major problems facing organizations of this type is that in different parts of the world, they operate under and are regulated by the laws and cultural traditions of other countries, as well as those of their own. Thus, the nature of managerial responsibility and ethical behavior takes on a new dimension. Richard Eells and Clive Walton have expressed the dilemma as follows: "Is the corporate domain of the multinational corporation to clash permanently — and perhaps in vain — with the sovereign claims of the international systems of nation-states? Or will the sovereign states give way at length to a more comprehensive worldwide political economy in which both nations and corporations will play their respective roles in harmony?"[24]

This distinction between the operating policies of the multinational firm and the local political, religious, and social values of the nation-state is nowhere more manifest than in attitudes toward bribery. To most Western business executives, bribery, payoffs, and kickbacks are reprehensible and in many cases strictly illegal, but elsewhere in the world, people regard them as natural tools of negotiation. Thus, it is sometimes argued that if the only alternative to indulging in such behavior is not to do business at all, it is perfectly legitimate when in Rome to do as the Romans do. By this argument, the end justifies the means, since the end is the contribution made by the multinational corporation to the economy of its parent state and the subsequent effect upon its balance of payments. Yet to take this attitude is to choke on the question; it suggests that business organizations exist purely as cogs in the national economic machine and that multinational companies are the instruments of government foreign policy. It sets patriotism on a higher level than personal ethics.

There are times, however, when the argument works the other way. Multinational firms sometimes find that to be "patriotic," in the sense of adhering to their parent country's foreign policy, acts to their detriment. Coca-Cola had such an experience in 1975 when one of its distributors, Tempo Bottling Company of Israel, asked for a Coca-Cola franchise. If Coca-Cola granted this franchise, it would antagonize its Arab customers who were at the time technically at war with Israel. Also, according to the unwritten rules, if any company violated the United States' foreign policy of doing business in one or the other of the two markets (Israel or the Arab world) by doing business in both, it would be in trouble. The Anti-Defamation League of B'nai B'rith conducted an extensive investigation into the issues and reported in 1966 that the reason for Coca-Cola's reluctance to grant the franchise was that it was cooperating with the Arab League's boycott against companies doing business with Israel. Coca-Cola denied this vigorously and offered counterarguments based on the lack of future profitability and the unreliability of the Tempo Company in observing the Coca-Cola trademark.

The repercussions were momentous. Mount Sinai Hospital in New York canceled its order for Coca-Cola. New York theaters and Nathan's Hot Dog Emporium of Coney Island threatened to do the same, and the New York City Human Rights Commission called for an investigation of the firm. Within a week, despite Coca-Cola's denial of the charges, it issued a franchise for bottling its products in Israel to Abraham Feinberg, a New York banker, president of the Israel Development Corporation, and a promoter of Bonds for Israel. The Arab League, at the initiation of Iraq, banned Coca-Cola. Coca-Cola opened for business in Tel Aviv in February 1968.[25]

The issues here are both clear and confused at the same time. James Farley, chairman of Coca-Cola Export Corporation, had to ask himself whether his company had any ethical responsibility to oppose or to support U.S. government policy at the cost of its responsibility to its stockholders. He also had to weigh the consequences of making economic decisions that could be viewed as racist. His problem was one of patriotism, and it raised very thorny questions of company decision-making processes, not only at the time, but also for possible future cases of a similar nature.

A more clear-cut example of the conflict between multinational company profitability, ethical norms, and the national interest is that of the Northrop Corporation of Los Angeles. In November 1974, Northrop settled out of court a civil action brought against the company by a stockholder on a charge of illegally using company funds for political contributions, employing false accounting practices, and making false and misleading reports, in violation of SEC regulations. The suit centered on a $1.2 million secret political slush fund, in existence from 1971 to 1973, which was used not only for illegal campaign contributions to Richard Nixon, Hubert Humphrey, Ronald Reagan, and others, but also for payments to certain consultants and sales agents for the company's foreign sales.[26]

The company apparently successfully "laundered" this money through a Northrop consultant in Paris, who, by a series of overpayments for his services, was able to transfer it to another Northrop consultant in Washington. It was then used to persuade prominent Europeans (including General Galland, a former Luftwaffe hero, and General Paul Stehlin, erstwhile chief of the French Air Force) to promote Northrop sales. When these facts became known, Northrop was penalized financially and subjected to severe restraints as to its future action. It was suitably contrite, but noticeably annoyed that the stockholder who brought the suit owned but two shares.

A stark contrast to the issues raised by the Coca-Cola and Northrop examples is the notorious attempt by ITT to interfere in the internal political affairs of Chile and to plot, with the knowledge of the U.S. government and the CIA, against the election of Salvador Allende to the Chilean presidency in 1970.[27] Allende was a Marxist, and ITT feared that he would nationalize the company's operations in Chile. The details of the affair are too well known to be recounted in detail, but from the evidence presented at a Senate Judiciary Committee hearing, there can be little doubt that the company received substantial support both from the CIA and other government representatives at all levels to prevent Allende's election. They failed, but Allende was overthrown and killed in September 1973; he was replaced by a military junta. The company's involvement in this coup was never proved, but that of the CIA was.

ITT had reason to be concerned about protecting its own interests in Chile, but the lengths to which it was prepared to go in doing this raised some serious questions. The line betweeen official U.S. foreign policy and the activities of multinational corporations has never been so dimly drawn. In its Israeli experience, Coca-Cola acted under severe political pressure, but in Chile, ITT not only worked hand-in-glove with the U.S. government, but also actually prompted government policy itself. In this, the company was acting out of a desire for self-preservation and a natural apprehension about an increasingly hostile political environment. Any organization in a similar situation would be similarly motivated, but it is questionable how far other chief executives would have matched the policy advocated by ITT's chairman, Harold Geneen, and senior vice-president, Edward Gerrity, who were prepared to support an anti-Allende candidate with up to $1 million of campaign funds from ITT.

Other multinational corporations have been influenced by government policy. British firms in South Africa are a good example. They were persuaded to limit their investment in a country that follows racist policies and in some cases even to withdraw altogether. But ITT, caught inescapably as it was in the mesh of international politics and economics, overstepped the limits of allowable action in its apparent collusion with the CIA and in its direct interference with the host country's affairs.

One of the arguments often advanced in favor of multinational corporations' subjugating the ethics of their parent nation to the practical realities of a different cultural environment is that if they did not, they would be placing themselves in a weakened position in international markets where they could be in competition with foreign firms who *were* prepared to compromise their business behavior. It is a difficult argument to refute, and as far as individual companies are concerned, there would appear to be a need for precise directives from senior management indicating what practices can be tolerated in business conduct and to what extent executives can deviate from parent-nation norms and at the same time remain within the bounds of legality.

The emergence of the developing nations of the Third World, newly aware of their natural resources and their consequent ability to redress the international economic balance, is a significant factor in the cultural and ethical differences facing multinational corporations. In such societies, religion and politics often go hand in hand, as, for example, in Islamic nations. To a very large extent, Third World countries have lacked the experience of an industrial revolution and the concomitant gradual movement toward a sophisticated democratic political system, which is seldom, if at all, influenced by religious dogma and power. Their political past has been essentially tribal and their economy peasant, and at all points in their history, politics and economics have been the materials with which their cultural edifice has been constructed, firmly cemented with the mortar of religion.

Western society, on the other hand, has its behavioral norms rooted elsewhere. It is true, as will be seen in Chapter 3, that much of Western society's ethical framework is based on the Judaic-Christian experience, but the values contained in that experience are not necessarily associated in the public's mind with the existence of the church and a belief in God; they have become social, commonsense values, which have been accepted as a means of ensuring a peaceful and safe coexistence with our fellow citizens. Furthermore, as we shall also see, they have been modified and refined by many social and philosophical thinkers, not a few of whom have been totally removed from religious belief of any kind.

Thus, while it is easy to criticize multinational organizations that are discovered in the transgression of traditionally accepted ethical norms, critics have to realize the very real problem that these companies face. It would appear that to some extent, allowances for compromise have to be granted if these organizations are to be able to operate in the competitive environment, but how such rules are established, and by whom, is a difficult question. Until some international code of business behavior is established — a utopian dream that seems unlikely to become reality — the onus will rest upon the values of chief executive officers and the supervisory powers of the state. Sadly, as we have seen from example, trust in those powers has not always been justified.

DILEMMAS: SOME EXAMPLES

A necessary prerequisite for any conceptual analysis of ethical behavior in business is an awareness of the practical problems that typically face individual business managers every day. Although it is not possible to produce an exhaustive taxonomy of such situations, we can, through an examination of selected examples, construct for ourselves a general understanding of the real nature of the dilemmas and conflicts involved.

Earlier in this chapter, we introduced the all-pervasive concept of ethical duality, the battle in the human conscience between responsibility to one point of reference or another — employer, family, colleagues, friends, or state. When distilled to their essence, all the ethical decision-making problems with which executives are confronted reflect this duality. They present the manager with a choice of options that can be resolved only through an ability to establish priority of responsibility. The focus of the problem, however, ranges over a broad spectrum.

Some executives find it easy to deal with such decisions, in some cases because they have a clearly defined conceptual framework of business behavior, and on a few occasions because they have no framework at all; but most people experience considerable difficulty because they possess no guidelines of personal behavior. The consequence is that they will frequently either pass over the issue altogether or decide on a totally inappropriate course of action. Chapter 6 will attempt to suggest a suitable value system that can help in the solution of ethical problems, but for the moment we have to examine the problems themselves.

Dilemmas of Profit

First, there are decisions about money, or, more specifically, profit. Business as the Western world knows it, exists for profit; if it did not, it would not exist at all. Its responsibility to its stockholders is paramount. Yet there are good ways and bad ways of making profits, either corporate or personal. What, for instance, does a branch manager in a chemical company do when faced with the problem of the pollution of a local river into which the company's industrial effluent is discharged?

Corporate management has said that only a certain amount of effluent is permissible as a matter of company policy, but at the same time the manager knows that his productivity bonus is in direct ratio to the effluent generated by the plant. Perhaps at the stipulated effluent level, his bonus will be insufficient to provide some of the things he is anxious to buy for his family, such as a new car, a better house, or a vacation on which his children have their hearts set. Perhaps, on the other hand, the manager is not as keen as the rest of his family on spending money on these things, but nevertheless feels that it is his duty as father and husband to do so. What is he to do? Where do his loyalties lie? How is he to reconcile the priorities of self, family, and employers (who are probably in any case perfectly aware that they have avoided their own responsibility)?

Take another example. A senior salesman for a company has the chance to make the biggest sale of his career and, on the strength of it, will stand an excellent chance of promotion to sales manager. His prospective customer, however, is notoriously susceptible to the charms of women and has said on many occasions that the ability and willingness of a supplier to accommodate this interest is a major factor in his allocation of contracts. The customer, in agreeing to meet the salesman to discuss the possibility of doing business, has hinted that during his visit to the salesman's company he will be looking forward to agreeable female companionship at his hotel. The salesman is torn between his own moral values, the prospect of promotion and financial betterment, and the profit or loss to his company in the event of the contract's being signed or not. It is another case of the conflict of responsibilities.

One of the thornier problems of money-making is what is known as "insider trading," or buying and selling shares of stock on the basis of privileged information. A typical example is contained in the research study in the final chapter, in which a director of a corporation is made aware of her company's intention to make a takeover bid for a competitive organization. She knows that if she buys stock before the bid is made public, she will be able to make a large profit when the stock price rises after announcement of the bid. The SEC's definition of an insider trader, as laid out by the Securities Act of 1933, is any officer, board member, or stockholder with at least a 10 percent share of the equity. Such individuals are not allowed to trade in their company's securities when they are in possession of information that has not yet been made public.

Technically, therefore, the director in this case, who is in possession of privileged information, is free to trade stock if she owns less than 10 percent, but she has a decided advantage over the small private investor.

Is acting on that information, although perfectly legal, ethically responsible? The problem received considerable airing in the celebrated cases of Texas Gulf Sulphur in 1963 and Merrill Lynch and Douglas Aircraft in 1966, in which employees and fund managers exploited tips given by Merrill Lynch.

There are many examples of stated (or unstated) company policy designed to improve profitability that have presented employees with ethical problems. One case is that of a California corporation in the fruit canning business that regularly employed illegal Mexican immigrant labor at wage rates below the minimum level. One executive of this company decided that the ethical complexities of this situation were too much to bear and complained to top management. He was promptly dismissed, and the company refused to give him a reference. The question to be asked is, was his action lacking in responsibility to his dependents and, if so, what alternative course was available to him?

Furthermore, take the case of the company director in a British advertising agency who chose to resign because he discovered that the president of the company was doctoring the books in order to create the impression that payoffs to prospective clients, amounting to several thousands of pounds, were legitimate business expenses. His resignation was a reflex decision, a spontaneous reaction, an emotional protest; he had no other employment in the offing, and his family's lifestyle was significantly curtailed until he was able to put the pieces of his career back together. Did he do the right thing? Could he have achieved his ends more effectively? Did he overreact to the moral question?

Perhaps the most frightening example of the conflict of responsibility is to be found in the case of the Ford Motor Company's 1971 cost-benefit analysis of the desirability of building certain safety features that would prevent loss of human life into the Pinto car. Any Ford executive who was aware of what was happening must have been placed in a most distressing ethical dilemma. It is a horrifying and somewhat macabre scenario, which requires rather more extensive analysis.

On October 14, 1979, the *Chicago Tribune* ran an exclusive investigative story, which in many ways was more stunning than the *Washington Post*'s exposé of Watergate. It suggested, through the evidence of Ford Motor's internally distributed documents, that Ford was prepared to trade the cost of the loss of human life against the cost of installing an $8 part into its Pinto car to reduce the chances of the gas tank's bursting into flames in the event of a rear-end collision. The cost analysis apparently influenced a decision not to improve the safety of the car.

Now it is quite possible that other automobile manufacturers do the same thing, but what complicates the Pinto story is that in 1978 Ford was indicted on a criminal charge of reckless homicide. The case involved three young women whose 1973 Pinto burst into flames in August 1978 as the result of its gas tank's exploding after a rear-end collision. The *Tribune*'s story strongly suggested that Ford knew before the production of the Pinto that its gas tank was more susceptible than other designs to fire and explosion in low-speed crashes.

In addition, at least twenty-three people died between 1973 and 1979 in fires resulting from rear-end crashes involving Pintos. Numerous civil lawsuits were brought, including one in which the jury awarded damages of $128.8 million to a teenager who had been burned over 95 percent of his body. This figure was later reduced by a judge to $6.5 million. The National Highway and Traffic Safety Association (NHTSA) stated that in 1976 and 1977 alone, thirteen Pintos — more than twice the number that might be expected according to the Ford calculations — were involved in rear-end burn crashes.

Ford's 1971 decision not to install the part was expected to save $20.9 million by 1976, by which time the company intended to add the part, but it did not do so until 1977. In 1978, Ford recalled 1.5 million Pintos on the orders of the government, and by 1979, 800,000 had been returned for conversion.

The cost-benefit analysis, developed by estimating the cost to society when a person dies or is seriously injured, was intially conducted because reducing the fire risk would have apparently reduced the Pinto's luggage space. The cost of the part and its installation would have been $11 per car, and by 1976, Ford expected to sell 12.5 million Pintos; thus, the savings achieved by not installing it would have been $137 million. On the other hand, the company estimated that deaths and injuries from burns would cost only $49.5 million by the same date, a difference of $87.5 million; this figure was based on individual deaths at $200,000 each, serious burn injuries at $67,000 each, and burn damage to cars at $700 each.

At the trial, this evidence was ruled inadmissible since it was held to be not germane to the specific 1978 incident. Ironically, the prosecution in the case admitted that had they brought a class action suit against Ford instead of a criminal charge, the documents could have been introduced into court. In March 1980, twenty months after the proceedings began, Ford was acquitted of the charge, for which the maximum fine would have been only $30,000 and for which no member of the company could have been imprisoned.

Dilemmas of Human Relationships

The second major ethical problem area has to do with human relationships, the management of people, and other issues removed from immediate financial significance. Note that the focus is still the possibility of conflict between corporate policy and individual conscience, which is felt most strongly by managers not having responsibility at the highest level.

A survey directed by C. E. Evans of Wayne State University and designed to determine how middle managers rank such ethical conflicts produced some interesting findings.[28] At the head of the list comes the difficulty of complying with a superior's requirements when they conflict with one's own code of ethics; this is a very general statement, as is the second conflict listed, which cites job demands infringing on obligations to the manager's home life. Third on the list is the problem of the methods sometimes used in competition for advancement (in the research described in Chapter 7, one example used is the case of a group head taking credit for work that had been done by a subordinate).

The fourth-ranked problem is the avoidance of responsibility or hedging on difficult decisions. Perhaps out of fear of the consequences of accepting responsibility themselves, managers will often pass an issue to their superiors, an act closely resembling the sin of omission in the Christian liturgy. Next comes the conflict of maintaining integrity and wanting to be well liked; at times, managers have to subjugate popularity to unpleasant decisions, such as the dismissal of subordinates for reasons that other employees do not understand or that are better not made public.

Sixth is the difficulty of maintaining impartiality with regard to race, religion, or personal prejudice in the treatment of subordinates or recruitment of new staff. An example contained in the research discussed in Chapter 7 concerns an executive who faces the dilemma of whether to hire a black as personnel manager. The executive knows that the applicant's qualifications and experience are superior to those of any other candidate, but cannot be sure that the applicant's color will not be an obstacle in negotiations with white labor leaders, who have in the past displayed tendencies toward racial discrimination. Is the idealism of equal opportunity to be discarded in favor of practical reality?

Seventh is the moral concern that one's job does not fully utilize one's capacities. Frustration in management, often the result of lack of perspicacity on the part of superiors, is perhaps the most morally hurtful of all emotions and can prompt disagreement, anger, and, at times, open rebellion.

Eighth is the tendency to condone poor quality, either in workmanship or in ideas, which is closely linked to the ninth problem area, that of knowingly giving one's less-than-best performance. Tenth and last comes misrepresentation of facts, strangely low on the list; this covers a wide range of possible conflicts, from knowingly indulging in untruthful or misleading advertising to laying the blame for personal failure on someone else who cannot offer an adequate defense.

W. L. LaCroix identifies three major pressure sources on the ethics of middle managers.[29] First is the pressure from business superiors, which in turn is subdivided into three types: "produce or else," "act questionably," and "do the right thing but also produce." In the case of "produce or else," the ethical dilemma is that the responsibility for results is shifted from top to middle manager, and yet those applying the pressure do not specify the limits of their demands. The point is that unless it is made clear what ethical boundaries exist in achieving specified goals, such as increased sales or market share or profit, the middle manager might well be tempted to employ unethical means to reach those goals.

The "act questionably" pressure refers to top management's directing middle management to act in ethically dubious ways; in situations that do not present obviously clear-cut ethical alternatives — that is, the "gray areas" — the middle manager will be most likely to succumb to this kind of pressure. A good example is the policy of controlled disclosure: The middle manager is pressured by superiors to omit from reports significant information that might cause the reader to think less of the company or individuals within the company.

"Do the right thing but also produce" echoes the dilemma of the chemical plant manager described earlier. LaCroix cites the electrical price-fixing conspiracy of the 1960s as an example of how the attitudes of top management are perceived by middle managers. He concludes, "The pressure to produce simply does not contain adequate provision to allow for ethical actions in the real circumstances of the time, even if top management 'wishes' ethical actions and recommends them overall. When general norms are not updated along with new policy directives, the middle manager is split in weighing how to apply both."[30]

The second major pressure source identified by LaCroix is the pressure from family-related obligations. The middle manager may succumb to the temptation to cooperate in unethical practices out of a sense of family responsibility and a fear of losing the job. It is a kind of psychological infidelity, which involves the confrontation of two contractual loyalties with each other.

The third pressure indicated by LaCroix is from peers within the company. It consists, on the one hand, of maneuvering behind the scenes and, on the other, of not speaking out when faced with an ethical problem. With regard to behind-the-scenes maneuvering, there is a widely held view among managers on their way up the promotional ladder that the way to the top involves several legitimate tricks, such as stealing others' ideas and undermining a superior's authority and reputation. Sabotage of authority results from a Theory X type of top management, which holds that people dislike work and must be coerced and that middle managers only need to *feel* that there is pressure to be silent and ethically compromising in order for feelings of resistance to emerge. The behavior of others in a particular peer group may also induce such feelings.

Dilemmas of Top Management

In this discussion, the spotlight has been entirely focused upon the situational dilemmas of managers operating at the middle level, removed from the ultimate policymaking responsibilities of the chief executive officer or the executive board. Yet it has to be remembered that higher levels of management face ethical problems also and that they have the additional responsibility of policy implementation; not only do they have to construct what they honestly believe to be an ethically respectable pyramid of policies, strategies, and tactics, but also they have to ensure that proper organizational structures allow for effective communication of these plans and that subordinates are well motivated to carry them out.

If their policies are indeed honest, and if they stem from responsible stewardship, such individuals are entitled to expect cooperation and support from their subordinates as a necessary part of any employment contract. However, because questions have been legitimately raised as to the degree to which subordinates can be forced to exercise obedience, loyalty, and confidentiality, there is now a feeling in some top management quarters that the debate has produced a tendency toward deliberately destructive behavior (typically called whistle-blowing, boat-rocking, or sabotage), which reflects the growing modern cult of doubt, criticism, and disregard of authority of any kind — parental, political, or managerial.

It is thus also the responsibility of top management to attempt to

differentiate as fairly as possible between proper subordinate protest
stemming from genuine ethical conflict and truly dysfunctional behavior,
which is frequently manifested in badly produced merchandise, dangerous pollution, excessive costs, discrimination, low quality control, and
the like. It is not always an easy task.

SUMMARY

In this chapter, we have introduced the concept of individual responsibility as distinct from the traditional view of the responsibility of the
corporation. In law, a corporation is a "synthetic" person, a myth or
fiction given the legal "attributes of a personality."[31] It can sue and be
sued, own property, pay taxes to appropriate authorities, and be given
privileges. In contrast, our thesis is that the acts and intentions of a
corporation are in the final analysis the acts and intentions of the executives who hold positions of power within it. The "responsibility" of the
corporation is the collective responsibility of its members.

A second concept fundamental to the discussion of business responsibility is that of ethical duality, which is the source of many of the
conflicts of conscience that permeate those situations in which an individual feels bound by obligations to two loyalties. The distinction is
broadly that between the social-political-economic universe, on the one
hand, and the personal-religious-moral perspective, on the other; in the
case of the executive and employee, this ethical duality is manifested in
the potential conflict between the values of the person as citizen, spouse,
parent, and member of an organization that provides a livelihood.

This chapter has also attempted to establish an acceptable taxonomy
of the language of business responsibility. *Business* is held to be any
industrial or commercial enterprise; it does not include government,
though discussion of the relationship between business and government
is essential to our study. *Society* is the entire framework or system of
which business is a part; thus, business's responsibility to society is
partially responsibility to itself. *Responsibility* needs a focus — a person
or a group to act as auditor or judge; you cannot be responsible if there
is nobody who holds you to account. In the present context, the auditor
is society. *Ethics* and *morals* are terminologically interchangeable for the
purpose of our discussion, though it is acknowledged that at times they
are invested with distinguishing implications. The *individual*, a central
figure in our study, is not John or Jane Doe; this person is you or I.
Authority is more than naked power; it has to be clothed in the vestments

of responsible action. Its power is not total, but conditional on its acceptance by others and the degree to which it minimizes dissonance on the part of subordinates.

We have also discussed the nature of the modern business enterprise and have traced its historical development through its several stages, from the age of the classical economists, through the transitional period of the late nineteenth and early twentieth centuries, to the more recent managerial view of "trusteeship" and the trend toward a partnership between business and government to attack social problems.

Arguments in favor of and antagonistic toward the concept of business's social responsibility have been presented. Supporters of the concept claim that since business exists because of an unwritten mandate from society, and since society's values are changing and creating new and different expectations of business, business must respond to those changes if it is to keep its mandate.

Other arguments for business responsibility are that it will produce a better community in which to conduct business, that it improves the public image of business, and that if business avoids the issues, government will apply increasing weights of legislation, which will limit freedom of action.

Opposition to the concept comes from Levitt and Friedman, who maintain that profit maximization is the sole purpose of business. In their view, social responsibility may have started as a defense against public criticism, but it has now become an end in itself; business decisions should reflect the interests of shareholders within the constraints of the law. Other criticism centers on the costs to society and possible damage to the balance-of-payments position.

The specific dilemma of the multinational corporation has been analyzed to illustrate the problems involved in situations involving a conflict of cultures, and it has been suggested that some compromise seems necessary to reduce such conflict.

The chapter has also presented some practical examples of problems in business ethics; these provide a background for the conceptual framework for ethical decision making suggested in Chapter 6. The examples fall into two categories, money-related and people-related, but they both arouse conflicts of individual conscience, particularly at the middle-management level.

Thus, this first chapter has attempted to establish the nature of the subject of this book; it leads naturally to the examination of historical, moral, cultural, religious, and social influences on modern business and personal behavior in the following two chapters.

NOTES

1. Bertrand Russell, *Authority and the Individual*, BBC Reith Lectures, 1948–1949 (London: Allen & Unwin, 1949), p. 83.

2. Ibid., p. 84.

3. The projective aspects of the study owe much to the questionnaire designed by Frank S. Leonard and published as an addendum to Albert Z. Carr's "Is Business Bluffing Ethical?" *Harvard Business Review* 46 (January–February 1968):150–53. The published results of the study can be obtained from the University of Wisconsin - Eau Claire.

4. Richard Eells and Clive Walton, *Conceptual Foundations of Business*, 3rd ed. (Homewood, Ill.: Richard D. Irwin, 1974).

5. Otto von Gierke, *Political Theories of the Middle Age*, trans. F. W. Maitland (Boston: Beacon Press, 1958).

6. W. H. Hamilton, "On the Composition of the Corporation Veil," *Publications of the Brandeis Lawyers' Society* (1946):46.

7. Chief Justice John Marshall, *Trustees of Dartmouth College* v. *Woodward*, 4 Wheaton 518 (1819).

8. N. H. Jacoby, *Corporate Power and Social Responsibility* (New York: Macmillan, 1973).

9. James W. McKie, "Changing Views," in *Social Responsibility and the Business Predicament*, ed. James W. McKie (Washington, D.C.: Brookings, 1974).

10. Adam Smith, *The Wealth of Nations* (Chicago: Encyclopaedia Britannica, 1952), bk. 4, chap. 2, p. 193.

11. Stephen Leacock, "Adam Smith," in *Hellements of Hickonomics in Hiccoughs of Verse Done in Our Social Planning Mill* (New York: Dodd, Mead; London: The Bodley Head, 1936). Reprinted with permission.

12. R. Ackerman and R. Bauer, *Corporate Social Responsiveness* (Reston, Va.: Reston, 1976), p. 3.

13. Milton Friedman, *Capitalism and Freedom* (Chicago: University of Chicago Press, 1962).

14. R. Townsend, *Up the Organization* (New York: Alfred A. Knopf, 1970), p. 62.

15. Theodore Levitt, "The Dangers of Social Responsibility," *Harvard Business Review* 36 (September–October 1958):49.

16. Quoted in M. Anshen, "Changing the Social Contract: A Role for Business," *Columbia Journal of World Business* (November–December 1970).

17. D. B. McCall, "Profit: Spur for Solving Ills," *Harvard Business Review* (May–June 1973):180.

18. J. B. Quinn, "Next Big Industry: Environmental Improvement," *Harvard Business Review* 49 (September–October 1971):120–31.

19. K. Davis and R. L. Blomstrom, *Business and Society: Environment and Responsibility*, 3rd ed. (New York: McGraw-Hill, 1975), p. 27.

20. Milton Friedman, "Milton Friedman Responds," *Business and Society Review* (Spring 1972).

21. Milton Friedman, "Does Business Have a Social Responsibility?" *Bank Administration* (April 1971):13–14.

22. G. Brooks, "Ethical Responsibilities of Labor," *Stanford Business Bulletin* 31 (1963):62–69.

23. Andrew Schonfield, *The Times* (London), February 2, 1971.

24. Eells and Walton, *Conceptual Foundations*, p. 202.

25. The details of this case history are taken from S. Prakash Sethi, *Up Against the Corporate Wall,* 3rd ed. (Englewood Cliffs, N.J.: Prentice-Hall, 1977).

26. Ibid.

27. Ibid.

28. C. E. Evans, Appendix B in Thomas McMahon, "Moral Problems in Business Management," *Catholic Theological Society of America Proceedings* 20 (1965).

29. W. L. LaCroix, *Principles for Ethics in Business* (University Press of America, 1979).

30. Ibid., p. 111.

31. C. I. Barnard, "Elementary Conditions of Business Morals," *California Management Review* (supplement) 1 (1958):7.

2 SYMBIOSIS AND CONFLICT:
Political and Ethical Contrasts

There is not a more mean, stupid, dastardly, pitiful, selfish, spiteful, envious, ungrateful animal than the Public. It is the greatest of cowards, for it is afraid of itself.

— William Hazlitt[1]

THE SHRINKING UNIVERSE

Perhaps the most startling phenomenon of the twentieth century is the exponential growth in worldwide communications. It took a week for the news of Nelson's death and victory off Cape Trafalgar to reach the London *Times*; television audiences in Europe knew of the assassination of John Kennedy minutes after the event.

The importance of this communications explosion has sometimes been ignored or, at best, understated; yet, whether we like it or not, we are now much closer, both in enmity and understanding, to people living in different cultures and different political systems than we ever were before. There is thus a greater obligation on us to accept that "no man is an island unto himself" than there would be if we were still separated by time and distance.

34

In this new global environment, pressures and influences from other cultures and societies have assumed larger dimensions. The growth of international trade and economic blocs has forced big business to regard foreign operations in the same light as domestic activity, and this changed perspective has brought with it its own special ethical problems, as was seen in the discussion of multinational corporations in the previous chapter. In politics, too, we have had the phenomenon of a president of the United States visiting China and a Russian prime minister dining with the queen of England.

This chapter is devoted to an analysis of the symbiotic implications of the new international political-economic and social-ethical alignment that has been the result of communications growth. The twentieth century, characterized by new "world" concepts both in war and peace, is proving to be the watershed of our civilization.

POLITICAL-ECONOMIC CONFLICT

Revolution is not new. For centuries, people have rebelled against oppression, tyranny, and exploitation; they have even attempted, successfully or unsuccessfully, to overthrow established authority in the pursuit of personal power and wealth. From Julius Caesar to the Ayatullah Khomeini, we have seen sovereignty transferred by violence and bloodshed.

In the last six decades, however, the nature of rebellion has changed. Until the Russian Revolution of 1918, the result of such protests was traditionally the exchange of one form of capitalism for another. While the motives for revolt were not infrequently socially rooted, as in Britain in 1688 or France in 1789, the effects on the economic system were marginal. This is not to say that the economic strength of the nations concerned was not changed, but that the basis of those economies remained the same, founded on freedom of exchange and personal ownership. Before 1918, the three most notable revolutions of postmedieval times took place in countries that are today still capitalist nations: Cromwell's Commonwealth, though admittedly short-lived, did not alter the economic structure any more than did the First Republic of France or the Declaration of Independence. However, the replacement of Czar Nicholas by Lenin's Soviets brought a new form of political economy into being and was the beginning of a different kind of relationship between East and West.

The new totalitarianism, extended after World War II to other nations in Eastern Europe, as well as to China and Cuba, has been built upon a system that involves every element of personal and social life. For a time, it polarized at two extremes, with fascism on one side and communistic socialism on the other, but the former was largely destroyed by war. As far as the liberally democratic West is concerned (the adverb is necessary since both capitalists and socialists lay claim to the adjective), there can be no complacency that totalitarianism can spread no further; it is a product of the machine age, with its emphasis on efficiency and organization, the two main requirements of successful government. The influence of communism in some Western European countries, notably Italy and France, is a warning to capitalism that totalitarianism could be just around the corner.

This fundamental confrontation of opposite political and economic ideologies is the backdrop to a wider and more complex scenario in which other smaller and less developed nations are beginning to decide on their alignment of affiliation. There is a third (and increasingly more important) sector of civilization, which until comparatively recently did not enter into consideration in the discussion of social, political, or economic affairs. The so-called Third World, composed of underdeveloped and developing nations, most of them former colonies of Western powers, has traditionally not only been taken for granted as a cheap supplier of such basic commodities as sugar, minerals, and oil, but has also been largely ignored as a social and political force.

Since the decline of colonialism and the emergence of these new nations, sometimes through the peaceful and constitutional granting of independence and sometimes through bloody warfare, new forces have emerged in the balance of economic and political power. Africa has become the focus of the world's attention as it struggles to find a new identity; powerful influences from both East and West are behind the new African nations' attempts to resolve the problem stemming from the presence of a white government in a black continent. The black African states themselves, through the Organization for African Unity, are striving to present a united front to the rest of the world.

Similarly, although the Middle East Arab states have a cultural heritage spanning centuries, it is only since the withdrawal of British and French interests that these nations have begun to make their economic strength felt in no insignificant way through the use of their major weapon, oil. The effects have been shattering on the economies of the Western powers. At the same time, with Israel in their midst, the territorial inroads made by the Israelis in successive wars have inspired a new desire for Arab solidarity, evidenced through the formation of the

Arab League and the less official, paramilitary Palestinian Liberation Organization.

These developments have changed not only the international political scene, but also the economic orientation of the world. Commodities that previously were cheap are now expensive, and the industrial nations place increased emphasis on productivity for export to achieve a satisfactory balance-of-payments position. Such nations as Taiwan, Korea, and Thailand are in the production race; others control the supply of sugar and bauxite. The lessons it took the industrial nations two centuries to learn are being assimilated by the newly emerging states in a decade.

Furthermore, this growth in political influence and economic power is presenting new social problems. The mobility of the world's population is increasing. In some of the new states, independence has resulted in a reduction in employment opportunities (notably in India and Pakistan) and a flow of immigrants to the West, many of whom are finding it difficult to become integrated into their new environments. In the United States, there has always been a significant black population as a result of the slave trade. Comparatively, though there have been problems, ugly moments, and even a civil war, and though in many ways blacks in America are still underprivileged, integration is now well advanced in that country. In Britain, however, which is the traditional destination of Commonwealth immigrants, the problem is more acute; on the one hand, the British government feels to a large degree bound by honor to give help and housing to these new citizens, but, on the other, powerful voices are being raised to warn against the danger of racial conflict, fewer jobs, and strained social services.

This potentially explosive situation is fueled by the competition between the Western democracies and the Marxist bloc for the favors of the Third World. The Western business ethic, founded on pluralism and the competition of group interests, is in no way similar to Marx's economic theory. "The West believes that negotiation and compromise are the appropriate methods for resolving differences among various groups, whereas Marx's insistence on violent conflict is too well known to need detailed elaboration. . . . Marx also concluded that the political behavior of men was determined by their economic interests, whereas Western pluralism recognizes that men often act to further the interests of their church, their country, their province, or their leader."[2]

Therefore, unless nations like Britain and Canada, who are the recipients of immigrants from different ethnic groups and social environments, can demonstrate by their own attitudes and values that they understand and are sympathetic to the problems that pervade the traditionally deprived nations, and unless some way is found to strike the proper balance between protecting the interests of indigenous populations and helping the people who come from elsewhere, the conflict of ideological values will extend beyond Africa and Asia.

Nowhere is this new population mobility felt more strongly than in employment. Both the government that admits immigrants and the organizations that are their potential employers need to tread a careful path, government because it needs to preserve jobs for the existing work force and potential employers because the law penalizes them for discrimination against minority groups. One of the problems facing organizations today is that of being accused of racism for making decisions on purely economic grounds.

It is strange that the postwar alignment of national interests has produced three major forces of quite different types in the world economic struggle. The United States is clearly the strong power in the West, and Japan, a country that defies analysis in industrial history because of its capacity to learn in a decade what other nations accomplished only over centuries, is the paramount competitor in the East. Between these two lies the European bloc. Britain, France, and Italy (participants on different sides in World War II and each severely crippled as a result of destroyed manufacturing resources and economic starvation) have eventually come together in the European Economic Community, in which Germany, even though divided by political maneuvering, has emerged as the strongest productive unit in Western Europe. How two defeated nations, with their economies in ruins, have managed to impose their competitive power on the rest of the industrial world is remarkable enough; why the other great countries, with their tradition of productive superiority, have been powerless to stem the tide is a question economists the world over have been unable to answer. Yet the yen and the mark for the last fifteen years have been consistently stronger than the dollar, franc, or pound. Only Switzerland with its "gnomes of Zurich" has been able to match the strength of this international monetary cabal, and Switzerland has been neutral longer than any country in Europe.

The countries of South America offer a stark comparison to the economic power plays just described. In Buenos Aires, it pays to borrow money for a week because the rate of inflation makes any interest rate favorable. Yet the Western democracies are little better; the prime rate of borrowing in England rose to 15 percent in July 1979, and in March 1980, Americans could not obtain money from a bank at less than 20 percent; $100 borrowed over five years will cost another $100. No business can stand that.

This suggests that economists are no longer able to prescribe accurately for economic problems. Millions of students taking courses — all required by traditional educational programs — find that the book answers fit the real facts about as well as Simon Zylotes sitting on his pillar. Reality has become relative; things are not true or false anymore, merely more or less right or wrong, depending on where the arbiter happens to be. If the economists cannot find the answer, then it is fair to ask, who can?

A survey conducted by Donald Kantner from the University of Southern California suggests that American political and economic positions and policies are the subject of much cynicism and alienation.[3] The survey polled 2,200 respondents in England, Belgium, France, Holland, Italy, and West Germany on their attitudes to the present state of the world. The results are sobering: The general feeling is that there is little good in people and that the world is becoming increasingly intolerable. The implications are almost entirely negative for traditional institutions, such as the church or accepted political systems. The only exception is in England, where many more people apparently still subscribe, outwardly at least, to the innate nobility of man, a strange paradox in a nation that produced the Hobbesian view that life is "nasty, brutish, and short."

The survey (part of a commercial study of consumer products) probed into fundamental questions of belief about self and other people. It sought answers to the problem of trust in others, of individuals' ability to control their own lives, of hope for the future, of free will compared with fate and destiny, of anticipation and despair. It was a noble, if perhaps vain, attempt to take the temperature of world opinion.

Echoing the results of the study described in the final chapter of this book, the survey discovered that there is cynicism and pessimism about human nature almost everywhere. The question of governmental moralizing and increasing state involvement in corporate activity is the subject of skeptical contempt. Since more respondents in Kantner's survey labeled people as liars and reality as money, corporate bribery comes as no surprise, and American preachings about morality in government and human rights are held to be "naive rubbish."

In the political-economic arena, the responses also suggest that European socialism is unstable and ultimately unworkable; distrust of others does not provide the best atmosphere for a system calling for common goals and cooperation. Europeans are beginning to feel they are losing control over their lives and are rapidly becoming alienated by trends that make them fear for the future. In the survey, more than half of the Italians, traditionally a people with great love for children, thought it unfair to bring more children into a world with so bleak an outlook.

International political and economic conflict can arouse strange and sometimes totally unpredictable behavior in individuals who occupy positions of power and responsibility in corporations. The war in Vietnam, the violent and apparently irreconcilable struggle in Northern Ireland, the taking of American hostages in Iran, the Russian invasion of Afghanistan, and the continuing Arab-Israeli confrontation in the Middle East have all had repercussions in the corridors of corporate power. For example, on January 8, 1970, Jay Monroe, president of Tensor Corporation, placed a $2,000 advertisement in the *New York Times* to annouce that he was withdrawing the $50,000 Tensor account from the Chase Manhattan Bank, where the company had a $250,000 line of credit. Since Monroe's shareholding in the company was only 27 percent, the advertisement in effect was largely paid for by stockholders' money; yet the views contained in it were Monroe's own. The reason for the public statement was that Monroe, a Jew, strongly disapproved of the advice given to President Nixon by David Rockefeller, president of Chase, and John McCloy, former president, that Nixon should reduce his military support of Israel so as not to jeopardize American economic interests in the Arab world. The ethical questions raised by such behavior are complex, especially since Monroe himself is a strong advocate of business ethics and considers a preoccupation with return on investment to be antisocial.

All political decisions are economic, and all wars are economically motivated, but it has been the growth of modern capitalistic and socialistic business systems that has made it easier to identify the relationship between politics and economics. In earlier times, that relationship was not so obvious because economic life was subordinated to other aspects of the social culture, such as religion, the arts, and philosophy, as well as politics; yet the relationship was still regarded as the means by which the values of these other aspects were achieved. It has taken the emergence of the corporation as the accepted economic vehicle to make us more aware of the broader issues of life. Individual decisions now have to be made not only against a background of sometimes conflicting political, economic, social, and ethical considerations, but also within a time and space horizon much nearer than it ever was before.

Thus, although the political-economic developments of the past thirty years are important and significant, their implications cannot be fully understood without an examination of the concomitant social-ethical forces emanating from the cultural differences involved. Our discussion will now turn in that direction, a route that the third chapter will follow also, but with more frequent stops to photograph the scenery along the way.

SOCIAL-ETHICAL CONTRASTS

It will be demonstrated in Chapter 3 that the influences on modern ethical behavior in Western business derive not only from religious doctrine, but also from the thoughts and writings of philosophers and social commentators. In the context of world culture, differences in ethical orientation stem almost entirely from religion.

We can categorize religious affiliation into six basic divisions. First, the Western world subscribes largely to the Judeo-Christian tradition; second, Islam (or Muhammendanism) has an influence that has spread eastward as far as China and westward to Africa and even Europe; third, Hinduism is concentrated exclusively within the Indian continent; fourth, Buddhism is the connecting link between India and the rest of Asia; fifth, Chinese religion is a cultural mixture of three systems — Confucianism, Taoism, and Buddhism; and sixth, the national religion of Japan — Shintoism — consists of the dual influences of Buddhism and Confucianism. All these religions have both worthy and unworthy followers (witness the blood shed in the name of religion over the centuries), but the purpose here is to identify the general impact that each of them has had on ethical norms. Our discussion will, to all intents and purposes, ignore the isolated tribal religions of the world, based largely on magical content, as well as dead religions, such as those of ancient Mesopotamia. The important consideration here is the ethical problems that behavior founded on these six different beliefs brings in its wake.

A seventh category, which is not a religion but the lack of one, also exists. It includes the social-political-economic creed known as communism, as well as the so-called heresies of Darwinism, Frazerism, and Freudianism: the first, that human life has evolved from lower levels of animal life; the second, that all religions are of equal value (the name follows Sir James Frazer's classic taxonomy of comparative religions in his series of publications known as *The Golden Bough*); and the third, that all religion is a fallacy and a mere projection of human desires. None of the entries in this seventh category explains why people of different cultures and different nationalities behave in different ways, nor do they even begin to explain culture itself. They are biological, analytical, and psychological; faith, except in the case of Marxism, is absent, and faith is necessary to life because no moral decision can be made on rational grounds alone.

The influences of the Judeo-Christian ethic on the behavior of the Western world are discussed extensively in Chaper 3. At this point, the focus will be upon other cultures and their points of contact with, and divergence from, the culture of the West. We shall also include in our survey a discussion of the ethics of socialism and the ethical and social problems presented by the Third World.

Islam

Muslims, the devotees of Islam, have many affinities with both Jews and Christians. All believe in one supreme God, whose word is made manifest in a holy book and whose will has been communicated to his believers through his apostles; in the case of Islam, the greatest apostle of God was Muhammad (sometimes wrongly called Mahomet), who was born in 570 A.D. and died in 632. Muslims believe Muhammad received the Word and recited it to the people through the Koran, the bible of Islam, which does, however, revere other prophets, including Abraham, Moses, and Christ.

The five Pillars of Faith of Islam consist of prayer (facing Mecca) five times daily, fasting during daylight hours in the month of Ramadan, almsgiving (one-fortieth of personal income), at least one pilgrimage to Mecca in a lifetime, and faith in Allah (God) and his prophet. Like Christianity, Islam maintains that all men are brothers in God, who is the head of the state, and that earthly rulers are his deputies. The ethical content of the religion stresses, as did the Greeks, the need for a middle way between extremes; it also emphasizes the importance of social behavior, particularly hospitality, which is one of the greatest virtues. Lack of belief is the greatest sin. Murder and adultery are also high on the list of sins, but blood revenge, limited to one life to avoid feuds, is allowed. Polygamy is permitted, although most modern Muslims have only one wife; divorce is easy for a man, but not for a woman.

Holy men command great respect, as the authority of the Ayatullah Khomeini has shown. Wine, music, and representative art are frowned upon, but with the growth of the communications industry, the last two are now beginning to gain acceptance. Islam takes many forms in its different sects and the different areas of the world to which it has spread, as far apart as Africa and China. Also, the impact of Western culture has begun to modify Muslim behavior in ways that are liberalizing its beliefs, but that also at times provoke a conservative reaction. Iran is a perfect example of such reactionary sentiment, spurred partly by political, but also largely by religious, antipathy toward Western (and particularly American) values and economic pressures. British influences in Africa have resulted in a different political and legal structure, in which traditional Islamic religious values are now more or less limited to private and personal affairs. The consequence of this influence is that Islam is having to adapt to modern science and technology, sophisticated historical criticism, and twentieth-century religious skepticism. This is true of most creeds throughout the world. Some Muslim countries, like Pakistan with its forward-looking educational program, are finding the adaptation easier than others. Yet tradition dies hard.

As far as Western business managers are concerned, this coming together of cultures is often presented in warning terms; they are advised to beware of the danger of imposing their business values on people whose religious tradition is quite out of phase with their own. Yet many fail to realize the changes taking place on the other side and the concessions that have been and are still being made to Western ideas. The growth of Middle Eastern business economies, increased industrialization, and, above all, the power derived from energy resources have all contributed to a closer relationship with the West, even though this has been somewhat soured by the emphasis placed on oil.

Hinduism

Most Indians are Hindus, but it is difficult to describe Hinduism as an organized religion since it exists in so many different forms, rather like the multivariate creeds of the Roman Empire before Christianity became the official imperial belief. What binds its various parts together is that it is quintessentially Indian. (The words *Hindu* and *India* both derive from the same Sanskrit root.) Before the granting of independence to India and Pakistan, some 30 percent of the population of the continent was Muslim, but the separation of the two countries has left India predominantly Hindu. Buddhism, too, had its beginnings in India, but little of it remains there; it has moved to other countries, as we shall see.

The most prominent characteristic of Hinduism is the caste system, originally based on the distinction between the invading light-skinned Indo-Europeans (or Aryans) of about 1200 B.C. and the darker indigenous Dasas whom they enslaved. Nowadays, the caste of an Indian has nothing to do with the color of his skin; the difference between castes, while originally social, has now taken on a religious connotation, with the Brahmins, the aristocracy of the ancient priesthood, at the highest level. To be born a Brahmin, whether a priest or not, is still the apogee of Indian social standing.

There is a significant mystical element in Hinduism, handed down in the books of the Vedas, or priestly writings, in which there is a close similiarity to the cult worship of ancient Greece as it was given form in the mystery rites of Eleusis and elsewhere. Siva (the Mother Goddess), *soma* (the sacred alcohol), Agni (the god of fire, from the Latin *ignis*), Rudra (the bull-god), and Vishnu, who with Siva is of greatest importance in modern Hindu deism, all come together in the everyday Indian prayer (or *mantra,* sacred sentence): "Let us meditate on the most excellent light of the Creator; may he guide our intellects."[4]

One of the more important aspects of the caste system is the concept of the reincarnation of souls. One's status in a future life is determined by the quality of the life one now lives as exemplified by the acts (*karma*) one performs. It is a frustrating and inimical existence, fulfilled only when the ultimate level of life (Brahman) is achieved. At this level, from which there can be no descent, one is released from further striving.

Hinduism has always had a respect for nature, especially animal life. The cow is regarded as sacred. This attitude toward the preservation of life and the essentially nonviolent character of the religion are the two most obvious facets of India to strike a visitor from the West. The advent of British trade and government, and the accompanying Christian missions, had profound effects on the system, one of which was a revival of Hinduism; another was a movement to combat the caste system and the discrimination that it creates. Mahatma Gandhi was concerned about the problem of the outcasts, people who have no caste at all, and succeeded in having them admitted to temples from which they had been barred, but the caste system is such a powerful element of Indian life that it is difficult to change it.

Gandhi, who was the driving force of Indian independence, did much to bring India and the West closer together. He respected Christianity and used its precepts widely in his social reform. Perhaps it is he more than anyone who has enabled the New India, with its strong and easily identifiable British influence, to begin to construct a business system that appears able to work in close harmony with the industrialized nations. Of all Eastern cultures, India probably presents the fewest obstacles to such harmony. The values of Indian business match very nearly those of the West.

Buddhism

A religion born in India, Buddhism has moved elsewhere. It is like Christianity and Islam in having a historical person, Gotama, as its founder, and quite different from Hinduism in this respect. There is much uncertainty about Gotama's life, but he probably lived during the sixth and fifth centuries B.C. The legend of his birth (choosing his mother while in heaven and descending into her womb to be born a Buddha and chief of all) bears a remarkable similarity to the story of the Christian virgin birth. Gotama renounced all earthly commitments, found spiritual enlightenment in the "utter peace of Nirvana," and spent the remainder of his life teaching and traveling, in the process converting sixty followers who became his monks. Their livelihood depended on the alms they gained through begging.

The basic tenet of Buddhism is the selfless life and a spirituality that scorns material values. Five precepts are stipulated for the layman: to avoid taking life; to avoid taking what is not given; to avoid unchastity (i.e., infidelity, but not marriage); to avoid falsehood; and to avoid alcohol and intoxicants, which encourage sloth.

Buddhism is now the chief religion of Burma, where it has proved very resistant to communism, even though communism played a great part in the independence movement. It also exists in China, Tibet, Korea, and Japan. In China, it has the largest following of all religions, but since the communist revolution, it has lost many of its monasteries and lands, and it is uncertain what the future holds for it. In Tibet, the land of Lamaism, there is an uneasy truce between the Chinese, who invaded the country in 1950, and the spiritual leadership of the Dalai Lama. In Japan, Buddhism has had a significant influence on culture, notably in education. However, in contrast to the situation in India, where Hindu tradition and Western values have found common ground, in both China and Japan there is a stark contrast with the West, which is manifested at all points of contact — political, social, and commercial. We therefore need to examine the religious and ethical behavior of these two countries as an intrinsic part of the national character.

Chinese Religion

It is hard to say what effect the communist takeover in China has had on traditional Chinese ethical systems. Three religions exist side by side, and few Chinese subscribe exclusively to one; Confucianism, Taoism, and Buddhism are regarded as different ways of achieving the same goal — Tao, or the way of the world. All three have been added to and have built upon an ancient nature cult involving ancestor worship and an obsession with the elements of the perceived world, such as Heaven, Earth, Thunder, Wind, the Seasons, and the spirits of the House.

Confucius (the Jesuit missionary version of Kung Fu Tzu) was a contemporary of Gotama, the founder of Buddhism. His teaching was social rather than religious and, with its stress upon virtue and propriety, in many ways resembles the political writings of Plato. Rulers and their ministers, Confucius claimed, should be chosen on the basis of their ability rather than their birth. He adored the ritual of religion, especially that concerned with ancestor worship, but he was very selective in what aspects of the traditional religion he accepted or rejected.

The Chinese emperors, whose rule ended in 1911, derived much of their authority from the teachings of Confucius. The republic that followed the empire tried to make Confucianism the official religion, but this met with so much opposition from Buddhists, Taoists, and even Confucians themselves that the idea was not pursued.

Taosim is usually associated with Lao Tzu, who was born in 604 B.C., and it is thus slightly older than Confucianism. It is based on the unity and harmony of the universe, having as its goal oneness with Tao, the Way. It was much modified as its intellectual content was adapted for the common people, and its emphasis on simplicity has made it a significant underpinning of all Chinese culture. Characterized by a strong mysticism, it is concerned with the search for immortality and the fighting of disease. Its influence is so strong that it will probably survive the communist revolution that is in so many ways ideologically opposed to it.

Buddhism in China, coming as it did from outside, had the effect of changing the perspective of Chinese religious tradition. Although with its goal of world salvation, it caused people to look beyond China, Buddhism had much in common with Taoism; Nirvana and Tao were complementary concepts. In addition, despite considerable initial conflict between Buddhists and Confucians, the idealism of Buddhism eventually had a great influence on Confucianism.

In modern-day communist China, the Cultural Revolution of Mao Tse-tung has shown hostility and even contempt for religious values. The traditional educational emphasis on Confucius and the Chinese classics has been reoriented toward Marx and Mao himself. By communist decree, parents brought up in the Confucian tradition are not to be honored, a paradox that many Chinese must find frustrating and contradictory. Yet, recognizing the power of simple agricultural Confucian belief, the communist leaders are trying to reconcile the old with the new; Sun Yat-Sen (the architect of Chinese revolution), in an attempt to restore some kind of cultural harmony, pronounced Confucius to be an exponent of democracy. Taoism and Buddhism have fared worse than Confucianism; the wealth and possessions (temples, land, and religious ornaments) of these faiths have been commandeered by the state, and their priests ordered to contribute to economic life. Taoism can resist this pressure because of its Chinese essence and may well flourish, but Buddhism, like the Orthodox church of Russia in a similar maelstrom thirty years earlier, may not possess the resilience to survive the attacks made upon it.

Until recently, Western businesses had little to do with China except in a highly formalized relationship. Sales of American or European products to China were usually negotiated through some Chinese government purchasing agency, and imports from China were virtually nonexistent. The relationship between Peking and Washington or London or Paris (or even Tokyo) was essentially diplomatic. Few Western managers had the chance to discover what barriers or bridges existed to hinder or foster trade, and thus little was known of the cultural problem, if such a problem existed at all. Recent developments would suggest, however, that this situation may be changing.

Japanese Religion

In Shintoism, the national religion of Japan, we can once more see the coming together of Confucius and Buddha. Their impression on the ancient Japanese religion, which contained little moral teaching, was profound, especially the impression of Buddhism, which became the state religion toward the end of the sixth century. Shintoism is essentially polytheistic, and its gods range from natural powers that command reverence or fear, such as heaven and earth, seas, mountains, and trees, to strange animals and even (until 1946) emperors.

Buddhism adapted the old Shinto gods to its own structure and regarded them as manifestations of the Buddha's own godliness. The situation remained like this until the eighteenth century, which saw a revival of pure Shintoism and a new nationalism of which emperor worship was a central element, as was also (more recently) the cult of the war dead. Toward the end of the nineteenth century, however, Buddhism revived and, along with Christianity, was granted autonomy, but Shinto remained the official state religion.

State Shinto thus became more of a national obligation than anything else, and it was because of this that Japan's defeat in World War II resulted in widespread disillusionment; hundreds of shrines were disestablished by the allies, and the teaching of Shinto in schools was forbidden. It is difficult to say what the future holds for Shintoism in Japan.

Part of the cause of this rapid turn of events was the incredible development of Japan as an industrial nation at about the time of the Russo-Japanese War. In a few short years, Japan achieved an industrial sophistication that it had taken the Western world a century and a half to reach. Shinto ideals were incorporated into this new society, and even today they are still visible in the family nature of Japanese corporations, with their emphasis on employee loyalty and strong company values.

Since World War II, Japan has once more achieved an economic miracle and in the process has made significant inroads into North American and European markets, at considerable cost to the domestic producers in both areas. It is, however, beginning to count the cost. The growth of consumerist movements and successive pollution scandals have "forced both big business and government to make significant changes in their attitudes and conduct toward the public and the environment." [5]

Occidental business enterprises have found in Japan an attractive trading partner, as evidenced by various manufacturing agreements, notably in the automotive and electronic fields. Japanese capitalism is the only example of a non-Western religious and cultural background producing an economy and an industrial capability that operates on principles similar to those of the West, but that still contains within itself an ethos peculiarly its own; and it has done this with a commitment and a vigor that is derived directly from its hereditary values. Perhaps such a phenomenon deserves a brief but closer look.

Japanese Business Society.   One of the most obvious characteristics of the Japanese is that they are essentially a society of groups. Isolated and immune from Western culture for so long, they still find it difficult to accept individualism; yet, despite this, they are the only truly industrialized Asian country. In one sense, Japan has changed rapidly; in another, it has resisted change, particularly the violent revolutions that have accompanied much of Western industrialization. Japanese corporations to this day, though operating on modern technological and management principles, cling firmly to the very strict and traditional feudalism of household family structure; groups of companies, as well as their internal divisional and departmental organization, bear witness to this historical experience. Shintoism has much to do with this attitude.

In comparison to the West, where industrial innovation was mostly on a small scale and where, consequently, entrepreneurial ventures resulted in a sharp distinction between capital and labor, Japan moved on a much larger and faster scale; learning rapidly from European and American experience, it imported Western technology wholesale and, as a result, had less need for invention and entrepreneurialism. The initiative of the Japanese government made it possible for successful industries to be offered to private concerns, and the trappings of a sophisticated industrial mechanism were thereby quickly created; financial and banking institutions, which in the West had prompted industrial development, were the product of Japan's new commercial awareness. Thus, modern Japanese debt-equity ratios seem unbelievably high to Western ears; 80:20 is about normal for them. Also, the level of personal savings (around 20 percent of disposable income) is staggering.

High personal savings in Japan can be attributed to five factors: (1) further education costs a great deal, and nine out of ten children pursue it; (2) everybody wants to build his own house, which is expensive; (3) there are few pension schemes, and so employees save for retirement; (4) medical care is not free, except where the larger companies provide for it; and (5) the Japanese have an acquired fear of natural disaster, a fear related to their long experience of earthquakes, typhoons, and wars.

Because stockholder equity is low and bank borrowing high, the most important objective of a Japanese company is growth and increased market share; higher profits are not necessarily desirable and could well be indicative of high risk. Banks are more interested in the interest on the loan than the performance of the firm (which, in essence, is true of banks everywhere, but more so in Japan where capital is more than usually bank-derived).

Any Japanese company believes that its primary purpose is to provide employment for its labor force; it therefore feels that its fundamental responsibility is to society. This attitude stems to no small degree from the fact that few dividends need to be paid; there are virtually no investors to whom any responsibility is due, and retained earnings are therefore readily available for reinvestment. The result is that the level of reinvestment has been about double that of Western industry (roughly 40 percent of the GNP). The situation is a direct consequence of the historical Japanese belief in group activity; all industry is linked inextricably to the Japanese group ethos, where industry, commerce, and government act together to serve a common purpose. Hence, major company groups represent more than 40 percent of all capital employed, each of them owning thirty to forty enterprises.

There is a remarkable commonality of purpose between Japanese business and government. The universities produce graduates for both, and both combine on major projects; the consensus is aided to no small degree by the cooperation that exists between the civil service (remarkably free from interference by politicians) and business itself. Yet Japanese politicians are not insensitive to the requirements of industrial progress; Japan's oil bill in 1974, much increased over previous years, was more than funded by a massive government-sponsored export drive, a testament to a system that many Western industrialists find difficult to comprehend. Such is the enigma and the miracle of this unusual race of people.

The Ethics of Socialism

Mention was made earlier of the distinction between capitalist and socialist revolution. It was also suggested that Marxism differs from other so-called heresies in that it demands of its supporters some social driving force closely akin to faith. Because Marxist socialism can thus be regarded as a kind of religion-substitute, and because trade between the West and the communist bloc, which is increasing steadily, involves cultural contrasts and problems of a nature different from, but with implications similar to, those encountered in the interface between Muslim and Christian, it is deserving of a place in this analysis. It is sometimes forgotten that a Muscovite is just as much a European as a Londoner, and that his religious heritage, like that of the Copt or the Calvinistic Methodist, stems from the Carpenter of Nazareth and the first Bishop of Rome.

The classical Marxist view of moral behavior can best be summarized in the words of Engels: "Men, consciously or unconsciously, derive their ethical ideas in the last resort from the practical relations on which their class position is based — from the economic relations in which they carry on production and exchange." [6] From this, it can be inferred that all moralities and their theoretical bases have been the direct result of the economic and social stage of development that the society had reached.

Until the modern revolutions of the proletariat, the social and economic systems of the civilized world had traditionally been characterized by a differentiated class structure. Therefore, states Marxist theory, all morality has been and is of necessity class morality. As long as there is a powerful and dominant ruling class, morality will be in the best interest of that class; but as soon as the proletariat gains sufficient strength to overthrow its opressors, morality will represent the spirit of that protest.

Thus, the socialist concept of a classless society is held to result in the perfect morality, since it serves all people alike.

In this way, Marxism produces a dramatically new approach to ethics; it changes fundamentally the ground rules for the discussion of ethics and moral behavior. The stance resembles the Marxist view of law, which is held to be an offense against the very idea of justice. Justice is regarded as being an unadulterated expression of the working class. Distilled to its essence, what the Marxists say (and this was one of the ideological cornerstones of the Revolution) is that if people desire a world in which everyone can exist in harmony, they can achieve it only if they strive and fight for a certain kind of social structure; furthermore, such a challenge becomes real only when the means of realizing it are available.

The obvious first argument against such a theory is the thesis of this book — that all ethical values are subjective and that the way in which we each perceive our ethical responsibility depends essentially on the many environmental and experiential influences to which we have been exposed over time. Therefore, it is unrealistic to prescribe a morality that by definition is common to all people.

The Marxist rebuttal to this argument is that the private conscience must be seen for what it really is — unconscious group allegiance to the cause of the proletariat. When members of the working class fully realize that they truly are workers and that their values are the values of their own class and no other, they then become a class-for-itself. Only then can they become a revolutionary force and commit themselves to a collective conscience that will resolve conflicting individual moralities into one morality in a classless society. Ethical decisions must therefore now be made on the basis of whether one's allegiance is to the oppressors or the oppressed, the exploiters or the exploited, since all people know what the issues are and cannot claim ignorance as an excuse for not facing their moral responsibility.

Closely allied to this doctrine of proletarian morality is the dogma that the end justifies the means. The "end" here is to increase the power of humanity over nature and to abolish the power of one person or class over another. It is not the first time that the argument has been used, but it is perhaps the most distressing example that can be found because the "means" in the Russian Revolution involved the massacre of thousands of victims, including the Czar and his family. The guillotining of French aristocrats after 1789 was based upon the same argument, but in that epoch, the thesis was never articulated philosophically, as it was by Marx, Engels, and Lenin.

The disturbing aspects of the belief in justification by ends center mostly in a basic attitude that finds little favor in the West. Logically, the two totally discrete premises that tyranny is bad and that murder is bad do not permit one to be ignored in the context of the other. Yet that is what the killing of Czar Nicholas amounted to; murder was condoned in the belief that it was justified because it resulted in the removal of an oppressor. The murderers did not, however, satisfactorily answer the question of whether the killing was *necessary*; the Czar's power had been taken from him, and he was therefore no longer the oppressor. The end in its turn needs to be justified.

Trotsky, answering the question of whether in the class struggle against capitalism, all means (lying, framing, betrayal, murder, etc.) are permissible, wrote:

> Permissible and obligatory are those and only those means, we answer, which unite the revolutionary proletariat, fill their hearts with irreconcilable hostility to oppression, teach them contempt for official morality and its democratic echoers, imbue them with consciousness of their own historic mission, raise their courage and spirit of self-sacrifice in the struggle. . . . Dialectical materialism does not know dualism between means and end. The end flows naturally from the historical movement. Organically the means are subordinated to the end. The immediate end becomes the means for a further end.[7]

This does not really answer the question. Hobbes and Spinoza, as will be seen in the next chapter, never answered it either, but they faced it without trying to hide behind self-delusion. Trotsky was uncompromisingly sympathetic with Irish, Russian, Polish, and Hindu terrorists in their struggle against "national and political oppression." Moral absolutes are futile, he claimed, even in the sharpest question — killing of human by human.

In the strange circumstances of post–World War II international relations, we have the spectacle of two superpowers blowing hot and cold in their dealings with each other: Berlin, Cuba, space cooperation, SALT, Afghanistan, and who knows what next? Neither side, it must be believed, wants a third war and a nuclear holocaust, but one has to wonder how much the ethics of capitalism or socialism enter into the fencing and feinting. The Third World watches the struggle with interest; famine, overpopulation, and lack of industrial resources stand in stark contrast to the economic strength of Russia, Europe, and the United States. It sees the Western ethic dogged by recession, and the East hiding economic problems behind state subsidies. Perhaps, in the end, the Third World will seek its salvation in dialectical materialism rather than democracy, but there will be hard questions, including ethical ones, to be answered in the process. The topic perhaps needs special consideration.

The Third World

It is difficult to imagine the feelings of those involved in political or commercial activities in the developing nations of the Third World as the modern international scenario unfolds. On the one hand, they have only comparatively recently acquired any form of world awareness. Their past has been the history of cultures dominated by the West, of religions subordinated to imperial necessity, of natural resources exploited and turned to the advantage of colonial powers, of an ignorance of their political strength and an awe of the economic and technological influence and experience of the industrial nations.

On the other hand, the nations of the Third World have seen major upheavals in the alignment of two diametrically opposed political and economic systems: The colonial powers, including the United States as the newest member of the club, have since World War II shown a willingness to allow their former dependencies the opportunity of governing their own futures and fortunes; at the same time, a new kind of colonialism, born of the abandonment of grand imperial strategy by Britain, France, Germany, Holland, and Belgium and the infiltration of the socialist ethic discussed in the previous section, has begun to beguile developing nations with the promise of economic and military support in this readjustment of international power. Cuba, the Middle East, Korea, Vietnam, and a host of African nations bear witness to this polarization of political and economic positions.

A culturally strong, but industrially weak history has been both the bane and the blessing of such societies. When technology mattered little, Islam overran Spain, and Christianity, in the form of the Holy Roman Empire, colonized South America. Japan, however, threatened by Russia, pulled itself up by the bootstraps and astonished the world by rapidly turning into an industrial nation. The rest did not because they had neither the innate inventiveness nor the experience of national identity that is the peculiar Japanese experience. Consequently, the "developing" nations remained underdeveloped until a bigger and broader opportunity — a place in the economic power game — presented itself.

Now the developing nations see themselves at the crossroads of choice. The oil-hungry Western nations are torn between the need to devote all their energies to the improvement of their own economies and the call for help from the underdeveloped countries (Mrs. Thatcher, for the United Kingdom, in July 1980 successfully blocked discussion about the economic world imbalance on the grounds that inflation in the industrialized world was a bigger problem). The communist bloc offers the Third World an alluring alternative.

CONCLUSION

It has been shown that within our world society, there exist different types of relationships between cultures, some of them bringing us closer together, others forcing us further apart. The ethics of contrasting religious backgrounds and political ideologies, combined with the growth in technology and the evolution of modern business corporations, have brought the world community to the threshold of a decision that experience suggests will be the most significant decision in all history: Which direction must we take, as we move toward the end of the twentieth century, if we are to have a world in which people can not only live together in peaceful coexistence, but can also redress the economic imbalance of today?

Traditionally, we have been taught that the future can be foreseen only as a continuation of the present and the past; yet we forget that change, which is the factor that identifies the transition from one age to the next, is rapidly accelerating. This makes it less easy to predict where the future lies. There have been more dramatic changes in political, social, economic, and technological activity in the last fifty years than in the whole of previous history; we are no longer surprised by change. There is thus a danger that unless we make calculated decisions about the future, we may well be overtaken by events.

Several factors need to be considered in this decision-making process. The first is the problem of growth brought about by change. The resources of the world are limited, as is the destruction that those resources can bear, the pollution that the world can tolerate, and the productivity that industrial human beings can achieve. Seen in the light of an explosive growth in the world's population, which, if it continues, will produce 6 billion people by the turn of the century, the seriousness of the situation becomes evident.

The second factor is the complex relationship between international political rivalry, universal inflation, and the unequal distribution of wealth and resources among nations. The disillusionment produced by the Vietnam War, the shock of Watergate, and the economic effects of the oil crisis have all in their different ways brought home to people the need for a different kind of thinking about the future. The most important objective is to achieve a world community in which differences of culture and political systems can still exist, but in which there is a strong consciousness of the interdependence of world society.

The third factor, which compounds the first two, is the complacency of human beings themselves. It can be seen at all levels and in all walks of life. Governments think in terms of national self-interest, business communities remain committed to corporate growth and ever-increasing profits, economists worship the GNP, and society at large, shocked and bewildered by the ravages of inflation and shrinking purchasing power, is not aware that to improve a nation's health calls for effort and sacrifice from each of its citizens. Yet it is the people who elect governments, it is people who manage corporations, and it is people, not land masses, who have to learn to live together.

The central problem is that virtually no nation is self-sufficient, except at a very basic level. Exchanges of trade are necessary if we are to enjoy the comforts of life or indeed anything beyond mere subsistence. This reliance on others has given people a convenient target; accusing fingers are pointed at other countries — at the oil sheikhs of the Middle East, the cheap labor of Japan, and the coffee exporters of South America. People somehow resent the fact that world resources are not equally distributed, but in the industrialized nations, they fail to realize that technology and productive ability are the greatest resource of all. Most Arabs and coffee workers are far less affluent than the average American, British, or French factory worker. It is not the geographical size of a country that enables it to support itself, as the differences between small European nations and India will bear out, but the sophistication of its technological base.

The equitable harnessing of the world's resources is a pressing priority. At the moment, according to Jean Mayer, a leading nutritionist, the food consumed by 210 million Americans could feed 1.5 billion Chinese. Other calculations demonstrate the huge contrast in the energy required to produce one calorie of food in different parts of the world. In industrialized economies, it takes between five and ten calories of energy; in underdeveloped countries, it takes about .04 calories. It would appear that energy wastage compounds famine.

Only by international cooperation can the remedy for this economic imbalance be found, but before such cooperation is possible, people from all nations and all cultures are going to have to realize that the future problems of their countries will have an international, not a domestic, root. Once the cause of the disease is properly diagnosed, the treatment can begin. The morality of the twenty-first century will be based on learning how to live with others. Strong leadership, supported by responsible business management, will be the prerequisites for the realization of this morality. Without them, the world may find that the opportunity has passed, never to return.

NOTES

1. William Hazlitt, *On Living to One's Self.*

2. Richard Eells and Clive Walton, *Conceptual Foundations of Business,* 3rd ed. (Homewood, Ill.: Richard D. Irwin, 1974), p. 44.

3. "In Europe, the Sullen Eighties?" *Wall Street Journal,* March 11, 1980, p. 6.

4. G. Parrinder, *Introduction to Asian Religions* (New York: Oxford University Press, 1957), p. 37.

5. S. Prakash Sethi, "Why Japanese Business Is Losing Its Halo," *Business and Society Review* (Winter 1974–1975).

6. Friedrich Engels, *Anti-Dühring* (London: Lawrence & Wishart, 1975, for Progress Publishers, Moscow), p. 114.

7. Leon Trotsky, "Their Morals and Ours," an essay written in Mexico in 1938 (Menit, 1969).

3 PHILOSOPHICAL ANTECEDENTS TO MODERN THOUGHT

Two things fill my mind with ever-increasing wonder and awe, the more often and the more intensely the reflection dwells on them: the starry heavens above me and the moral law within me.

— Immanuel Kant[1]

THE FOUR PERSPECTIVES OF THE INDIVIDUAL

Self, state, law, and church offer four different perspectives of the individual. In each of these lights, the individual is a different type of being.

Behavioral scientists talk much about "self" and people's perceptions of their own personalities, and it is true that we tend to think of ourselves more in terms of our own "self-concepts" than as we believe others see us. This self-view is, of course, modified by what others tell us about ourselves, but the modification is the result of another person's *individual* perception, the view of someone whom we know and who knows us; it is a personal thing based on the relationship that exists between individuals, the desire to be accepted by friends and peers in our daily encounters. Much of modern philosophy, from Descartes to the present, is about perception and the evidence of our own senses, about the relationship between our own minds and the people and things around us, about the verification of the world in which we live. It is difficult for us to escape from ourselves because our senses and our brains are our only link with things outside us, a kind of telephone switchboard through which all messages come.

Self-orientation is manifested not only in our perception of physical things; our "cognitive map" (to borrow a psychological term) also includes our ideas and beliefs about intangible concepts. And just as we sometimes find it difficult to describe physical things without stating the absurd, such as saying that we have seen a train growing smaller, we can entertain the concepts of justice, or goodness, or beauty without necessarily being able to define them articulately. The basis of our understanding of such concepts is that amalgam of philosophical, religious, political, and social experience built up through the centuries. Interestingly, however, the legacy has not come to each of us in the same form; variations of upbringing, education, and environment have meant that we all differ, sometimes only infinitesimally, from each other in our perception of the ethical or moral order of things. Sometimes the differences are not sufficiently strong to represent a problem in our dealings with others, which is why it is possible for groups of people to subscribe to a common cause, such as a political party or a religious denomination. At other times, however, the problems caused by the conflict between two sets of ethical criteria can be traumatic. In any event, our ethical values tend to change only slowly and as a result of much experience.

All this is at a very personal level. Yet the individual's self-perceived identity is lost when he is viewed impersonally from elsewhere. To the state he is a citizen, one of millions; he is required to pay his taxes if he is employed, and he receives a certain amount of state assistance if he is not. If he leaves the country, he needs a passport; if he is injured in a road accident, he is taken to a hospital; if he travels by public transport, he pays a fare; if he casts a vote, it is counted along with thousands of others. In short, unless he achieves fame as a movie star or notoriety as a murderer, unless for some reason he becomes the sort of person whose face or name is featured regularly in the media, he is unknown except for his acquaintance with a relatively small circle of people.

While governments may claim that they have the welfare of their citizens at heart, this can be only a very general concern. Because governments necessarily have to consider either the population as a whole or its larger subgroups, they cannot be concerned with individuals. To a government, the more people there are of a certain group type, the easier it is for the system to deal with them; by and large, deviations from the average are not welcome to bureaucracy.

Thus, the immediate contrast between the individual as seen by himself and as seen by the state is one of extremes, from entirely personal to entirely impersonal. He is noticed by the state only if he fails to observe his responsibilities, such as paying his taxes, fulfilling obligatory military service, or sending his children to school. In principle, he has a say in the decision about who shall run the state, but if too few of his fellow citizens vote the way he does, his voice is unheard. In the sense that he has the right to vote, he is a "political animal," though not in the way that Aristotle meant.[2] Unlike his moral responsibilities, his responsibilities to the state, though real and socially congruent, are frequently externally imposed; moreover, they are not always welcome.

Whether the executive and legislature are inseparable, as in the United Kingdom and Canada, or discrete, as in the United States, the effects upon the individual are similar. The law exists primarily for the protection of the individual, but it protects only through the deterrent it represents to, and the punishment it inflicts on, those who might be disposed to contravene it or have actually broken it. The law is thus a safeguard against the breakdown of social order and the disruption of the smooth operation of the state. Citizens who observe the law go unnoticed; those who break it are brought to account.

The law is not particularly interested in one's morals unless they fail to satisfy the legal code. If a person believes it is not immoral to kill and acts on that belief, the law will punish him. In the context of business, there are those who say that any activity is permissible provided that it does not break the law; there are others who disagree, and this, as we saw in Chapter 1, is largely what the debate on social responsibility is all about. The law thus overlaps the individual's own cognitive framework of behavior, even though it is not basically concerned with it. Much of such individual frameworks may well derive extensively from the Christian ethic, or "commonsense" morality, as do many of the fundamental laws of the land. However, these frameworks of belief are held not so much because certain kinds of behavior are legally wrong as because they are morally offensive.

In this context, it is worth noting that some of the greatest people in history have been those who have contributed to the development of moral thought, despite the fact that in many cases they were reviled during their lifetimes by their own societies. It is through such people that slavery was abolished and the exploitation of child labor deplored. Today, it is perhaps less easy for such figures to stamp their imprint on society, since the growth of state (and thus legal) power tends to leave such innovation to the government.

The fourth perspective of the individual is that of the church. (The term *church* here is not intended to describe any particular faith or denomination, such as the Christian or Jewish religions or the Roman Catholic, Anglican, or Baptist connections; rather, it is used to refer to that influence on man's behavioral framework which uses faith and unquestioning acceptance as its cornerstone.) The loyalty of creed has, throughout the ages, gradually become a stronger stimulus to the unification of individual belief, though since the end of World War II, it appears to have lost much of its strength. We still see evidence of political-religious strife: in Northern Ireland between Catholic and Protestant, and in the Middle East between Jew and Muslim. These different factions, though identified largely with traditional religious affiliations, are really no longer fighting on the basis of the rights or wrongs of the tenets of their faiths, but on the political and economic circumstances resulting from their historical ideological incompatibility. It is remarkable how often God is apparently supporting both sides at the same time, an astonishing testament to the influence of religious group membership.

The teaching of the church, in particular the love of one's neighbor preached by both Christianity and Buddhism and used on occasion as the justification for warfare and massacre, has, perhaps unintentionally, forced people to regard their fellow humans as either friends or enemies; toward the former we have feelings of association, toward the latter feelings of competition. These feelings can be manifested in different ways and at different levels, and the distinction between friend and foe is constantly changing. Two business competitors can unite through a merger or a takeover and attack a third; the same shift can take place on a personal plane. As Bertrand Russell has commented, "In times of safety we can afford to hate our neighbour, but in times of danger we must love him. People do not, at most times, love those whom they find sitting next to them in a bus, but during the blitz they did."[3]

Ideally, if God is father of us all, all are brothers. Yet this very credo has been distorted to mean that those who believe in God are "brothers in God" and that those who do not believe in God are out of bounds and will go to Hell. Thus, the friend-and-enemy distinction is created. "Men will wrangle for religion; write for it; fight for it; anything but — live for it."[4]

The important characteristic of the responsibility of the individual as seen through the eyes of the church, as opposed, for example, to the perspective of the law, is that moral behavior based on religious belief is not *primarily* socially motivated; rather, it is an investment in the life hereafter. The Sermon on the Mount is heavily oriented toward salvation: "Theirs is the Kingdom of heaven. . . . they shall inherit the earth. . . . they shall see God. . . . great is your reward in heaven."[5] In other words, what we do now is but a preparation for the Day of Judgment. The statute book, on the other hand, is concerned with a different kind of judge and a different kind of sentence; to some, the prospect of six months in prison is a greater deterrent than eternal damnation.

Furthermore, people can choose their religious beliefs; they can even choose to discard them all. It has been said that the Thirty-nine Articles of the Anglican church allow one to believe more or less anything one likes. In the words of George Bernard Shaw, "There is only one religion though there are a hundred versions of it." [6] We thus have considerable latitude in defining the boundaries of our moral territory. In contrast, though Bumble might protest that "the law is a ass — a idiot," [7] the law has a tendency to concentrate our minds on peaceful behavior.

One is therefore at once the person one perceives oneself to be and a different person when viewed through different eyes. It may be possible to classify an individual as a group member, as perceived by state, law, or church, but the individual remains essentially a mind isolated, doing what he does because he feels it is right to do it. The influences on his behavior, on his ethical code or moral framework, are absorbed gradually but significantly into a system that, consistently or inconsistently (it matters little which), governs his decisions about what course of action he should take in different situations. The result is a person who is not quite like any other; to condemn him because his standards are not the same as those of others is to declare him guilty before he is proved innocent. He deserves a hearing before such a verdict.

We now move to an examination of the historical sources of influence on the individual's social and ethical values. As will be seen, it is a complex and interesting story, but two points need to be established before embarking on the analysis. First, in philosophical terms, although much attention has been devoted by many learned scholars through the ages to the study of morals, surprisingly few advances have been made for the simple reason that, as we have seen, individuals are discrete and separate storehouses of ethical criteria. Second, the developments that have taken place have been developments in the treatment and alleviation of social problems rather than steps forward in the basic theories of right and wrong.

PRE-CHRISTIAN THOUGHT

The Classical School

Throughout the development of social and moral thought, there have been those thinkers who have favored the tightening of social bonds and those who have wanted to loosen them. The former have usually held that "good" consists not of happiness, but of something nobler and more self-sacrificing; the latter, taking a more liberal view, have favored science, utilitarianism, and reason in an attempt to promote the social "good." The contrast, still to some degree evident, certainly existed among the early Greeks.

When discussing the philosophical contribution of classical Greece, we have to take care to distinguish, if we can, between the views of those individuals who expressed their views in writing and the commonly observed morality of the day. While Greek philosophers down to Aristotle were dominated by religious and loyal devotion to the city-state, and while their ethical thought was consonant with the political life of the citizen, it is questionable whether their actual moral teachings had any significant effect on the average Athenian merchant or soldier. The Greeks were, and always have been, strongly politically oriented (it is said that if you listen to two Greeks discussing politics you will hear three political opinions), and the *social* cohesion produced by their city membership was undoubtedly of more concern to them than the ethical philosophizing of the scholars.

Although it is customary to associate Greek philosophical thought primarily with the teachings of Plato (c. 427–348 B.C.) and Aristotle (384–322 B.C.), they were but two in a long line of scholars. They themselves owed much to the influence of the so-called pre-Socratic philosophers, notably Pythagoras, Heraclitus, and Parmenides (all of the sixth century B.C.), each of whom deserves some mention in this historical overview, not least because some of the principles they established in other fields (notably mathematics) still hold good today.

Pythagoras believed in the immortality of the soul and reincarnation; he supported the equality of the sexes and the common ownership of property. In all this, he preempted both Christianity and communism. He was an intellectual mystic, though more mystical than rational, "putting all value in the unseen unity of God, and condemning the physical world as false and illusive, a turbid medium in which the rays of heavenly light are broken and obscured in mist and darkness."[8] His ethic, which praised the contemplative life, was based on the Greek system of aristocracy and slavery; it differs from more practical modern attitudes, which were inspired by the rise of industrialism.

Heraclitus, probably slightly later than Pythagoras, possessed a vigorous contempt for his fellow human beings, believing that only force would compel them to act for their own good. A strong advocate of war, he was ascetically aloof, which prompted Russell to compare him with Neitzsche;[9] he was certainly very hostile to the religions of his day.

Whereas Heraclitus is perhaps best known for his claim that everything is always changing ("in a state of flux"), his successor Parmenides believed that nothing changes. Parmenides is said to have had a great influence on Plato's Socrates, and although he made no contribution to the development of ethical thought, he serves as a useful link between the pre-Socratics and the two great Athenians in that he was responsible for inventing arguments based on metaphysics, which have been common to most philosophical thought ever since.

Plato is a less than satisfactory ethical guide since many of the questions he raised, particularly in his major work, the *Republic,* went unanswered. Because their political community was so small and intimate, the Greeks, as has already been suggested, made less of a distinction than we do between morals and politics. In the Greek view, the law of the city-state was the basis of all moral standards, and the individual was equated with the citizen. This is not to say that the Greeks were not strongly individualistic in practice, but they did link morals and politics very closely. The *Republic* is therefore as much about morals as about politics in our narrower sense, and since Plato's ideal state was a serious suggestion that he one day hoped to see established in practice, we have to attempt to understand his moral teaching.

Because of this close link between morals and politics, Plato's discussion of the concept of justice rapidly changes to an inquiry into the basis of social and moral obligation, and thence, more simply still, to the question, "Is there a standard of 'good' and 'bad,' except whatever we each mean by these words?" Plato's devil's advocate, Thrasymachus, maintains that enlightened self-interest is the answer: If you like something, it is good for you; if you do not, it is bad for you; in the event of disagreement, the decision can be resolved only by authority, power, and force. Thrasymachus's stance comes remarkably close to the theme of this book, but for Plato the question did not really exist; he was convinced that there is something called "the Good," which does not change with the individual's own opinion of it, and that the "goodness" of his ideal state could be proved.

Plato's theory of "ideas" (or ideals) is fundamental to his doctrine, and it has had a profound effect that is recognizable even in business values today. Just as every table is a version of the ideal table and can be recognized as a table because of the existence of such an ideal, so a just or good act is identifiable because of the existence of the ideas of "justice" or "goodness." This theory is the first example of the concept of universals in philosophy, and as such, it is an important development, but unfortunately Plato did not realize the real difference between universals and particulars (i.e., "man" and "George Washington"); as Russell has pointed out, Plato's "ideas" are really just other particulars, ethically and aesthetically superior to the ordinary kind.[10]

Socrates, the central figure of the Platonic dialogues, is something of an enigma. On the one hand, he is devoted to the pursuit of what he believes to be the truth and is totally indifferent to material things; on the other, he is frequently notoriously unscientific in his approach, particularly as he appears to try to explain the nature of things in a way that fits his own standards rather than vice versa. How much he reflects Plato's own personal attitudes is a question that has taxed commentators throughout the centuries, but it is interesting that one of the philosophically least important (though historically most influential) of the Platonic dialogues, the *Timaeus,* does not include Socrates in its list of characters.

The *Timaeus* is the story of the Creation. It differs from the Judeo-Christian version in that it describes God as bringing order out of chaos rather than making a universe out of nothing. Although the work is in many respects utterly fantastic, it does have a basic aesthetic appeal in that it postulates a supreme being who is more concerned about an ordered arrangement of things than about a spectacular manufacturing achievement. In this respect, the dialogue commanded a great deal of attention and support among the adherents of Neoplatonism in the days of Plotinus, and it was the only Platonic work known in western Europe during the Middle Ages. Also, perhaps unknowingly, modern management philosophy owes much to the argument expounded in the work.

In comparison with Plato, the uncompromising idealist, Aristotle is essentially much more down to earth. His influence is still felt; indeed, much of the quality and strength of British nineteenth-century public school education can be traced to the importance attached to the Aristotelian tradition. Far more likable than Plato, less intolerant and bigoted, more realistic and relevant to everyday life, Aristotle, like Shakespeare's Caesar, bestrides philosophical thought like a colossus, while lesser thinkers "walk under his huge legs, and peep about."[11]

Aristotle's moral philosophy, unlike Plato's, is fairly representative of the attitudes of educated persons of his day. It is, in a sense, the morality of everyday life. Good is happiness, and virtue exists in two forms, intellectual and moral; intellectual virtues result from teaching, moral virtues from habit. Every virtue is a mean between two extremes, the extremes being vices. This idea of the "golden mean" works well enough in most cases (courage is the mean between cowardice and rashness, modesty between bashfulness and shamelessness), but unfortunately it cannot satisfactorily be applied to truthfulness. As far as justice is concerned, Aristotle's view differs from the modern one. According to Aristotle, justice involves not equality, but right proportion, which is only sometimes equality.[12]

Also, Aristotle's definition of the good individual does not match the Christian ideal. The good individual should be properly proud and be aware of his own merits; he should not be reluctant to despise those who deserve to be despised. Here, again, the mean is applied, for pride (or magnanimity — *pride* in the original Greek did not have the sinful Christian connotation) falls between vanity and humility, and Aristotle considered it the crown of all the virtues.

Aristotle's view further differs from the Christian view in that it regards as satisfactory a community that by its nature confines the best things to a few (the virtues of magnanimous men depend on a high social position) and the second-best things to the majority. This view stems from the Greek subordination of ethics to politics, and Greek politics could never countenance a situation in which virtue is as possible for the subordinate as for the master, as it is in the Christian view. Yet, in many ways, this Aristotelian stance is not all that far away from our modern picture of the business enterprise; company presidents are not expected to be quite the same as Aristotle's magnanimous individual, but they are expected to be rather different from the majority of their employees and to possess abilities, privileges, and merits in keeping with their position. Aristotle would have defined such merits as "ethical," meaning "appropriate to the situation." One would suspect that Ayn Rand is a fan of Aristotle.

In Aristotle's view, virtue is the means of achieving happiness, which is the end and the good. Christian morality, on the other hand, regards virtue as good in itself, to be valued for its own sake and not for its effects. Aristotle believed that the important requirement of behavioral philosophy is that it define the good; he also believed that human virtues are those activities that produce that good. Perhaps there is some kind of lesson here for modern industry: If a chief executive is to be ethically responsible, he has to decide first what is to be achieved by such conduct. Can virtue for virtue's sake really be satisfactorily applied to management? For Aristotle, virtue for virtue's sake was an incomprehensible concept.

The decline of the Athenian city-state, with its own very special version of "democracy," had significant effects on philosophical thought. The Hellenistic age, dominated first by the Macedonian empire of Alexander and then by the Roman republic, produced the Cynics and Skeptics (the former seeking virtue and moral freedom and spurning worldly goods, the latter adding moral doubt to doubt about the evidence of the senses) and later the Epicureans and Stoics. The overall trend was away from the political-social focus of Plato and Aristotle toward questions of individual morality.

Both the Epicureans and Stoics have been somewhat misrepresented in popular modern interpretation. Although Epicurus (341–270 B.C.), whose philosphy was illuminated largely by the Roman poet Lucretius two hundred years later, maintained that pleasure was the good, he devoted his life and his teaching to the search for tranquillity. He was not an out-and-out hedonist; rather, he felt that the truest pleasure is the absence of pain. Justice, for instance, consists of acting in such a way that other men feel no resentment, a concept not unlike Rousseau's social contract. Unlike Rousseau, however, Epicurus advised men to avoid public life because power increases envy and hatred; the wisest course is to live unnoticed and thus to have no enemies. It is an attractive idea, and one that is particularly appealing at times of increasing social stress and bureaucratic pressure. Epicurus regarded religion as undesirable since it encourages the fear of death; thus, it does nothing to reduce pain.

Zeno, the founder of Stoicism, believed that everything is determined by natural laws. Virtue is the only good; health, material possessions, and happiness are unimportant. Virtue is the result of an individual will that is in harmony with nature, which is the overriding system ordained by the supreme power — the Lawgiver or God. Whatever the uncomfortable vicissitudes of life, people can remain virtuous; they always have perfect freedom providing they avoid worldly things. A philosophy that advocates a virtuous life without prospect of achievement or reward is depressingly bleak, and it is surprising that Stoicism should have prevailed until the days of Marcus Aurelius. Zeno was born some five hundred years earlier.

The early Roman Empire was a marvel of social cohesion and military organization. Under its rule, a single civilization evolved under a single government. It produced a systematic legal code that still has an influence today, and its language helped to shape that of almost every modern Western country. Nevertheless, it was philosophically barren; what philosophy existed was borrowed from the Greeks, while the Romans themselves preferred to channel their energies into the more pragmatic skills of architecture and engineering.

In the third century after Christ, however, when the Roman Empire was experiencing one of the most disastrous periods of its history, there emerged one figure who has been described as the last of the great philosophers of ancient history: Plotinus, who founded the school of Neoplatonism.

At this time, Christianity was widespread, although it had not yet been officially adopted as the Imperial religion. Plotinus, like the Christians, turned to the eternal world of truth and goodness and away from the misery and destruction around him. In this, he was reviving the Platonic world of ideas, and since such a philosophy had much in common with the Christian theology of his day, he is frequently credited with having done much to mold the later development of religious thought. St. Augustine spoke of Plato's system as "the most pure and bright in all philosophy" and described Plotinus as a man in whom "Plato lived again." Had Plotinus lived a little later, St. Augustine wrote, he would have "changed a few words and phrases and become Christian." He was certainly a link between classical philosophy and the Christian world.

Judaic Law

Apart from Greek philosophy, notably that of Plato and the Neoplatonists, a second major influence upon Christian thought has been that of Judaism, especially in its moral and historical traditions. Russell has identified the most important Jewish elements in Christianity as follows:

1. Sacred history from the Creation to a future consummation;
2. The selection of a group specially favored by God (for the Jews, the Chosen People; for Christians, the elect);
3. A new conception of righteousness (i.e., practical philanthropy);
4. The Law (the Christians having retained the Decalogue);
5. The Messiah (to the Hebrews, a future champion; to the Christians, the historical Jesus Christ dying and rising again as their savior and redeemer);
6. The Kingdom of Heaven, the Other World in the future, when the virtuous enjoy everlasting bliss and the wicked suffer everlasting torment (a "revenge psychology" intelligible to all and sundry).[13]

The Old Testament is part history (though exactly how much of it is legendary we cannot be certain) and part prophecy. The history is that of the Jewish people, their persectuion and their heroism; from it comes the idea that all other religions are wicked, especially idolatry. The prophecy looked forward to the destruction of the Gentiles under the leadership of the Messiah.

Jews thought much about sin, as well they might, bearing in mind the strictures of the Law and their jealous God, but they rarely thought of themselves as sinners; the Christian concept of humility was generally not practiced. Nonetheless, it was among Jews that early Christians found their first converts. However, as orthodox Judaism became narrower, and as Christianity in the second century became more formal, relations between the two became more distant and even hostile; anti-Semitism in its worst forms has been more prevalent in Christian societies than elsewhere, and it is only in recent times that it has begun to be regarded as undesirable.

It is impossible to analyze the influence of the Christian ethic on modern moral attitudes without acknowledging its significant Jewish content, even though today Judaism and Christianity appear to be wholly separate creeds. Yet apart from certain requirements of religious belief, such as the divinity of Christ, or certain behavioral impositions, such as circumcision or abstinence from pork, the average modern Jew and Christian have very similar moral codes. It is important to remember that in most Western societies these are the only two religions; all other influences are the result of social and philosophical thought.

THE CHRISTIAN ETHIC

Without doubt, Christianity has made the single most important contribution to modern ethical thought and behavior. Yet one may with justification ask whether if Christ (even the purely historical figure) had not existed, the particular characteristics of the Christian ethic would have developed in any case; for Christianity is in many ways a "common-sense" code, and while it is sometimes regarded as the cause of Western moral standards, it is also often viewed as their result. Debate upon such hypothetical speculation has been extensive and to a large degree fruitless. Within the terms of the present discussion, we have to examine the influence that Christian thought has had on our society and the extent to which it has added new dimensions to earlier philosophical attitudes.

One of the most significant features of the very early Christian period, as well as the centuries we somewhat quaintly label the Middle Ages, was the tremendous power of the Christian church, which brought philosophy, politics, and social thought much closer together than they had been before, and in the process, the church acquired prodigious wealth and influence. Until the later Middle Ages, almost all intellectual thought stemmed from churchmen, and their philosophical outlook, particularly politically, reflected the interests of the church. While the Christian ethic was to some extent modified to suit the temporal structure of the Roman

Empire, there is no doubting its rapid and overwhelming effect on the pagan Roman world, especially after the conversion of the emperor Constantine.

As we saw in our reference to Neoplatonism, the hope of a better life hereafter that Christianity offered to people troubled by an unhappy world was the factor that ensured its speedy acceptance. The passport to this eternal bliss was a life of virtue and goodness; this world had nothing else of value to offer. The contrast with earlier Greek appreciation and enjoyment of the beauties and pleasures of the physical world is marked, and although the Christian preoccupation with life after death is less intense in the twentieth century than it was in the fifth, it still lingers in some of the more austere and puritanical sectors of the modern church in the form of strict sanctions against worldly pleasures.

Both the power of the church and its emphasis on the Kingdom of Heaven produced yet another example of that ethical duality discussed in the previous chapters. Indeed, the injunction to "render unto Caesar the things that are Caesar's, and unto God the things that are God's"[14] could be said to encapsulate the particularly Christian distinction between church and state, a distinction that neither existed in earlier pagan philosophy nor appears in much twentieth-century political theory.

The Christian religion, in recent years much modified in its dogmatic detail, can broadly be described as a belief in an omnipotent being who was so concerned about the errors of humankind that he sent his "son," parthenogenically born of human parents, to die and rise again for the sins of the world and to offer eternal life in heaven to all those who believe in God, love their neighbors, and generally live virtuously. It is partly a creed of comfort, reassurance, and reinforcement through reward, partly a disincentive against misbehavior. It allows significant latitude of interpretation, as indicated by the many sects throughout the world; the church is now more motherly than militant, more discussive than dogmatic, more therapeutic than theological. People have killed and pillaged in its name, and people have martyred themselves rather than deny their faith in it.

Gibbon offers five causes for the rapid growth of Christianity: inflexibility and intolerance on the part of its first adherents, which are more exclusive and threatening traits than those found in most other religions; the doctrine of a future life; miracles (though Gibbon does not explain why Christian miracles should be any more credible than those of Greco-Roman mythology); a pure and austere morality (for which there is much evidence in pagan literature); and "the union and discipline of the Christian republic, which gradually formed an independent and increasing

State in the heart of the Roman empire."[15] Unfortunately, however, political acceptance and subsequent power brought about a change in the focus of early Christian enthusiasm. No longer was its main task to convert and evangelize, but rather to punish the "heretics" whom the new Christian establishment was not slow to discover and whose execution provided a convenient outlet for religious fervor.

Between the adoption of Christianity as the official religion of Rome and the invasion by the barbarians, one man by his writings confirmed the new relationship between church and state. St. Augustine (345–430 A.D.), in his *City of God*, made it clear that the state could only be part of God's order of things by deferring to the church on all religious matters, a rationalization necessary in Imperial Christendom and unquestioningly accepted until the Reformation.

MEDIEVAL SCHOLASTICISM

In the twelfth century, a new intellectual movement began. It was concerned with orthodox beliefs and a philosophical shift from Plato to Aristotle, largely as a result of the two philosophers' disagreement on the question of universals. The Scholastics tended more toward dialectical reasoning than traditional Christian mysticism, especially on topics upon which church dogma made speculation safe.

The greatest figures in the movement appear in the thirteenth century, and the greatest of them all was undoubtedly Thomas Aquinas (1225–1274). In his two major works, the *Summa Theologica* and the *Summa contra Gentiles*, Aquinas set out to prove the truth of the Christian faith by adapting the philosophy of Aristotle for the purpose. In this, he displayed much originality and organization, for which his works are justly renowned, but it cannot be said that he displayed the same spirit of philosophical inquiry as Aristotle himself; one senses that instead of employing philosophical arguments to seek out Christian truth, he already knows the truth and uses rational Aristotelianism to support it when convenient to do so. If no such support is available, then there is always divine revelation to fall back on.

Other important figures in the Scholastic movement were Roger Bacon, Duns Scotus, and William of Occam. The last, a Franciscan who died in 1349, followed Aquinas closely in his adherence to Aristotle, but whereas Aquinas adopted a largely theological outlook, Occam was much more of a philosopher and recognized, where Aquinas did not, the difference between arguments based on rationality and those based on faith.

He managed a nice compromise between the attitudes of Augustine and the new Scholasticism.

By the fourteenth century, the authority of the Papacy was becoming diminished, a phenomenon by no means unconnected with the work and writings of an English Schoolman, John Wycliffe. A secular priest, he tended toward the philosophy of Plato rather than that of Aristotle. Throughout his life, he became increasingly less orthodox in his religious attitudes, beginning with attacks on the temporal power and wealth of the Papacy and ending by calling the pope Antichrist, translating the Bible into English, and finally denying transubstantiation as blasphemous. To Wycliffe must go much of the credit for releasing religious belief from its choking dogma and introducing a new moral liberalism into the modern world.

MACHIAVELLI AND MISUNDERSTANDING

The Renaissance substituted the authority of the ancients for that of the church and in so doing encouraged the development of humanism. In the field of political philosophy, it produced one preeminent figure. Niccolò Machiavelli.

No philosopher has been more reviled and at the same time more misunderstood than Machiavelli. He is popularly regarded as the Devil Incarnate, since his pragmatic, empirical concern is for the proper means to ends, irrespective of whether the ends are good or bad. (In this, he stands in stark contrast to Marx.) *The Prince,* written as a political handbook for Lorenzo de' Medici, gives us only partial understanding of the author; it is necessary to include the *Discourses* in any appreciation of his doctrine.

Machiavelli, perhaps more than any other philosopher, has a direct relevance to modern management. Indeed, one commentator has gone so far as to identify him as the first management scientist, since "the great modern corporations are so similar to independent or semi-independent states of the past that they can only be fully understood in terms of political and constitutional history, and management can only be properly studied as a branch of government." [16] It is certainly true that if Machiavelli's political advice is translated into business terms, the behavior of today's firms is easily recognizable.

Machiavelli's greatest sin, in the eyes of his critics, is that he was not afraid to discuss political dishonesty and human error as a fact. In this, he was merely reflecting the values of fifteenth-century Italian city-states, all of which were riddled by corruption; if it comes to that, modern politics are not entirely free from blame, with the memory of successive coups d'état so recent and the specter of Watergate still stalking the corridors of American power.

Apart from his political theory, Machiavelli's ethical outlook is interesting. He rates eminent men on a scale of excellence; founders of religions are the best, then founders of monarchies or republics, then literary men. Destroyers of religions, subverters of kingdoms and republics, and enemies of virtue or literature are bad. Significantly, he thinks religion should be prominent in the state, not necessarily because it represents the truth, but because it helps to bind society together. He is very strongly critical of the misconduct of the church of his day and of the temporal power of the popes.

Despite his comments about the ethical hierarchy, Machiavelli is very willing to let his model ruler ignore conventional morality, since if he is always good, he will fail. He should only keep faith when it pays to do so, but should not let it be seen that he is faithless; above all he should *appear* to be religious.

Machiavelli was essentially concerned with power, and his comments are particularly relevant to business. A policy is worthless unless it is accompanied by the authority to implement it. "Right is might" not because of its rightness, but because of its power; the quotation might be more accurate if reversed. The argument is difficult to refute, especially in the light of twentieth-century industrial development, and we shall examine it in greater detail in Chapter 5. It is enough to observe here that it is a question less easy for us to answer now than it was for the moralists of the last century.

SOCIAL PHILOSOPHY

The Reformation

The Reformation and Counter-Reformation, the one basically German and the other Spanish, were largely directed against the intellectual power of Renaissance Italy (Italians in the literature of the time are frequently portrayed as villains). Luther, Calvin, and Loyola all protested in their own ways against the church as it existed, the first two founding prominent Protestant sects and the last creating the Jesuit order. Doctrinal unity was abandoned, and a new liberal movement, more concerned with the secular side of philosophy, began. The Reformation, though philosophically barren, led to the rise of science in its broadest sense.

Francis Bacon pioneered the scientific method and inductive reasoning. He was an orthodox religious believer, but held that everything in theology except the existence of God, which he thought could be proved by reason, depended on faith. Philosophy was the search for truth; thus, in matters of religion he believed in the "double truth" of reason and revelation.

Empiricism

Bacon was the precursor of Hobbes (1588–1679) and the empiricists, Descartes (1596–1650), Locke (1632–1704), Berkeley (1685–1753), and Hume (1711–1776), as well as Spinoza (1632–1677), who followed Hobbes closely. Empiricism was essentially based on the scientific approach to philosophy; its specific characteristic was the tenet that all true philosophical knowledge is derived from the evidence of the senses, that unless facts are verifiable through experience, they cannot properly be called facts.

Like Machiavelli, but for different reasons, Hobbes was fundamentally interested in power and sovereignty. In his major work, *Leviathan,* he maintained that whatever government is in power has the absolute right to rule. The first law of human nature is to seek peace; there is nothing for which it is worthwhile to risk one's life. The laws of nature are only binding when they are also commands of the sovereign: "The Diseases of a Commonwealth proceed from the poison of seditious doctrines; whereof one is *that every private man is Judge of Good and Evil actions.* . . . Another doctrine repugnant to Civill Society, is *that whatsoever a man does against his Conscience, is Sinne*; and it dependeth on the presumption of making himself judge of Good and Evil."[17] Morality rests on law, not law on morality. We must obey even a bad law, because we only make matters worse (i.e., we diminish our security) by disobedience.

It is here that the problems of Hobbes's thesis begin, for although he went on to say that "the obligation of subjects to the sovereign is understood to last as long as and no longer than the power lasteth by which he is able to protect them,"[18] Hobbes did not indicate who is to say when the sovereign is not protecting them. Spinoza's answer was that wise men in the community will decide which social system gives greatest security to its citizens, but this does not really resolve the difficulty. .

It is a difficulty not unusual in business. Commentators have tried, unsuccessfully, to distinguish between power and authority. Jacques Maritain maintains that they "are two different things. Power is the force by means of which you can oblige others to obey you. Authority is the *right* to direct and command, to be listened to or obeyed by others. Authority requests power. Power without authority is tyranny. Thus authority means right [and] since it means right, it has to be obeyed by force of conscience, that is in the manner in which free men obey and for the sake of the common good." [19]

This is an uncomfortable contrast. Clearly, authority is necessary if order is to be maintained, but is power therefore to be equated simply with a thief holding a gun at one's head? Hobbes asserted that since men are rapacious, reckless, and combative, authority armed with power is a necessary evil, for without it, they would destroy themselves. Maritain would appear to be saying that even if human beings were all goodness, sweetness, and light, they would still need authority. Bertrand de Jouvenel, on the other hand, writing at the end of World War II, puts forward the modern version of Hobbes: "Power is authority and makes for more authority. It is force and makes for more force. Or, if a less metaphysical terminology is preferred, ambitious wills, drawn by the lure of Power, expend unceasingly their energies in its behalf that they may bind society in an even tighter grip and extract from it more of its resources." [20] It is interesting that modern versions of Hobbes sound more and more like Machiavelli.

The argument is difficult, but not necessarily important. We shall investigate the structure of power in Chapter 5, but two points should be stressed here. First, most people who choose a business career do so because it offers the power to put their own values into practice (see Chapter 7). Second, if a semantic distinction is to be made, we have to admit that without power, there can be no authority.

The parallel between Hobbes's political theory and modern business practice is very close. The role of the company president consists of stewardship of the affairs of the corporation through the authority vested in the president by the stockholders. In theory company presidents can, and in practice frequently do, act unilaterally without the formal approval of the board of directors, and providing they stay within the law, their rule is absolute and their word must be obeyed on pain of dismissal. The only way in which they can be removed is through a stockholder vote, and that vote is usually instigated by a motion of the board. For "board," substitute Spinoza's "wise men," and the parallel is complete.

While it is fashionable in tracing the development of philosophical thought to move chronologically from Hobbes to Descartes, it is more logical to seek the conclusion of Hobbes's ideas in the writings of Spinoza, that likable Hispanic-Dutch Jew whose ethical outlook is perhaps the most agreeable of all the philosophers'. His political and psychological thinking owed much to that of Hobbes, his metaphysics were a mild variation of Descartes', but his ethical outlook was entirely his own. Fundamentally he believed that all sin is due to ignorance and that one should, like Christ, "forgive them for they know not what they do." Hatred can be overcome by love, the world is ultimately good and is getting better, and one's own misfortunes are really only a part of eternity, which they do not affect, being merely "passing discords heightening an ultimate harmony." [21] It is an attractive thought, even though it may be hard to maintain in practice. As Russell has written, "Such reflections may not suffice to constitute a religion, but in a painful world they are a help towards sanity and an antidote to the paralysis of utter despair." [22] And as Stuart Hampshire has observed, "Perhaps, in the last resort, no one will fully understand and enjoy Spinoza who has never to some degree shared the metaphysical temper, which is the desire to have a unitary view of the world and of man's place within it." [23]

Modern social thinkers owe more to Spinoza's contribution to philosophy than perhaps they realize; certainly, business could benefit from a knowledge of it. It would be interesting to see whether the outcome of business negotiations would be any different if they were based on a more optimistic view of human nature instead of on suspicion, mistrust, and ambivalence; in any event, the negotiators would leave the table happier people.

The Beginnings of Modern Philosophy

Descartes, the "father of modern philosophy," brought a freshness and originality to philosophical thought not encountered in any thinker since Plato or Aristotle. His approach was to discount what had gone before and to start afresh. Beginning from the point of ultimate subjectivism by deciding that the only entity of which he could possibly be aware was his own being (*je pense, donc je suis* — *cogito, ergo sum*), he laid the foundations for that essentially logical and consistent intellectual discipline that has been the glory and limitation of French education ever since. What Descartes is to France, the classical authors and the nineteenth-century moralists are to England and Thomas Jefferson to the United States. The Cartesian method is at once both excitingly liberating and frustratingly rigid. All philosophy derived from "Cartesian doubt" follows the same path: the subjective view that matter can be known only through what is known of the mind. This tendency exists "both in Continental idealism and in British empiricism — in the former trium- phantly, in the latter regretfully."[24]

From his basic premise, Descartes proceeded to build his entire system of knowledge. There are sometimes doubts as to the existence of external things as a result of three sorts of sense perceptions (those that are innate, those that come from without, and those that one invents), and we can dispel these doubts only by proving the existence of God. This Descartes did with little trouble and less conviction; once done, the rest was easy.

Although it is fashionable these days to find fault with Descartes' starting point of "I think" on the grounds that the existence of thoughts does not mean the existence of "I," this fundamental subjectivism is the basis of much modern so-called realistic philosophy. It is also very germane to the thesis of this book — that one is answerable only to one's own conscience and that one's behavior is governed exclusively by the latitude or constraint dictated by that conscience. Moreover, it is another example, and a very important and influential one, of the duality referred to in Chapter 1; in this case, the duality is one of mind and matter, like the other dualities of God and man, of the individual and the corporation, of private and public behavior. The tradition that imbued Descartes' work is clear: The new science of his day and the Scholasticism of his early education combined to give his philosophical thought an influence that is felt even today.

This influence has been evident in two directions. First, Locke, Berke- ley, and Hume fostered the Cartesian approach and in turn prompted the utilitarian philosophy of Bentham; through Voltaire (1694–1778), the lib- eral tradition was transmitted back to France, where it was eagerly accepted in the years leading to the Revolution. This stream of thought was eventually to give rise to the dialectic materialism of Marx (1818– 1883). Second, through Kant (1724–1804), Descartes' influence bred the school of German intellectual idealism, and thus it was that the heirs of the founder of empiricism became philosophical antagonists in the form of Marx and Nietzsche.

Empiricism is essentially individualistic. *Cogito, ergo sum* made the cognitive starting point different in different people and produced both the theological ingenuity of Berkeley and the atheism of the French; these two attitudes are similarly founded on the reliability of clear and distinct ideas and on the individual's ability to recognize that reliability.

This is an important point in the discussion of business responsibility, since it stresses once again the salience of individual perceptions and values. Situation ethics, recommended in Chapter 6 as the most appropriate vade mecum for modern business people, stems almost directly from the inherent subjectivism of the empiricists.

The British and the continental schools deriving from Descartes differed in a number of ways, in large measure because of a difference of method. British philosophy, in particular that of Locke or Hume, tended to draw cautious conclusions from a broad examination of many detailed facts. Leibniz, on the other hand, whose contribution to ethical thought was negligible, and Kant, to whom ethics were supreme, constructed huge frameworks of deduction from one single a priori principle. Leibniz was not as directly influenced by Descartes as he was by Spinoza, but Descartes' influence on Kant was certainly direct, and it is thus interesting to note the similarity of Leibniz's and Kant's methods.

The difference between metaphysical argument and pure empiricism is seen also in different philosophical approaches. Descartes proved the existence of God by metaphysical argument. Locke and Berkeley followed him in this, the latter using a totally new argument, but Hume abandoned metaphysics completely, claiming that no useful purpose is served by reasoning on metaphysical matters. In this, he can be contrasted with Kant and his followers, who saw everything to be gained by metaphysical contemplation.

As far as views on ethics are concerned, Locke and the empiricists believed pleasure to be the good. The continental (and particularly the German) approach was different: Pleasure was deemed ignoble. Kant himself held that there is no moral merit in a kind act born of friendship; the only moral merit exists in the fact that the action is prompted by the moral law.

Locke, the arch-empiricist, put forward the doctrine that all our knowledge is derived from experience. He argued against the Platonic view of innate ideas; ideas come only from our perception of the world and our understanding of the operation of our mind. In ethics, as has been indicated, Locke believed that people must be motivated by desire for their own happiness or pleasure: "Things are good or evil only in relation to pleasure or pain. . . . Happiness, in its full extent, is the utmost pleasure we are capable of. . . . The necessity of pursuing true happiness is the foundation of all liberty." [25] He held that since one's self-interest and the general interest coincide only in the long run, people should be guided by their long-run happiness; thus, the pursuit of happiness should be tempered by prudence.

Locke's political philosophy, which was influential in the drafting of the American Constitution, is based on the idea of a "natural law," which is a set of moral rules independent of legislation. Without such rules, one could not distinguish between good and bad laws. For Locke, the natural law was the Bible, but when removed from religion, the concept is much more difficult to explain and brings us back to individual values. Locke also favored the idea that civil government is the result of a social contract, since government is accepted as a means of preserving individual liberty and therefore happiness.[26] However, governments should not be absolute, and the judiciary should be independent of the executive. The power of government by contract never extends beyond the common good, but Locke did not acknowledge, as Hobbes and Spinoza did, that there is a problem here, for who is to be the judge of the common good? We shall return to this question in Chapter 5 in our discussion of the structure of power.

Of all the ingrained values of the modern American business manager, the notion of the natural moral law is perhaps the strongest. Its pedigree is pure Locke, and it can be traced directly to the significant Lockean content of the American constitutional ethos. It has produced that view known as "current ethics," which is examined in Chapter 6. Too little importance is attached to the fact that businessmen played a major role in the founding of the United States; the Constitution has a strong business orientation, and much of the theory of the American system of representative goverment was developed by Locke and others in their roles as directors or consultants to stock companies. The Declaration of Independence, with its specific reference to "life, liberty and the pursuit of happiness," might have been written by Locke himself. It is ironic, however, that Montesquieu, who was born some fifty years after Locke and through whom Locke's theories were incorporated in the American Constitution, should have misunderstood his predecessor's statement about the independence of the judiciary and the executive to such an extent as to have caused an element of one of the great political systems of the world to be there by mistake.

Berkeley, who followed Locke, based his philosophy on the denial of matter. In essence, he held that things exist only through our perception of them. However, since God always perceives everything, objects will still exist even if nobody is perceiving them, and since our common sense tells us that things have a continued existence, this is proof of the existence of God. As a link between Locke and Hume, Berkeley is important in the development of empirical philosophy, but his orientation is more toward the theory of knowledge than toward moral thought.

Hume, on the other hand, took empirical philosophy to its logical conclusion and in the process achieved a level of skepticism that has never been surpassed. By taking nothing on trust and by seeking to substantiate everything by experience and observation, he arrived at the conclusion that experience and observation prove nothing and that there is no such thing as a rational belief. "In all the incidents of life we ought still to preserve our scepticism."[27] Unlike Locke, Hume carried his skepticism to nature; he argued that natural law has no claim to universal validity since people and nations (and, we might add, business managers) usually disagree about its content. The only law that could certainly be shown to exist is the law in the statute book laid down by authority. This view tends to predominate in our own time, but it raises problems when examined in the light of executive power in the massive modern corporation.

Toward the end of the eighteenth century, and after Hume's destruction of empiricism, a revolt against traditional ethical and aesthetic standards produced a wave of feeling that had an influence on all aspects of philosophy, art, and politics. The romantic movement, as it was called, is in many ways still going on. It was based on the traditional French inclination toward emotion removed from all rationality. It was in this sense nothing new, for yearnings for the simple life and quiet contemplation are to be found in the literature of all ages. To the cultivated eighteenth-century Frenchman, poverty was something beautiful to contemplate, but not to experience, something virtuous and free of problems. This romantic idealism perceived the world through a glass tinted with roses, and it was Rousseau (1712–1778) who articulated the vision. He was, in his political and philosophical writings, expressing the mood of a Europe ready to abandon the utilitarian attitudes of the previous hundred years. The romantic movement really began in Germany, but it is most closely associated with Rousseau. Born a Swiss, he spent most of his time in France, and his influence on social thought has been immense.

In his essay *Discourse on Inequality,* published in 1743, Rousseau maintained that "man is naturally good and only by institutions is he made bad." Some commentators on managerial behavior might make the same comment. Rousseau claimed that though nature, as a state, existed no longer, it was necessary to have an idea of it to serve as a means of judging the present situation. Natural inequality — of age and ability, for example — is acceptable, but inequality of privilege is not, and privilege owes its origins to the possession of property. The essay marked the beginning of Rousseau's quarrel with Voltaire.

Rousseau's religion was consistent with such thoughts. Unlike his philosophical predecessors throughout the centuries who attempted to prove the existence of God by intellectual argument, he preferred to rely solely on his innate belief in the presence of God in nature. As for moral law and rules of conduct:

> I do not derive these rules from the principles of the higher philosophy, I find them in the depths of my heart, traced by Nature in characters which nothing can efface. . . . Thank Heaven, we have now got rid of all that alarming show of philosophy; we may be men without being scholars; now that we need not spend our life in the study of morality, we have found a less costly and surer guide through this vast labyrinth of human thought.[28]

According to Rousseau, we should follow the guidance of our conscience at all times. Our natural feelings prompt us to serve the common interest, but our reason leads us to selfishness; therefore, following feeling makes us virtuous.

As proof of the existence of God and a universal code of conduct, following feeling is unsatisfactory since it is essentially very private, and the fact that Rousseau believed it is no guarantee that others will do the same. Yet, in this overview of moral thought, nothing else has illustrated the theme of this book more effectively; ethical management behavior depends in the end on individual perspectives and cognitive maps. Within his lifetime, Rousseau upset many people with his beliefs. He offended both traditional Protestant and Catholic principles (he belonged to both religions in turn), he quarreled with Voltaire, he was expelled from France, and in his final insanity, he broke his long-standing friendship with Hume; even his native Geneva would have none of him. And, yet, he was in all things guided by his feelings, his sensibility, and his conscience. It is a fitting testimonial to the strength of his beliefs.

He is best known for *The Social Contract,* which contains his political theory. His statement of the problem is straightforward: "To find a form of association which will defend and protect with the whole common force the person and goods of each associate, and in which each, while uniting himself with all, may still obey himself alone, and remain as free as before." Again, this is an echo of the problem of individual responsibility. To Rousseau, the answer is quite clear; it lies in the idea of a social contract that involves "the total alienation of each associate, together with all his rights, to the whole community; for in the first place, as each gives himself absolutely, the conditions are the same for all, and this being so, no one has any interest in making them burdensome to others."

Lest this be interpreted as a total rejection of individual freedom, Rousseau went on to say that the will of the sovereign (i.e., the community) is always right and is the "general will." Everyone shares in this general will, but each citizen, as an individual, may also have a particular will running contrary to the general will. Whoever refuses to obey the general will is forced to do so and is thus "forced to be free." This is difficult to understand, and it seems to suggest a form of totalitarianism. The answer is probably that Rousseau thought that self-interest, which governs every persons's political opinion, has two aspects, one of which relates to the individual and the other to all members of the community. All the individual interests will cancel each other out, and the common interest, or general will, remains. The idea of the general will is the direct ancestor of the theory of consensus ethics discussed in Chapter 6, where its limitations are pointed out.

It is hard to say what positive influence the political theory of Rousseau has had on modern thought; certainly it was popular among French revolutionaries. It could be said also to have led in the end to the different forms of totalitarianism found in Stalin's Russia and Hitler's Germany, but it would be unfair to label it as being so unequivocally undesirable. Rousseau was nothing if not genuine and would no doubt have been mortified to think that he was indirectly the cause of dictatorship and tyranny. Indeed, on many occasions in *The Social Contract,* tyranny is condemned. Perhaps the closest parallel to Rousseau's ideal is the ancient Greek city-state, which, significantly, was a small political unit incapable of existing on a large scale; to have attempted to extend such a system to the size of modern states may well have been Rousseau's fundamental mistake.

In Germany, romanticism took a different, though associated, course. There, also, philosophers — Kant prominent among them — reacted against Hume and developed a school of thought, usually described as German idealism, that was intended to maintain knowledge and virtue against the subjectivist attack they had suffered from the writings of Descartes, Locke, Berkeley, and Hume. The German idealists held knowledge to be the way to truth, and mind to be more important than matter. Utilitarianism was replaced by abstract philosophy, but the abstractions were anything but irrelevant.

Kant, the greatest philosopher of the German school, died in the fourth year of the nineteenth century. He thus serves as a link with more modern schools of thought that have exercised so much influence on current business attitudes. Although his best-known work is his *Critique of Pure Reason,* it is the *Metaphysic of Morals* that presents his ethical philosophy. In this work, he introduced the celebrated concept of the categorical imperative, which is a familiar phrase even to those unfamiliar with philosophical thought.

The categorical imperative is a command of reason: All moral concepts are entirely a priori in the mind, and moral worth exists only when one acts from a sense of duty. This imperative has nothing to do with self-interest; doing good things out of self-interest is not virtuous, but doing good things because they are objectively necessary is. "Act only according to a maxim by which you can at the same time will that it shall become a general law."

Kant's ethical standpoint is attractive and has resisted many attempts to disprove it. Certainly, it is relevant to the dilemmas of executive behavior described in other chapters of this book. It does, however, have limitations, not least of all that the maxim quoted at the end of the previous paragraph is not enough to justify certain types of action. As Russell commented, "While the categorical imperative can be used to show the wrongness of murder it cannot be used equally satisfactorily to show the wrongness of suicide."[29] Nevertheless, the categorical imperative is not unusual in business decision making.

The nineteenth century saw a rapid growth in science, and with the rise of industrialism, scientific technique began to influence social thought. The romantics condemned the ugliness created by industry and opposed the trading classes who supported it. This tradition persisted until later in the century when socialist thinkers spearheaded the revolt against capitalism that was implemented by the Russian proletariat in 1920. That revolt is still manifesting itself in various parts of the world.

The growth in industrial technology brought a corresponding growth in human power. Power is now the creed of business. "To formulate any satisfactory modern ethic of human relationships it will be essential to recognize the necessary limitations of men's power over the non-human environment, and the desirable limitations of their power over each other."[30]

Before proceeding to the twentieth century, we must examine one more school of thought, which we have already referred to in passing. The utilitarian movement, essentially a British phenomenon led by Jeremy Bentham (1748–1832), was derived basically from Locke. It was a development wholly divorced from the German idealistic school of the same period. Through his belief in the "association principle" (the association of ideas and language, of ideas and ideas), Bentham was seeking a social system that would automatically make men virtuous, and to define virtue, he adopted the principle of "the greatest happiness." Basically, what is good is pleasure or happiness, and what is bad is pain. Although this view had been held by different philosophers through many centuries, Bentham was the first to propose its practical application. In particular, he campaigned for the abolition of the death penalty for everything but the worst crimes and advocated the equal division of a man's property among his children. A radical, he gradually came to maintain that nothing was believable except on rational grounds, and he thus opposed monarchy, hereditary aristocracy, and religion. He espoused democracy to such a degree that he proposed votes for women long before they received them.

James Mill (1773–1836) and his more celebrated son, John Stuart Mill (1806–1873), carried on where Bentham left off. J. S. Mill's ethical doctrine was that those actions are good that end in producing general happiness, even though that may not have been the intention — not quite "situation ethics," but almost (see Chapter 6). In this, we see a fundamental distinction between utilitarianism and German idealism: The former is concerned with effects, the latter with reasons. It is interesting that both schools come together in the birth of socialism (articulated into a philosophy by Karl Marx), though the relationship of socialism with idealism is less obvious and more complex.

TWENTIETH-CENTURY MATERIALISM

Although Marx is a product of the nineteenth century, it is impossible to consider his impact on social thought without viewing him in the light of the revolution he inspired but never experienced.

Like Bentham and Mill, Marx would have nothing to do with romanticism. To him, scientific reasoning was paramount. His philosophy of dialectical materialism ("dialectical" because it is never completed) led him to believe that the driving force is the individual's relation to matter, of which the most important aspect is his mode of production. Marx claimed to have removed ethical considerations from his advocacy of socialism, although the discussion of Engels's interpretation of Marxist theory in the previous chapter suggests otherwise; the advent of socialism was inevitable, determined by the dialectic, and it must therefore be an improvement on what had gone before it. Nonetheless, Marx's political theory (that the injustices of capitalism, such as free competition leading to monopoly, must produce revolution of the proletariat) cannot be wholly divorced from ethical attitudes; certainly, the Russian acceptance of Marxism in the form of communism was as much the result of a rejection of feudalism in favor of a more equitable and just society as it was of Lenin's articulation of the Marxist dogma. Whether Marx believed it or not, his vision must have been inspired partly through his feelings of right and wrong. It was left to another Marxist, after another major revolution of the proletariat, to introduce the notion of cultural protest.

Lenin's Russia, Mao's China, and Castro's Cuba, the three most prominent examples of revolutionary success, succeeded not so much because of ideology as because of the social improvements the ideology promised. Liberalism and radicalism in Western Europe and North America also led to social upheaval, but of a different kind. In Britain, the growth of the trade union movement was part political, part social; in its present form, the British trade union is probably more political than unions anywhere else in the world. Unlike their colleagues in North America, British trade unionists are not closely wedded to the capitalist system, and the gulf between labor and management is due largely to political differences based on traditional class barriers. In the more class-less society on the other side of the Atlantic, the capitalist ethic is shared more equally, and the economic objective of the unions is more evident.

With the growth of totalitarianism in its various forms has come a decline in religious belief. Nazi Germany, a descendant of Rousseau's romanticism via Nietzsche, subjugated the church to the power of the state; Soviet Russia has no part for the church to play in its system of things and has suppressed religious thought in favor of party ideology.

Even in the British "welfare" state, spiritual comfort is valued less than the financial aid of the social services. In Europe and North America, new cults and trends advocating the overthrow of traditional values have been inspired by the innovative and sometimes bizarre inclinations of modern youth. The years since 1960 have been the years of the "youth culture," and they have witnessed a reaction against tradition as strong and as significant as the romantic movement itself.

The new society of the West is thus now a strange amalgam of influences, which have their roots in the philosophical and political stimuli of the past. It is more difficult now than ever for individuals to find an ethical "package" that will be entirely satisfactory. Consequently, in the complex and sometimes confusing atmosphere of modern life, few conceptual frameworks of ethical behavior will be the same.

Therefore, if there is one thing that characterizes ethical decision making today, it is the multiplicity of criteria upon which it is based. The study of the development of moral thought uncovers many interesting theories, some powerful and influential, others relatively insignificant and frequently odd. Political and economic factors now influence moral thought more than ever before, and religious beliefs are often relegated to a lower level, or, indeed, ignored altogether. Even as recently as Locke, Rousseau, and Kant, views on moral questions were strictly orthodox; God existed, whatever the proof of his existence. Innovations in theology were made in the interests of religion. Today, religion has to fight hard for consideration.

CONCLUSION

It is a long way from Pythagoras and Heraclitus to Pepsi-Cola and Hoover, but the historical excursion serves to illustrate what a complex scenario of ethical thought surrounds the social and moral decisions faced by modern management. Most of the philosophies that we have examined carry some meaning for business today. "In a vague way, business as an institution is aware that a concern with intrinsic values — with good in its most essential sense — has to have a place in its scheme of things."[31]

The conceptual underpinnings of moral decisions are thus constructed from material emanating from both secular and religious sources. Every individual manager is influenced to some degree by one or both of these sources; some of the precepts are obeyed by managers even without knowledge of their origin. The human mind is a complicated mechanism at the best of times, even when dealing with simple matters of fact; when, however, it is faced with questions of value, its judgments call upon evidence from far beyond its own field of vision. What the philosophers and social commentators of previous generations provide is a storehouse of advice to help the managerial mind reach just and equitable decisions that will not only help the enterprise to prosper, but that will also satisfy the rightful demands of conscience.

NOTES

1. Immanuel Kant, *Critique of Pure Reason,* 2nd ed., trans. Norman Kemp Smith (London: Macmillan, 1933), Conclusion.

2. Aristotle, *Politics,* chap. 1, sec. 2.

3. Bertrand Russell, *Authority and the Individual,* BBC Reith Lectures, 1948–1949 (London: Allen & Unwin, 1949), p. 17.

4. Charles C. Colton, *Lacon: Or Many Things in Few Words; Addressed to Those Who Think* (London, 1820), vol. 1, chap. 25.

5. Matt. 5:3, 5, 8, 9.

6. G. Bernard Shaw, *Plays Pleasant* (London: Penguin, 1946), Preface, p. 8.

7. Charles Dickens, *Oliver Twist,* chap. 5.

8. F. M. Cornford, *From Religion to Philosophy* (London: Arnold, 1912), p. 201.

9. Bertrand Russell, *A History of Western Philosophy* (London: Allen & Unwin, 1946).

10. Ibid.

11. William Shakespeare, *Julius Caesar,* act 1, sc. 2, l. 134.

12. Aristotle, *Nichomachaean Ethics,* sec. 1131b.

13. Russell, *Western Philosophy.*

14. Matt. 22:21.

15. Edward Gibbon, *The Decline and Fall of the Roman Empire,* chap. 15.

16. Anthony Jay, *Management and Machiavelli* (London: Hodder & Stoughton, 1967).

17. Thomas Hobbes, *Leviathan* (London: J. M. Dent & Sons, 1914), p. 172.

18. Ibid., p. 175.

19. Jacques Maritain, *The Social and Political Philosophy of Jacques Maritain* (London: G. Bles, 1956).

20. Bertrand de Jouvenel, *On Power: Its Nature and the History of Its Growth,* trans. J. F. Huntington (New York: Viking Press, 1949).

21. Russell, *Western Philosophy,* p. 603.

22. Ibid.

23. Stuart Hampshire, *Spinoza* (London: Penguin, 1951), p. 225.

24. Russell, *Western Philosophy,* pp. 586–87.

25. John Locke, *Essay concerning Human Understanding* (Chicago: Encyclopaedia Britannica, 1952), bk. 2, chap. 20, p. 176.

26. John Locke, *Second Treatise on Government.*

27. David Hume, *Treatise of Human Nature* (London: J. M. Dent & Sons, 1911), bk. 1, part 4, sec. 2, p. 209.

28. Jean-Jacques Rousseau, *Emile,* trans. Barbara Foxley (London: J. M. Dent & Sons, 1911), bk. 4, pp. 249, 254.

29. Russell, *Western Philosophy,* p. 737.

30. Ibid.

31. Richard Eells and Clive Walton, *Conceptual Foundations of Business,* 3rd ed. (Homewood, Ill.: Richard D. Irwin, 1974).

4 ETHICAL MANAGEMENT:
Problems in Decision Making

We may give advice, but we can never prompt behavior.

— François, duc de la Rochefoucauld[1]

THE HARSH REALITY OF CONSCIENCE

In Chapter 1, we identified the focus of this book as the examination of the social responsibility of business through the perspective of individual managers in ethical problem situations. The historical analysis of the different moral and social influences on modern personal values presented in the preceding chapter showed just how complex one's ethical heritage can be. The situation is further complicated by the additional fact, easily observable, that the business executive of today faces problems and dilemmas not understood or provided for by earlier philosophical frameworks; there is something of a confrontation between traditional value systems and contemporary norms. Thus, the serious executive has to try to make sense out of the new and to reconcile it with the old.

The executive's response to a particular ethical problem may not be consciously founded on any historical influence, but it will nevertheless be consistent with the values that have become part of life. Managers may not, in other words, be able to articulate their perceptions of such abstractions as rightness, goodness, or justice, but they will recognize examples when they meet them. We are not as a rule philosophically contemplative, but the stimuli provided by historical value systems will to some extent determine our decisions, and those decisions will frequently have to be made without time to ponder upon grand concepts of morality.

While our thesis is that it is people rather than corporations who must bear the responsibility for social and moral decisions, it must not be forgotten that executives have to decide on appropriate courses of action within the context of the firms that employ them. This adds another dimension to the decision itself. Furthermore, in the modern corporation, a few people make decisions for thousands. Clarence Walton makes a telling point: "George Washington would have been more at home with the entrepreneurs of Aristotle's day than he would have been with either John D. Rockefeller or Henry Ford." [2] The comment illustrates how very new our present concept of the corporation is.

The fact that in such large organizations, the majority of executives are faceless and unknown to the outside world makes an analysis of the problems they encounter difficult, but not impossible. In this section, we will attempt to identify problems in different categories and to offer practical case examples, some real, some disguised, and some invented, to illustrate the conflicting forces that sometimes impinge on the individual executive conscience; in the process, an effort will be made to relate the specific situation to the discussions in previous chapters.

However, by way of a general introduction to the difficulty of evaluating the personal ethical dilemmas that lie behind the corporate curtain, we shall begin with a case that is perhaps as complex as any example can be. It deals with the development and introduction of the Concorde supersonic passenger aircraft. After reviewing this case, we shall proceed to examine other, more personal ethical incidents according to the order in which they are featured in the problem taxonomy that is presented after the Concorde example.

CONCORDE: AN ETHICAL CUL-DE-SAC

The Concorde project is not easy to analyze. It affects two countries, Britain and France; it affects two governments; it affects two large manufacturing organizations, in Britain the British Aircraft Corporation (BAC) and in France Aerospatiale; it affects the taxpayers of both countries, who paid for it but had no say in how their money was spent and who might have preferred it spent on schools or hospitals or pensions; it affects the workers not only in the two manufacturing companies, but also in the supporting organizations that supplied them with their raw materials, components, and technology; it affects air passengers, particularly business executives who do not have to buy their own tickets, who fly across the Atlantic for a meeting and get back in time for dinner because the aircraft flies at such a phenomenal speed; it affects two of the world's major airlines, British Airways and Air France, who between them have been forced by their respective governments to purchase nine Concordes at a cost of about $45 million each with taxpayer's money in the form of government subsidies and who operate them at a loss (as an exercise in marketing, it is a disaster); finally, it affects the population of the world in that, according to an American scientist's estimate, if there were as many supersonic airliners flying today as there are subsonic jets, at their cruising altitude of 60,000 feet, their kerosene-powered engines would so burn up the ozone layer in the atmosphere that in less than a year all animals in the world would be blinded and all plant life would die.

On January 31, 1973, came news from Pan Am that killed the enthusiasm of even the most fervent supporter of Concorde: Pan Am had decided to cancel its options to buy seven of the new supersonic airliners. An hour later, TWA canceled its six options, a month and a half before it needed to. On February 13, American Airlines followed suit, canceling another six options, and on March 29, Continental, Sabena, Qantas, and Lufthansa canceled theirs. Originally there had been seventy-two options; twenty-four were now left. On March 30, BAC and Aerospatiale, the British and French manufacturers, announced that the option system was at an end.

On Sunday, June 3, 1973, at the Paris Air Show at Le Bourget, Concorde's Russian cousin, the Tu-144 (Concordski), fell out of the sky, burst into flames, and disintegrated, killing all its crew and seven civilians in front of 300,000 spectators. Two days later, the Japanese government announced that no supersonic airliner would be allowed to fly in or out of Tokyo without absolute guarantees of safety. JAL had had options for three Concordes.

These events, following each other in rapid succession, were the anticlimax of many years of doubt, indecision, and error. The concept of an Anglo-French supersonic transport had first materialized in 1962, after a period of independent development in each country. Traditionally, the British had followed the Americans in civil aircraft design — except once: The first jet airliner to be introduced after World War II was a British airplane called Comet, which was a superb piece of work. Unfortunately, as the result of metal fatigue, two of them crashed, and the subsequent suspension of operations enabled Boeing to dominate the market with the 707. Thus, since 1955, Britain and France, whose Caravelle was also dominated by the 707, had been attempting to recoup some of their lost prestige.

In 1959, Britain recommended the start of detailed design work on a 100-seat medium-range and a 150-seat long-range supersonic aircraft at a cost of $190 million. In 1961, Sud Aviation (the predecessor of Aerospatiale) revealed a design for the "Super Caravelle" at the Paris Air Show. The British and French designs showed a marked similarity, which led to an agreement between the governments of both countries to collaborate on a joint project, estimated in 1963 to cost by 1970 some $300–$350 million in research and development and production tooling. These costs were to be shared equally between the two countries, and the manufacturing companies were to be almost entirely government-financed, the understanding being that the governments would recoup their investments from a levy on eventual sales revenue.

The agreement was not easily made. In the first place, the objectives of the program were not entirely clear; the overriding consideration seemed to be the rivalry between the European (particularly the British) and the American aircraft industries to be the first to introduce a "second-generation" jet airliner. Second, because the design involved breaches of the frontiers of technology in almost every respect and continuous experimentation, the specifications of the aircraft were constantly changing; thus, the "package" (payload, range, speed, size, cost) was determined not so much by what market conditions required as by what it was possible to produce. Third, Britain was at the time apparently on the brink of being accepted into the Common Market, following the meeting between Prime Minister Macmillan and President de Gaulle in June 1962, and it was imperative as an indication of British good intent that the supersonic agreement be signed as quickly as possible.

Thus, although no agreement on specifications had been reached, BAC and Sud Aviation, at the request of their governments, signed their Document of Cooperation on October 29, 1962, and on November 29, the two governments signed what was virtually a treaty (in fact, it was registered as such at the International Court at The Hague) to confirm the commercial agreement on technological cooperation.

Both documents had shortcomings. By stipulating exact work sharing between Bristol (BAC Filton) and Toulouse, the commercial agreement failed to observe the economics of production in that it ignored the extra costs involved in shipping parts across the English Channel. As for the "technological treaty," it was a document that successive British governments were to come to regret, since — as a token of good faith on the part of the United Kingdom — it was signed without any provision for either country to withdraw for technical or economic reasons. Andrew Wilson has called it a "blood pact . . . to allay French suspicions of 'perfidious Albion.'"[3]

De Gaulle, however, was not impressed. The following January he effectively vetoed Britain's entry into the Common Market. When the Labour government came to power in Britain in 1964 with the prospect of a balance-of-payments deficit in excess of $1.5 billion, it immediately examined the various "prestige projects" in hand with a view to cancellation. Four of these involved aircraft, and the government canceled three, the TSR-2, the P-1154, and the HS.681 (all military machines), despite violent objections from the military services and the manufacturers. It now seems certain that the Concorde project would have been canceled also, had the government been prepared to accept the protests of the French and the possibility of being sued by them at the International Court for nearly $400 million in damages (the escalated cost of Britain's contribution). It was an unattractive prospect.

After that, the Concorde program moved on inexorably, with ever-increasing costs, and, with the increased investment, governments became more reluctant to write off the money spent. By 1970 when Heath's Conservative government took office (once more with the Common Market in view), costs had risen to a staggering $1.65 billion, and although the Heath "think tank," headed by Lord Rothschild, came to the conclusion that anticipated revenue was unlikely to cover the remaining costs of about $500 million, it recommended that the project continue for the sake of entry into the Common Market. By the end of 1973, costs were over $2,000 million, and only sixteen aircraft had been authorized, of which only nine were firm orders (five for British Airways and four for Air France). The airlines had reluctantly placed these orders only after guarantees from their respective governments that their operating losses would be made good.

Meanwhile, on the other side of the Atlantic, the Americans had taken a different course. Following President Kennedy's authorization of a development program for a supersonic transport (SST) in 1963 under the auspices of NASA with a cost ceiling of $1.5 billion, Boeing, Lockheed, and North American Aviation were asked to submit preliminary designs. In 1964, Boeing and Lockheed were given contracts for further airframe designs, and General Electric and Pratt and Whitney for engines. The anticipated in-service date was 1971, a year after Concorde's originally scheduled service date. In 1966, preference was given to the Boeing 2707 swing-wing design and the General Electric GE4 engine.

In comparison with Concorde, the 2707 was to have 250 to 350 seats (versus Concorde's 118), a speed of Mach 2.7 (versus 2.2), and a range of 4,000 miles (versus approximately 3,500). Its weight was to be prodigious — 635,000 pounds (versus 350,000) — and was the cause of a series of design problems that necessitated a total reevaluation and an investment of $45 million of Boeing's own money. After a long and painful reappraisal of the economic and environmental considerations and much bitter argument in Congress, the SST project was canceled in 1971 after relatively little expenditure. This encouraged Concorde's supporters to feel that Europe would at least have the edge in the airliner battle. However, the arguments that persuaded the Americans to abandon the SST were in essence those that caused the U.S. airlines to turn their backs on Concorde.

Concorde's one advantage over previous jet airliners is that of speed (1,400 miles per hour compared with less than 600). However, the Concorde passenger obviously has no advantage over the passenger of the subsonic jet in terms of travel time between city center and airport. Furthermore, Concorde involves more "seat-belt time," since it has to climb to and descend from higher cruising altitudes (60,000 feet).

Concorde's disadvantages are many. First, it is expensive, both to buy and to operate. Including spares and backup equipment, each aircraft (on the basis of the British Airways and Air France purchases) costs $45 million, and its direct operating costs have been estimated to be two and a half times higher than those of the latest subsonic jets. This is true in spite of the fact that with its structure of exclusively first class fares at a rate much higher than normal, it should in principle be able to break even with a lower load factor.

Second, it is not particularly comfortable. Its cabin width is only 110 inches, compared with the Tri-Star's 237 and the Boeing 747's 257. There is no room for many of the amenities now common on the large subsonics.

Third, it is noisy. The Local Authority Aircraft Noise Control (LAANC), which represents fifty-two local councils affected by Heathrow noise, announced in November 1975 that its decibel monitors at the airport showed that, at its worst, Concorde was seven times louder than the legal limit and passed the threshold of pain. In general, the council claimed, Concorde was three times noisier on takeoff than the Boeing 707. In the United States, a four-volume environmental impact statement on Concorde by the U.S. Federal Aviation Administration (FAA), issued at the same time as the LAANC report, stated that Concorde was "at least twice as loud" as the relatively noisy 707; the FAA statement pointed out that the 707 belonged to an older generation of jets and that Concorde was four times as loud as the newer Boeing 747 and eight times as loud as the DC-10. Despite this, the British government has exempted Concorde from the Heathrow noise regulations.

Fourth, it still has to be proved that its kerosene-burning engines will not pollute the atmosphere. Scientists have predicted frightening consequences.

Finally, two major factors need to be stressed. The first is the rapidly rising cost of fuel, which makes it virtually impossible to calculate exactly how large Concorde's costs and fares will be in the long term. The second is the current state of the world's airlines and the type of traffic they must serve. Traditionally, airline passenger traffic has been increased by the introduction of faster aircraft; the "first-generation" jets are a case in point. However, when the "jumbo" jets were introduced, although they offered no improvement in speed, they nonetheless increased passenger traffic because they provided greater comfort and space, as well as other amenities; they also enabled the airlines to reduce fares substantially and thus to compete more successfully with the charter services. Concorde is now offering greater speed, but with many qualifications and at much higher cost.

The implications of these cost factors are fairly clear. The airlines have only recently invested a vast amount of money in "second-generation" subsonic airliners (about $20 million for each plane). This has not only made a large hole in their pockets, but has also created excessive capacity, which has made the prospect of Concorde more unattractive, especially as its operating costs are so much higher. Wilson has estimated that "in 1970 the airlines were flying the equivalent of 100 empty 707's every day" across the Atlantic,[4] and that was even before the 747 was put into service. The time slippage on Concorde's original development schedule (eight years plus six)[5] meant that the 747 (which was first announced by Boeing in 1965 and put into service in 1971) took much of the money that the airlines might originally have earmarked for Concorde. BAC, however, claims that Concorde can be operated as a complementary, rather than a replacement, aircraft.[6]

The total cost estimate for Concorde so far is $2,500 million. This is likely to be increased to cover further work on the noise problem. In addition, a member of the House of Commons Committee of Public Accounts, which examined the cost of Concorde in July 1973, estimated that each of the first thirty Concordes built would involve a production loss of $12 million; the British government has already loaned BAC $500–$700 million for production. Also, $260 million in "public dividend" capital was given to BOAC (later to become a division of British Airways) for its Concorde purchases, and operating losses are now accruing. Wilson estimates the total joint bill at more than $4 billion.[7]

At BAC in Filton, 25,000 jobs were involved and almost as many at Aerospatiale in Toulouse. Filton's MP in 1976 was Anthony Wedgwood Benn, Labour's minister of aviation.

Questions

It might justifiably be asked after an examination of the Concorde case: Whose responsibility was it? How do personal ethics enter into the problem? Where does the blame lie?

It is important to think of the forces involved here. The manufacturing companies wished to preserve their national industries, and the British government was anxious to save its face and to gain entry to the European Economic Community, a fact little known in the Concorde story, certainly very little appreciated. The French, seldom a nation to sublimate national pride to economic forces, could sometimes be relied upon to display (at least to outsiders) an insouciance when reason, despite Descartes, suggested otherwise.

However, in the matter of personal ethics, certain central questions need to be put. Had you been the prime minister of Britain, or the president of France, or the managing director of the British Aircraft Corporation, or the president of Aerospatiale, or a worker in one of the plants, or a British or French taxpayer, or the president of an international airline (most of which have refused to buy Concorde for one reason or another), or a businessman with work to do on the other side of the Atlantic, what would your views have been, and how much could they have affected the issue?

It might be argued that the matter is not personal, but corporate. This avoids the question, since, as we have already pointed out many times, corporate problems are often the result of personal decisions, and the resolution of such problems involves personal values. It is therefore perfectly legitimate to analyze the Concorde story from the standpoint of personal responsibility.

At the industrial and manufacturing level, key managers at both BAC and Aerospatiale faced decisions about whether or not the project was worth continuing at several points in the program; the factors affecting those decisions were partly financial, partly commercial, and partly political. Technology was not a problem; it became evident that the development of Concorde was within the state of the art, but its cost could frequently be called into question as the commercial potential of the airplane gradually diminished. Successive British and French governments voted more funds as cost estimates soared, and executives at both companies knew that this would continue until the development program was completed. Yet, surprisingly, the first passenger marketing studies were not conducted until 1973, and irrespective of whether or not the results were encouraging (rumor had it that they were not), one has to suspect that Concorde's disappointing commercial viability was being subjugated to considerations of political expedience. Government money could come from one source only — the public purse provided by the taxpayers — and the executives concerned could have taken this fact into account in their deliberations involving other factors, such as possible technological spinoffs, the provision of employment opportunities for a large labor force, environmental problems (like noise and pollution), national pride, and the international prestige derived from the achievement.

The taxpayers themselves, of course, had no opportunity to make their views felt, even though they were the ultimate providers of the money. The politicians, on the other hand, had a wide variety of options. It is not at all uncommon for politicians holding government positions to resign on matters of principle, but this never happened in the case of Concorde. In view of the circumstances, this is surprising, for the debate about the project was at times heated; on more than one occasion in the British House of Commons, aviation ministers were hard pressed to defend the continuation of the program in the face of strong pressures from both sides of the House. Personal values were, it seems, being suppressed by international political maneuvering.

Individual workers at Filton and Toulouse had the choice of accepting employment there or not, but if the alternative was unemployment it is fairly safe to guess that the decision would not be in doubt. Matters of company profitability, international politics, and pollution are less important to the labor force than the paychecks that support families and provide life's comforts.

Concorde will never make money; British Airways and Air France need government support to operate the Concordes they have, and the chief executives of these state-owned organizations must feel somewhat disillusioned after having been told that the nationalized industries are expected to make a profit. Perhaps this, too, is a case for individual protest.

A PROBLEM TAXONOMY

It is not enough simply to state that the ethical dilemmas executives face almost always stem from the incompatibility between their roles as employees (with contractual responsibilities to their employers) and their roles as private individuals (with equally important responsibilities focused elsewhere), though this is, of course, true and is frequently painfully obvious. Besides, this kind of moral conflict is not restricted to the business milieu, but occurs in all walks of life; everybody has experienced problems in choosing the best, or most honest, or most just course of action. Thus, we need to identify and classify situations involving ethical problems in a way that will facilitate discussion and analysis.

In the broadest sense, ethical problems can be categorized as relating to (1) matters external to the organization or (2) intraorganizational issues. However, this distinction hides the fact that some problems affect both areas. In the former group, we can unhesitatingly place the control of pollution and the ecology, product safety, honest advertising, pricing probity, truthful accounting, and fair dealing with suppliers and customers; in the second, we can locate the treatment of employees, conflicts of interest, professional codes, and the more general and many-faceted continuing phenomenon of the divergence between personal and corporate values. Spanning the two categories are the treatment of minority groups and equal opportunity employment policies, but since by definition such policies concern prospective employees, it seems logical to allocate problems in this area to the second category.

For the purposes of our analysis, therefore, we shall examine problem situations according to the following classifications and include in each discussion a realistic case that calls for an ethical decision from the personal perspective:

Extraorganizational Issues
1. The environment, pollution, and ecology;
2. Product safety;
3. Advertising;
4. Pricing and profiteering;
5. Fair dealing and consumerism.

Intraorganizational Issues
1. Employment policy;
2. Conflict of interest;
3. Legislation for company ethics;
4. Personal ethical conflict;
5. Minority groups and equal rights.

EXTRAORGANIZATIONAL ISSUES

The Environment

The problem of environmental pollution and the destruction of the ecological balance is nothing new. It has been a subject of debate for centuries, though not in the context of technological growth and industrial development. However, it is only in the last twenty years that people of all types and in all walks of life have begun to understand the real importance of maintaining a proper ecological balance and environmental quality. This understanding is largely the result of space technology and exploration, which showed dramatically how small and vulnerable the earth is in the hostile universe. The protection of its vital life support systems rapidly became perceived as essential.

Business, and in particular those industries involved in extracting resources from under ground or using those resources in chemical or equipment-manufacturing plants, has been a highly visible environmental offender. The evidence is ubiquitous and worldwide: Ugly scars on the earth's surface remind people of the ravages of the mining industry, polluted rivers in which no fish can live give testimony to the price that has been paid for the benefits of production, and city smogs, created largely by automobile exhaust fumes, are the trade-off for the convenience of personal transportation. Yet business executives themselves are among the most vociferous supporters of pollution control and environmental improvement. The eyesores produced by ugly housing, unkempt gardens, and unthinking littering of public places are caused by faceless people who can only generically be blamed.

Too much has been written about the seriousness of the environmental problem to warrant repetition here, but it has to be pointed out that tackling it involves cost and, to a large degree, government involvement and regulation. In those cases in which industries have not put their own houses in order, the state has ordered them to do so. Hazel Henderson quotes the examples of Royal Dutch/Shell's being refused permission to build a supertanker terminal in Wales and Gulf Oil's being ordered to close its new ethylene plant in Rotterdam until it meets pollution control requirements.[8] On another level, the pea-soup smogs of London, so beloved of Hollywood in its reenactments of the works of Dickens and Conan Doyle, have virtually disappeared as a result of clean air acts that permit only smokeless fuel to be burned in industrial furnaces and home fireplaces.

The cost factor (the pun is unintentional) is a burning issue. One school of thought holds to the belief that the cost of environmental preservation is a public cost since the industries that create the cost are serving the public and if the public were unable to benefit from the goods produced by those industries, its standard of living would be reduced. The other school accepts the thesis that business should bear the cost itself, but, as was observed in the first chapter, increases in operating costs are invariably passed on to the public in the form of higher prices.

Incident 1: Greg Doyle and Capital Chemicals, Inc. At eight o'clock on a warm August morning in 1979, Greg Doyle, a plant supervisor at Capital Chemicals, pulled out of the driveway of his new $50,000 home in his 1978 Impala to drive to the company's manufacturing facility three miles away at Dennington, Texas, a small town with a population of 12,000.[9]

Capital Chemicals had built its plant at Dennington five years before. Its business was processing liquid chemical by-products through vaporization and condensation and selling them to other industrial users. Greg Doyle, an industrial chemist with a B.S. degree from a well-known East Coast university, had joined Capital in 1977 at an attractive salary significantly higher than the one he had been earning in his previous job in Detroit. He and his wife found the Texas climate pleasant and the air much more agreeable than that in the big city.

This morning he was feeling worried, and during the drive to work, he was thinking about his wife's health. She had recently been experiencing inexplicable bouts of nausea, had been suffering from insomnia, and sometimes seemed uncoordinated and confused. The family doctor, who had been unable to diagnose any specific complaint, had suggested that she had probably been overworking (she worked at home writing encyclopedia topics for a popular publisher) and had given her medication, which had had little or no effect.

As he stepped out of his car at the company parking lot, Doyle was greeted by a colleague, Jack Olson, who had pulled into the next parking space. Olson, a research chemist in Capital's R and D division, and Doyle walked the short distance to the building together. The troubled look on Doyle's face prompted Olson to ask whether there was a problem, and Doyle told him about his concern for his wife; he said he was thinking about taking her to a specialist, but since the doctor had no idea of what was wrong with her, he did not know what kind of a specialist to see.

Olson looked thoughtful, and then, to Doyle's surprise, asked whether her symptoms included nausea, insomnia, lack of coordination, and confusion. Doyle replied in the affirmative and asked Olson how he had been able to describe the symptoms so accurately. Olson told him that the situation fitted with some other things he had heard around the town, and he was wondering whether they were all part of a pattern with a common cause. As they were about to part company in the reception lobby, Olson invited Doyle to stop by at his apartment that evening for a drink so he could explain what he was talking about.

Doyle hesitated, but after a moment's thought, he agreed to be at Olson's place at six, saying to himself that he would not have to leave his wife alone for too long. Throughout the day, his thoughts constantly returned to their conversation, and by half-past five when he left the plant, he was really eager to continue it.

He reached Olson's apartment shortly before six o'clock. Olson poured drinks, and they settled down in armchairs to talk. Over the next half hour, Olson told Doyle a story that both shocked and scared him.

Olson was not a medical doctor, but he had majored in toxicology for his degree in chemistry, and he had learned enough to know something of the relationship between the inhalation of certain chemical fumes and different types of illness. He had been told of several cases similar to that of Doyle's wife within a few miles of the plant, and he had begun to suspect that they were all cases of pancreatitis. The cause could be the fumes expelled by the plant as part of the vaporization and condensation process. He had conducted four tests on the chemical content of the ambient air at different distances and in different directions from the plant, but his equipment was rudimentary and could not give him conclusive proof.

He had been to see the plant's general manager, Al Hoffman, and had told him what he suspected. He had also given Hoffman his opinion that the company should either install filter devices on the plant's extractor fans (the fans were large, and there were twenty-four of them) or call in experts from the Texas State Health Department with the proper equipment to measure the extent of the air pollution. Hoffman had scoffed at him and told him he was worrying about nothing.

Doyle was deeply troubled. He knew that the installation of efficient filter devices was a complicated and expensive business. He also knew that it would take a great deal of persuasion to get the health department to come and make proper and accurate tests. Even if the health department did make tests, there was no certainty that they would confirm Olson's suspicions about the level of pollution or, even if they did, that the relationship with the illnesses would be proved; Olson would put no more than a 50 percent probability on the outcome. Doyle told Olson that only Hoffman could authorize the installation of filters and that the cost would be offset against Doyle's budget; in addition, Doyle said, Hoffman would do this only if positive proof of the pollution were available, but he would never agree to a visit from the health department.

All this aside, Doyle's wife was definitely not well. She liked Dennington and hated moving. Doyle drove home pondering on what he should do. If he talked to Hoffman, he would get the same reaction as Olson had; if he approached the health department, he would be going over the head of higher authority; if he told his wife, he might frighten her unnecessarily; if he told the doctor, he might be laughed at; and if he made too much trouble, he might lose his job.

Product Safety

It is easy to say that a product should be safe. It is not so easy to say what safety consists of. In real terms, the safety and reliability of an automobile might be doubled, but only by putting on it a price tag that nobody could afford; similarly, the safety of two cars of the same manufacture and model can be very different in the hands of drivers with different degrees of driving competence or sobriety.

In the area of product safety, as in pollution control, government regulation is significant. Not only in the automobile industry, but in other industries, too, official safety specifications regulate manufacturing standards. Nor is such regulation concentrated solely on industries producing goods that are by definition dangerous in the wrong circumstances, such as chain saws or painkilling drugs in the hands of children; the strictures placed on companies selling products that in principle are harmless are sometimes severe — flammable garments, cooking utensils, and adhesives are good examples.

In most nations, a governmental body legislates safety standards. In the United States, it is the Consumer Product Safety Commission (CPSC); in Britain, it is the British Standards Institute. All have basically the same objectives: to protect consumers and the public at large from the consequences of unsafe products or substandard manufacture. Their regulations cover design standards, quality control, and testing procedures. Yet, because of the different perceptions of risk in the minds of different consumers, it is difficult to establish precisely what the safety standards should be; most people will accept that there is some degree of risk inherent in almost any product, but at the same time they know how to avoid harming themselves. The pen with which I write could blind an eye, but I am sufficiently conscious of that fact to see to it that it will not do so. The fundamental ethical problem is raised when I buy a product with an inherent risk that I do not recognize because it has a fault or an unsafe component that I cannot see.

Incident 2: Bob Grant and Elmtree Steel Castings.   As he put down the telephone after a conversation with the vice-president of operations of Centurion, Inc., makers of motorbikes of all types, Frank Hemming, senior project engineer of Elmtree Steel Castings, sat pensively looking at the instrument.[10]

The conversation had been on the subject of a component in the brake mechanism in a new model recently introduced by Centurion. The component was produced by Elmtree and was delivered to Centurion ready for assembly. Since the introduction of the new bike, several customers who had bought it had complained of excessive brake noise, which Centurion, through tests, had traced to the component in question. It had been discovered that the component was not accurately aligned and that this was due not to incorrect assembly, but to the fact that the part was slightly misshapen. While the complaints had been about noise and not about braking efficiency, this misalignment could conceivably cause brake failure and accidents, although the probability was slight. Hemming had been asked by Centurion to investigate the problem.

Elmtree had a number of projects in progress at the time, and Hemming was not happy to have to take on yet another. The company could not spare the time, nor could it afford the expense if the problem was a complicated one that required redesign or other high costs, which Elmtree, according to its contract with Centurion, would have to bear.

Hemming picked up the telephone again and called Tom Stewart, vice-president of Elmtree's engineering division. He explained the situation to Stewart, who, after thinking about it for a moment, said that it was unlikely to be anything serious; he told Hemming to look into it with his project team and to check first for tensile stress, which is what both he and Hemming were convinced the trouble was and which, if proved, could easily be rectified.

Hemming allocated the job to one of his assistants, Bob Grant, and a technician. Grant had recently joined Elmtree just after graduating from college with a metallurgical degree. He was pleased with his job and found the problems he had to solve interesting and challenging. He got on well with people in the company, especially those on his project team, but he disliked Hemming because, being of a very practical outlook, he found Hemming's rather superficial theorizing somewhat irritating. As a result, he also disliked Stewart, who was particularly friendly with Hemming; the two were often together socially.

Testing for tensile stress is not difficult, but it does involve some basic dirty lab work. Hemming left this to Grant and the technician, and after about a week of experiments, they proved to themselves that tensile stress was not the cause of the problem. They therefore began testing for other possible causes.

Taking a coffee break one morning soon after having found the cause, Grant was surprised to be told by another member of the lab that a report had already been sent to Centurion over Hemming's signature identifying tensile stress as the cause of the problem. When Grant obtained a copy of the report, he found that the data of his tests had been changed to disprove his conclusions.

He was distressed, but he knew that nothing he said to Hemming or Stewart would have any effect. He wondered about the possibility of accidents, injuries, and deaths. He slept badly that night and the next morning was no nearer the solution of his dilemma.

Advertising

There has been perhaps more debate on advertising than on any other function of business. The reason is fairly obvious: Advertising is the one visible element of a company's total marketing strategy. We are bombarded every day by advertising messages through every type of medium for every kind of product.

Two main complaints are made against advertising. The first is that it is wasteful and unnecessary and therefore immoral; the second is that it is often untruthful, misleading, or in bad taste, which is equally immoral. While a good argument can be made for the view that there is too much advertising and that a significant proportion of the money spent on it is directed at convincing people that there is a difference between products that are totally interchangeable, it is difficult to see how manufacturers and service organizations could otherwise reach their markets and create volume sales, thus reducing unit costs.

It is not the purpose of this discussion to question the economics of advertising, but to examine its morality. In so doing, we need to remember a few salient facts. First, an advertisement is never all things to all people; that is, an advertised product is almost always directed at only a segment of the total population. The growth of the mass media, particularly television, has provided the opportunity for mass communication, but such media also involve a degree of wastage. A company promoting female products, such as cosmetics or panty hose, on television is "wasting" half its expenditure on men; yet the medium is still an efficient method of reaching women. Selective perception of only those advertisements that are related to our needs is a common phenomenon in the communication process; we screen out those messages that we find dull, in bad taste, or irrelevant because they are not meant for us.

Second, the criteria upon which the public judges an advertisement are usually whether it is "clever," whether is is amusing, or whether it displays skills of technical production. Judgment is rarely passed on whether it is likely to achieve its purpose; advertising, like politics, makes everyone an expert.

Third, if advertising is concerned with one objective above all others, it is concerned with attitude change or attitude reinforcement. To achieve this, the meaning of the message perceived by the receiver must be consonant with the meaning intended by the sender. This would appear to be self-evident, but it is remarkable how often advertisements fail to communicate because messages are misinterpreted or misunderstood, and large amounts of money are spent on exhaustive pretesting of advertising campaigns to minimize such risks. Thus, to accuse advertising of being misleading or in bad taste may be the result of wrong interpretation, since not all people associate the same meaning with particular words or phrases.

Fourth, specific advertisements tend to be couched in the language of the audience for which they are intended. Therefore, if an advertisement offends you because it does not talk your language, it is likely that it was never aimed at you in the first place; you are one of the "wasted" audience. If one compares the language of advertising in the *New York Times* with that in the *National Enquirer*, the point becomes very obvious.

Advertising has come a long way from the days of the hucksters and the barnstorming antics of the nineteenth and early twentieth centuries. Legislation and regulation, both external and self-imposed, have placed heavy constraints and penalties on the advertising business. This restraining influence makes it extremely difficult for any advertisement that is dishonest or that promotes dangerous or harmful products to be published. Regulation falls broadly into four categories: consumer protection groups, the advertising industry itself (consisting of advertisers, advertising agencies, and the media), governments (both state and federal), and government agencies, such as the U.S. Federal Trade Commission. However, despite such regulation, we can identify anomalies, such as the advertising of cigarettes, which are sold with a government health warning on their packs; thus, the constraints are far from perfect, largely because of vested governmental interests (in this case those of tobacco duty).

Consumers, either singly or in groups, have a number of options in protecting themselves against advertising to which they take exception. They can write to the company involved, they can inform the press, they can sue the offending company, they can complain to an official regulatory agency, or they can consult one or more consumerist associations, such as (in the United States) the National Consumer League and the Consumer Federation of America or (in Britain) the Consumers' Association.

As for the self-policing measures formulated by the advertising industry, several sets of regulations are published by different formal organizations representing the different aspects of advertising. The American Advertising Federation, consisting of local advertising clubs, produces the *Advertising Code of American Business,* which sets standards in the areas of truth (revealing facts that if concealed would mislead people), responsibility (being willing to substantiate claims), taste and decency, guarantees and warranties, price claims, and unprovable claims and testimonials.

In addition, the American Association of Advertising Agencies publishes its own *Standard of Practices,* as does the Association of National Advertisers, the British Institute of Practitioners in Advertising, and the British Advertising Association. Better Business Bureaus, sponsored by advertisers, agencies, and media, handle consumer complaints and in many cases obtain redress for complainants. Their national body, the National Council of Better Business Bureaus, has established the National Advertising Review Board, which acts as an appeal court for the review of complaints not settled by the council's National Advertising

Division. The board can exert considerable pressure on miscreant advertisers, including making their offenses public and reporting them to the Federal Trade Commission. Comparable organizations exist in most Western democracies.

The media, both individually and through their associations, have wide powers not to accept offending advertisements or to insist that they be amended. In accepting advertisements, magazines, for instance, use such criteria as the protection of readers from exploitation or dishonesty, the known characteristics or tastes of their readers, and in many cases the personal ethical standards of the media owners. The television networks appraise and, if necessary, censor advertisements; advertisements for some products, such as cigarettes and hard liquor, are prohibited.

Media associations include the National Association of Broadcasters, which issues its *Television Code* and *Radio Code,* which are enforced by a special review board; the Direct Mail Advertising Association, which maintains a Standards of Practices Committee to prevent its members from mailing objectionable materials; and the Outdoor Advertising Association of America, which sets standards for billboard advertising.

Among the most prominent American government agencies involved in the regulation and supervision of advertising practice are the Federal Trade Commission, which, in addition to its many other responsibilities, takes action on false and deceptive advertising; the Food and Drug Administration, which controls the marketing of food, pharmaceutical products, cosmetics, and medical devices, and other potentially hazardous products; and the Federal Communications Commission, which supervises the granting and withdrawing of broadcasting licenses. Many other agencies also control advertising standards in different specific product or service areas, such as agriculture, securities, and airlines. The Federal Trade Commission's major concern is with prior restraint on advertising that might offend or cause harm to "the least reasonable man," as well as with the need for corrective advertising if claims made for a product over time have been cumulatively deceptive, as was the case with Warner Lambert's campaign for Listerine in which the product had been promoted as a means of killing all known bacteria; it is also very rigorous in its attitude toward testimonials and endorsements, comparative advertising, and advertising aimed at children.

It is clear that advertising has to negotiate many hurdles before it eventually sees the light of day. The controls described in the preceding paragraphs have been itemized at length not merely for the sake of information, but also as an indication of exactly how difficult it is for dubious advertising to survive. The fact that such governance prevents the publication of obviously untruthful or otherwise dishonest advertising is a measure of its effectiveness. Yet this is not what much of the criticism of advertising is about; the innuendo, the meaningless attribute used to substantiate a claim, and, not least, the very obtrusiveness of advertising's presence in our lives are all difficult, if not impossible, to control. Regulation in these things is largely a matter for the individual conscience, as is the often necessary compromise between professional competence and advertising objectives, which is illustrated in the following case example.

Incident 3: Mike Watson and McAllister, Collins Associates. McAllister, Collins Associates, or MCA, is a relatively new advertising agency.[11] It was founded in 1976 by Jack McAllister and Brian Collins, who until that time had been account director and chief copywriter, respectively, at the London office of J. Walter Thompson (JWT). The new company experienced rapid growth and gained several prestigious clients. Its billings (the advertising expenditure of its clients), initially a mere £200,000, increased to a phenomenal £5 million by April 1980, largely because the highly imaginative creative work McAllister and Collins had done on their accounts had begun to attract more big business.

Along with the growth in billings and profits came a growth in staff, mainly in the creative area, which was regarded as MCA's distinctive competence. Collins was highly respected as a man who could transform mundane products and services into scintillating advertising; he had been much sought after by other agencies when he was at JWT. The people whom Collins and McAllister brought into their company were all successful copywriters and artists from other large London agencies. One of them, Mike Watson, had been employed at Ted Bates, where his work had aroused a great deal of comment and admiration throughout the advertising business. He enjoyed his new job at MCA, especially the freedom he was given to exercise his imagination and even, at times, to suggest his own overall strategy for a particular client. McAllister and Collins felt fortunate to have been able to persuade him to join them and were very enthusiastic about his work and his contribution to the success of their venture.

At the beginning of May 1980, Jack McAllister received a telephone call from the Conservative party's Central Office. The Conservatives had formed a new government in the spring of 1979, and their economic policies, based on reduction of direct taxation, an increase of indirect taxation, public spending cuts, and a dramatic increase of the bank rate, were beginning to find disfavor with the public, since the result had been an increase in the rate of inflation from under 10 percent to nearly 20 percent within a year. With four years of their term of office still to run, they had decided to evaluate their present advertising agency along with other possible candidates, with a view to laying the groundwork for an eventual advertising strategy for the next General Election, due some time before the spring of 1984.[12]

McAllister was asked on the telephone whether MCA would be interested in making a speculative presentation, in competition with other agencies, for the Conservative party account. The agency would not be expected to give advice on party policy or strategy, but merely to devise means of presenting the Conservative party line as dramatically and as competitively (vis-à-vis Labour publicity and adverse public opinion) as possible. McAllister was delighted at the opportunity, since the account was sizable, and although there would be no significant expenditure in the immediate future, an election campaign would produce a bonanza.

Over the next three weeks, there were meetings between members of the agency staff, including Mike Watson who had been assigned to the presentation team, and the people responsible for the party's propaganda machine. At these meetings, the agency was thoroughly briefed on the objectives of the party's continuing campaign and the possible focus of eventual election publicity. The discussions were exhaustive, and the MCA people returned to the agency to begin preparing their presentation, knowing that four other agencies (including the party's present agency) would provide stiff competition.

MCA assembled an impressive presentation package, and after delivering it, they waited three weeks for the verdict. They felt that they had done as well as they could. Then, with great jubilation, they received a call from the Conservative Central Office informing them that they had won the account and that their presentation had, by a unanimous vote, been judged the best of the five. When McAllister and Collins discussed the question of who should work on the new account, it seemed logical to leave it in the hands of the people who had been members of the presentation team, and Collins called Mike Watson to tell him he would be responsible for the creative work.

Watson received the news with no enthusiasm. He had been perfectly happy to serve on the presentation team, since the account represented a significant potential profit for the agency. However, he was an active member of the Labour party, and he knew he would be campaigning for his local Labour candidate at the next election. He had said nothing about this when asked to help with the presentation, hoping that if the agency won the account, somebody else from the creative group would be asked to work on it. He wondered whether there was any difference between his writing copy for a brand of toothpaste he disliked and a political party for which he would never vote.

Pricing and Profiteering

Pricing policy determines the eventual profitability of the corporation. It is a commonly held belief that the purpose of business activity is to make a profit that will keep stockholders happy, that will maintain the financial security of the enterprise, and that will contribute to the health of the nation's economy. It can therefore be argued that the more profits a company makes, the better these ends are served. Most business executives would like to make more profit than they do; yet few of them have any idea of how much more profit or of what maximum profit is.

As Joseph McGuire has pointed out, the word *profits* implies a range from a maximum to zero, and the profit objective must therefore be located somewhere between the two.[13] From an ethical viewpoint, the ideal goal would be to achieve maximum profits consistent with the observance of social and environmental obligations, although it is not easy to calculate what the cost of such observance is. Some business executives would argue that being a good corporate citizen brings its rewards in the shape of higher future profits and that it is this, rather than the ethical obligation itself, that makes good works worth doing. Such a view would have offended Kant, whose categorical imperative made doing good things out of self-interest reprehensible, but today, despite the skepticism that attitudes of this type attract, most people would approve of ethical conduct even if it were prompted by the wrong reasons.

Administered pricing is the variable that controls the profit motive. Pricing policy is a broad subject, but here it is sufficient to examine its implications, rather than the specific techniques it involves. Clearly, decisions about price can have both good and bad effects. If the price at which products or services are offered produces revenues that satisfy stockholders, provide a reasonable profit, allow for adequate retained earnings for future investment, and contribute to the gross national product, and if the price is also at a level that customers are happy and willing to pay, then it can be said to be a fair price; but if a seller's greed makes it so high that customers find it difficult to pay it, the price is unjust.

Incident 4: A Bargain at Twice the Price.   Leonard Rosenthal, chairman and managing director of Rosen Tailoring, Ltd., prepared early for the entry of the United Kingdom into the European Common Market.[14] Although the union was not effected until 1972, Rosenthal was convinced as early as 1962 that it was inevitable and that Rosen Tailoring should take maximum advantage of it.

Rosen's was one of the largest multiple tailoring firms in Britain, with over 500 branches on main-street sites throughout the country. Because it could purchase cloth in volume, the company was able to offer made-to-measure men's clothing of good quality and style at prices no independent tailor could match. In 1962, a made-to-measure suit in high quality English worsted could be bought from Rosen's in any style for the equivalent of $20 to $50. The company also sold ready-to-wear clothing, such as overcoats, raincoats, sport coats, and casual pants.

When buying a made-to-measure suit at Rosen's, a customer first chose his cloth from hundreds of patterns and price levels. He was then measured in the store, and special styling details were noted. The measurements were sent to the company's manufacturing plant in Yorkshire, where the suit was tailored; it was returned for fitting about two and a half weeks later to the branch store where it had been ordered. After minor adjustments had been noted at the fitting, the suit went back to the plant for finishing. The final product was returned to the store for customer collection about four weeks from the date of the original order.

In his plan to enter the European market, Rosenthal chose France as his first target. He bought a large department store building in an excellent location on one of the main shopping streets of Paris, gutted it, and completely restyled and refitted the interior to suit the nature of his business. The name on the front of the store was displayed as "Rosen's of Regent Street, London." At the same time, he bought a new building in an industrial development complex on the outskirts of the city and began to fit it out with the machinery necessary for tailoring operations. He intended to bring to Paris experienced tailors and other operatives from his Yorkshire plant to start up the French production facility and to train French workers for the job. The plant would not be ready to start production until six months after the Paris store opened, and so initial manufacturing would have to be handled in England.

The grand opening of the Paris store was planned for June 1, 1963. The operation was to be identical to that of any Rosen's store in the United Kingdom, and the prices, quality, and cloth were also to be the same. Thus, Parisians had the opportunity to buy made-to-measure suits in the best English cloth (highly regarded in France) for exactly the same price charged at Rosen's stores in Britain. For the first six months until the French production facility came on line, unfinished and finished suits would be shipped by British Airways scheduled passenger services between France and England. Rosen's planned to expand their French operations, using the Paris plant as the central production unit, to other major cities, such as Bordeaux, Marseille, Lyons, Lille, Rouen, and Dijon, thus replicating their British system.

Shortly before the Paris store opened for business, Rosenthal held a meeting with representatives from his advertising agency (which had an affiliate office in Paris) to discuss the advertising that had been prepared for the opening. During the course of the meeting, which was attended by several members of the French agency, Rosenthal for the first time announced that there would be no difference between the prices charged in France and in England.

At this news, there were gasps of astonishment from the Frenchmen. It was crazy, they said, to charge British prices: There was no comparable tailoring service in France, except that provided by very expensive private tailors; British cloth was regarded as the best in the world, and Frenchmen associated it with high price, as they did a Rolls-Royce; and, finally, all that could be bought elsewhere in Paris at the prices Rosenthal intended to charge were ready-to-wear suits of very inferior French cloth. The Rosen's price, they claimed, would have no credibility, and sales would consequently suffer. Frenchmen were naturally suspicious of the British and would think there was a trick somewhere; Rosenthal should therefore double his prices.

Rosenthal was horrified. He replied that his company's profits, based on its current price structure, were already high and that doubling his price in France would result in astronomical levels of profitability. Also, he was a fair man and had never exploited his customers in his life. Value for money was his obsession. Ever since his father started the business in 1900, the chief executive had always personally dealt with customer complaints, and the fact that in 1961 Rosen's had made 90,000 suits and had received only seventeen complaints testified to the high standards of quality and honesty to which the company aspired.

The French were adamant. Emphatically they insisted that this was not exploitation, but good business; the low prices were the road to suicide. The meeting ended with the question unresolved, and Leonard Rosenthal called his chauffeur to take him home to his seventeenth-century mansion in the Yorkshire dales, a sorely worried man.

Fair Dealing and Consumerism

The so-called consumerist movement grew in the 1950s and 1960s out of a feeling that an effective social force was necessary to offset what people perceived as the unduly dominating power of big business. In the 1970s, the movement appeared to lose some of its impetus, due largely to the fact that business itself came to realize the effects that consumer pressure could have. Consumer protest groups emerged as a potent force because they had the power to prompt government legislation to control those elements of business appearing reluctant or unable to control themselves. As soon as business became aware of this power, the need for the protest itself, as well as for government legislation, declined.

The reasons why such consumer awareness and protest emerged are complex. F. D. Sturdivant has attributed the explosion of disenchantment to a growing consumer sophistication: Because of increased levels of education, the impact of the mass media, and more specialized consumer information services, people have become more competent in filtering and analyzing the information fed to them.[15] As a result, consumers are more wary and cynical toward business and its products and advertising.

Having witnessed the success with which Ralph Nader fought General Motors and eventually forced the withdrawal of the Corvair from the market and a change in the composition of GM's board of directors through the addition of members concerned with consumer affairs, business (and particularly big business) has been fairly eager to put its house in order. Aware that government intervention and regulation are already at a significant level, business is anxious to avoid more of the same and in many cases is actually turning consumer preoccupations to its own advantage. The introduction of low cholesterol and low calorie foods is a good example; the advertising emphasis on environmental protection, energy preservation and exploration, economy, and product safety is also indicative of the business response.

There is no doubt that the increase in articulate consumer protest has had a profound effect on both government and business organizations. Yet there have been recent instances in which no amount of consumer objection has had any effect. The entry of Britain into the European Common Market — ostensibly economically, but in fact politically, motivated — resulted in previously unimaginable rises in the price of consumable goods (most agricultural products) to a level that causes real hardship; this contribution to inflation was compounded by the move from a duodecimal to a decimal currency, hastily and inconsiderately perpetrated, leading manufacturers and retailers to round off prices in the new money, which senior citizens to this day have difficulty comprehending. The price of a refrigerator may have remained fairly constant, but that of a pound of butter doubled almost overnight. Efficient British agriculture was, in effect, required to subsidize inefficient Italian and French agriculture. Business organizations could do little in the face of political profligacy, and no consumerist group could force the government's hand as it could that of a Unilever, a British Motors Corporation, or a Dunlop Rubber Company. The people had no say in the Common Market decision, except after the event, which is a strange comment on the principles of the oldest democracy in the world and the home of the Industrial Revolution. Politicians frequently criticize business for misleading advertising; yet most political party manifestos would have a hard time with the truth-in-advertising concept.

If the concession theory of business is valid, then consumerism has a logical place in our society. (For a discussion of the concession theory, see Chapter 1.) *Caveat emptor* may be a phrase with a history, but in the second half of the twentieth century it has a hollow ring; whether modern business organizations like it or not, regulatory pressures are here to stay, and it is through the people that such pressures are born.

Incident 5: Anne Plummer and Stamps Unlimited. Anne Plummer graduated as a journalism major from a small liberal arts college in New York state in 1978.[16] While she was looking for a job where her writing ability would be an asset, she met a friend, Susan Stevens, who had graduated at the end of Anne's freshman year and whom she had not seen since.

Over coffee in a restaurant, Susan told Anne about her new job with a company selling postage stamps to collectors by mail order. Susan was assistant to the president of the company, Stamps Unlimited; as such, she was responsible for the general administration of the office and for processing customers' accounts. The company had been set up the previous year by John Frankel, who had owned and operated a stamp store in New York City for several years; he had found that he was able to do far more business by mail than over the counter and had therefore decided to concentrate entirely on that aspect of his operations. Accordingly, he had closed his store and taken a lease on a small office building for the mail-order activity. Business flourished, and at the end of his first year, his staff had increased from two to eight; he had hired Susan as his assistant so that he could spend more time buying stamps and could leave most of the administrative problems to her.

"I'm glad we met today," said Susan, "because you may be just the person we are looking for." When Anne looked puzzled, she explained that John Frankel had been talking of possible new methods of increasing his already flourishing business, including negotiating with other mail-order companies for joint promotions. This would mean looking for someone who could coordinate this new operation and who could also write good, hard-selling copy. "Why don't you come and talk to John about it?" Susan asked.

Anne thought it over and decided that the job sounded interesting. Susan called her that evening and arranged for her to meet Frankel the next day.

Anne liked John Frankel as soon as she met him. They talked for an hour, and at the end of their conversation, he offered her the job. Anne thought the salary was generous, and she accepted the offer. Frankel had already made agreements in principle with two mail-order photographic-processing companies for joint promotions, and so he was pleased when Anne told him that she could begin work immediately.

From the beginning everything went well. Anne designed attractive leaflets promoting the Stamps Unlimited selections and devised several promotional special offers to arouse initial interest. In return for a service fee, the photographic companies included this material in all packets of processed photographs they returned to their customers, and the offers attracted substantial new business. Using John Frankel's expertise, she produced a booklet that she called the "Frankel Finder;" this helped collectors locate the country of origin of stamps that were difficult to identify. The booklet was offered free, with no obligation to buy stamps, to new customers; it was a great success. In the majority of cases, customers asking for it ordered stamps also; even when they did not, Stamps Unlimited was able to add their names to the company's mailing list for future promotion.

Anne's job concentrated entirely on promotion. She had nothing at all to do with mailing the stamps or invoicing. Every day she received from the order department the quantity of orders produced by each promotional offer and was thus able to analyze the effectiveness of each offer in terms of the revenue it generated. Over time this made it possible to establish which type of promotions were likely to attract the greatest response. Consistently, the "Frankel Finder" worked well — so well, in fact, that after six months and the addition of five more joint mail-order promoters, Anne decided that further copies should be printed. Frankel approved her decision.

One day, just about a year after Anne had joined the company, and after many expressions of praise and appreciation from both John Frankel and Susan Stevens for what she was doing, she noticed a discrepancy on one of the order summaries. For some reason, the key number, which served as a reference to the promotion that had prompted the order, was missing. She went to the order department to ask why. It was lunch hour, and only one of the order clerks was on duty, a young man who had been with the company for only two weeks. He had not processed the orders in question, but he showed Anne the daily records file and, since he was working on something else, suggested that she look up the information herself. She did so and had a shock. On going through the file, she found that in hundreds of cases, orders had no reference numbers, and when she checked the invoices, she discovered that the reference numbers had been added by hand. She went back to her office, troubled and mystified.

The following weekend, under the pretext of catching up with unfinished work, she borrowed Susan's master key and made a more thorough examination of the orders and invoices. Her worst fears were confirmed. It was quite obvious that Stamps Unlimited was sending stamps to people who had asked for the "Finder," but who had not ordered any stamps. The money involved amounted to over $20,000. In most cases, it appeared that customers had adopted the line of least resistance and paid the bills for the unordered stamps. In a few, however, there were letters of protest on file claiming that no order had been made and indicating that the merchandise was being returned; Anne even found some records clearly showing that the company had continued to send stamps and invoices to people who had consistently refused to accept them. She discovered one bill for over $500, and the correspondence from that particular customer bordered on the hysterical. The average order was between $10 and $20; Anne was horrified.

First thing the next day, Monday, Anne went to see Frankel and told him what she had found. She insisted that he investigate the situation, dismiss the person responsible, and make sure that there would be no recurrence. The practice, she claimed, was an infringement of consumer rights. Frankel told her to calm down. Apparently he was fully aware of what was going on. "Nobody has sued us yet, Anne," he said, "and it brings in a lot of business. Just continue to do your job and the rest of us will do ours. We're dealing with stamp enthusiasts. They usually pay up after thinking about it a bit."

Anne enjoyed her job and felt she was contributing significantly to the company's success. She had also heard from some of her recent fellow graduates; they were finding it difficult to find employment that matched their qualifications. Furthermore, she liked Frankel. She decided to have a long talk with Susan and seek advice. She did not know whether Susan realized what was happening.

INTRAORGANIZATIONAL ISSUES

Employment

Few decisions involve more subjective criteria than those regarding promotions, appointments (i.e., employment of persons from outside the organization), and dismissals. The first and the third are usually based on one's past performance; the second is more directly concerned with one's future usefulness. Yet so often it happens that these criteria are reversed. Executives are promoted at times not because they have performed well, but because they are expected to perform well; they are appointed not because of what they are expected to achieve, but because of their track record; and they are dismissed not because they have not done their duty in the past, but because there appears to be no useful role for them to play in the future.

There is perhaps no aphorism more carelessly offered, yet more painfully true, than the one that claims that it is not what you know but whom you know that counts. Many executives in secure and well-paid positions have failed to achieve advancement, have failed to attract other employers, and have even lost their jobs because their present or prospective bosses have ignored them in favor of someone whose choice in clothing they preferred. The standards by which performance is judged are at worst prejudicial and at best unscientific.

Furthermore, every executive feels that he or she has some inalienable right to promotion. The old story that people are promoted to the level of their incompetence has an unfortunate foundation in fact. Why people should feel that because they do one job well, they can do another job better is sometimes difficult to understand; a salary increase — even a large salary increase — is frequently held to be an unsatisfactory reward for good performance if the recognition does not carry elevation to a higher level, even if such a promotion would mean that performance would be out of keeping with position and that ability would not match demand.

Unfortunately, despite the fact that most modern companies have some stated criteria (even if rudimentary) for the appraisal of managerial performance, with rewards or penalties to match, the application of those criteria is frequently confused and even abused by alliances or conflicts of personality. One of the "organizational overlays" suggested by J. M. Pfiffner and F. P. Sherwood concerns those personal relationships in companies that override and supersede formal channels of communication.[17] Friendships between individuals at different authority levels and with different functional responsibilities interfere with the stated means of getting things done and often result in alliances that produce unwarranted changes in status, totally unrelated to performance and not uncommonly inequitable and unjustified.

Pfiffner and Sherwood give the following five examples of such overlays:

1. *Sociometric network of private likes and dislikes for others.* Some investigators have included in this classification such attitudes as *prescribed relations* (those identical with the formal organization), *perceived relations* (people's interpretations of the official network), *actual relations* (those that in fact take place), *desired relations* (people's preferences regarding interactions they want with other persons), and *rejected relations* (relations with other people that are not wanted).
2. *Functional network dependent on special skills and knowledge.* Specialists often exert their influence on operations without direct responsibility for the work itself.
3. *Grid of centers where decisions are really made.* The power and authority network, together with the functional network, may cut across hierarchical channels.
4. *Pattern of power politics at work.* In this case, power is no longer viewed as synonymous with authority, but depends on personal political influence.
5. *Channels of communication.* The information process affects controls, decision making, influence, power, interpersonal relations, and leadership.

The existence of such relationship patterns within the formal hierarchy suggests the possibility of favor and prejudice overriding equitable performance assessment and reward. The effects of this discrimination will inevitably be felt and noticed most obviously by employees in management positions at a level lower than the very top, as the following example will show. The labor force is usually protected by its unions and senior management by its authority, but middle-level executives are frequently vulnerable and defenseless.

Incident 6: Harry Simmonds and Universal Insurance Ltd.   Harry Simmonds felt that he had done well.[18] After a checkered academic career that had reached no great heights, he had finally found himself a position as an estimator with Universal Insurance, a British national insurance company offering life and automobile insurance and other services in competition with other major companies.

Before obtaining this job, he had tried working in a bank, selling used cars, being a traffic warden (an occupation he particularly disliked because he felt sorry for the owners of the cars on which he stuck parking tickets), and working as a security guard in the Natural History Museum; he was not fond of museums or natural history.

His job at Universal seemed to be the beginning of a real career. His interest in cars and his sympathy with car owners (he drove a rather old but well-loved Mini) gave him the opportunity to make the most sympathetic settlements with motorists who had had the misfortune to have to make claims on Universal as the result of automobile accidents. His judgments were always fair, in his opinion, and in the best interests of both insurer and insured. His job consisted of going out each day to estimate the damage and costs of repairs to cars insured by Universal.

His new job had enabled him to settle down with his family (his wife, Jean, and his one-year-old daughter, Carol) in a pleasant suburb in southwest London, where he had moved into a house with a small garden on a mortgage he could barely afford but that he felt was worth it. He liked his neighbors, met friends in the local pub, and grew tomatoes, of which he was inordinately fond. Each year, he managed to take his family to the coast, where they rented a small cottage and had a quiet vacation. He had, in addition to a generous company pension scheme, a small life insurance annuity, and his mortgage was insured against death but not against loss of earnings.

He had joined Universal almost by accident. After apparently drifting for several years, he had met an old friend from his school days, John Faraday, who had done well for himself and was departmental head of Universal's auto insurance division. He and Faraday had come across each other in a pub, and Faraday had, after three or four drinks, offered Harry a job; Faraday did, however, stress that it was no sinecure and that the rewards would depend on what Harry made of it. Harry jumped at the chance, and his performance and subsequent progress in the company bore witness to his enthusiasm and application. He was paid a base salary and commission.

After three years with Universal, Harry was one of two estimators who, because of their past performances, were usually sent out on difficult and complicated jobs. The other was Tom Chester, who had been with the company for only six months and who seemed to live in Faraday's pocket. Harry did not dislike him, but he felt that he did not know him very well. There was little communication or socializing between the two.

Harry spent his seaside vacation as usual and came back to the office on the Monday morning after it ended, refreshed and ready to start work again. As always, he went straight to Faraday's office to pick up his estimating assignments for the day. Faraday's secretary handed them to him and, as he was about to leave, informed him casually that Faraday had suffered a heart attack the week before and that Tom Chester was in charge of the department.

Harry's first reaction was one of shock at John Faraday's misfortune, but then the full significance of what had happened struck him: Chester, who had been with the company for a mere half year, had been given preference over Harry as Faraday's temporary successor. His mind went back to a chance remark that Faraday had made several months previously, when he had mentioned to Harry that Chester's wife was an attractive woman and that he, Faraday, was interested in her. Harry wondered whether this had anything to do with the situation, and, if it did, what he should do about it. If he complained to higher authority, he might get Faraday into trouble, which he did not want to do under the circumstances; if he did nothing, he might find himself permanently answering to Tom Chester. Either way, he had missed promotion. Perhaps the best solution was to seek a position with another insurance company and to say nothing at all about his suspicions.

Conflict of Interests

Nowhere is there anything nearer to the problem of ethical duality than the conflict of interest that occurs when executives find themselves involved with forces that pull in opposite directions. Examples are frequently found in politics, where individuals have on occasion been required to resign from positions of political responsibility because their professional activities do not harmonize with their private financial involvements, or vice versa.

In business, the conflict is not so clearly defined. However, a company director who has a financial interest in another firm that supplies his own with raw materials or equipment might have difficulty in maintaining a credible position of impartiality. Similarly, an executive who has to deal with customers from whom he personally derives some financial reward would not be above suspicion. The important word is *personally,* since there is clearly nothing wrong with parent companies doing business with their subsidiaries. These examples could well refer to managers who are perfectly blameless; it is the doubts they raise that make it desirable to rectify the situations.

There are other cases, however, in which employees feel their jobs are in jeopardy when they engage in activities that are held to be detrimental to the firm. It is difficult, in such circumstances, to establish satisfactory guidelines; employee behavior outside the company is notoriously hard to legislate.

Much research has been conducted to examine to what extent influences exerted by organizations on the behavior and attitudes of individual employees may be regarded as legitimate. Broadly speaking, this influence is segmented into coordinative and substantive requirements. Coordinative requirements (i.e., those designed to coordinate activities within the organization to ensure smoothness of operations) are usually readily accepted. On the other hand, substantive requirements (those that relate more directly to the job, such as work quality) tend to be less acceptable as they become less job-connected (e.g., requirements regarding clothing, appearance, or political opinions). Substantive requirements are acceptable if they relate to actions on the job or actions related to it. Areas in which substantive requirements carry minimal legitimacy are those involving personal opinions and motives, such as religious or political beliefs.[19]

The problem with research studies of this type is that it is difficult to be specific in describing organizational influence. For instance, though religious opinion may be regarded as an area of minimal legitimacy, an employee may at times encounter conflicts of conscience in an on-the-job situation that stem directly from a fundamental irreconcilability between personal religious beliefs and the task that must be performed. Although religion may in general be regarded by research respondents as not particularly job-related, in specific cases it may be the cause of personal and organizational differences.

The topic is very closely related to those discussed in the next two sections of this chapter (the problem of legislation by companies for employee morality and the overriding dilemma of personal ethical conflict). No more therefore needs to be said at this stage. The following case makes the point.

Incident 7: Marcel Rostand and Industrie St. Pierre S.A.   Industrie St. Pierre S.A. (ISP) is one of the largest manufacturers of sheet metal in Europe.[20] Located on the outskirts of a big industrial town in northern France, it employs some 15,000 workers and is by far the most important employer in the area.

Marcel Rostand, thirty-seven years of age, had worked with ISP for most of his career as an information officer responsible to the Director of External Affairs. The Office of External Affairs was an important part of ISP's general publicity activity, since it was the means by which community and other social projects were initiated, implemented, and communicated to the public, both local and national. Such projects included pollution control and financial support for city development, community centers, the arts, recreation clubs for ISP employees, children's playgroups, and homes for senior citizens, among many others.

Between 1 percent and 2 percent of ISP's gross income was spent each year on these activities, and the company was frequently the subject of highly favorable comment in the national French media because of its attention to the social responsibilities of business. Several case studies had been written by researchers from well-known French business schools on different aspects of the company's social program. ISP was pleased with its record, since not only did management feel that it had a social duty to do these things, but it also appreciated the publicity value accruing from them. While no figures could be attached to the increased profitability directly generated by community involvement, it was felt to be considerable, and funds for social projects were always available.

Rostand enjoyed his work, and he was happy to be associated with a company that held social responsibility to be so important. His wife, too, was pleased to know that Marcel not only worked for such an employer, but also was directly involved with this aspect of its affairs. They had been married for ten years and had two children, both of whom received financial support for their schooling from ISP. Mme. Rostand (Félice) often accompanied Marcel on his frequent engagements to make public speeches or to represent ISP in other ways as part of the company's social program.

Of late, Félice Rostand had begun to involve herself energetically in the women's movement. She had read most of the authors who wrote about it and was a great admirer of Simone de Beauvoir. Of particular interest and concern to her was the significant discrepancy between the salaries and wages paid to men and women; she felt very strongly that the two sexes should receive equal pay for equal work. Marcel agreed with her, although he did not attend the meetings held by the local women's group, of which his wife was secretary; he did, however, take a great deal of interest in the topics discussed and talked about them with his wife.

ISP had not, in its social strategy, laid any emphasis on equal rights for women; whether this was because it was unsympathetic or because it felt there was little publicity value in the idea is uncertain. It was, however, a fact that no policy of "equal pay for equal work" existed in the company.

One morning Marcel was surprised to be called in to see the director. He very rarely met him, except at department meetings at which all his colleagues were also present. As he passed through the office of the director's secretary, he asked the reason for the summons, but received no enlightenment.

The director greeted him and asked him to sit down. After a few moments of small talk, the conversation became more specific. Management, it seemed, was concerned that the wife of one of its managers (and one who was a company spokesman, at that) was publicly expressing views that were not stated in the company policy; although no reference had been made to ISP in these utterances, it was felt that her relationship to one of the ISP information officers gave her statements the appearance of an official view. Furthermore, even if her views did reflect company policy, it should be left to ISP to state them. The director, in the most affable and charming manner, asked Marcel to see to it that she ceased publicizing her views forthwith.

Marcel was perplexed. He sympathized with his wife's opinions, and even though his company had no official policy on women's rights, he could not believe there could be any objection to what she felt. He said this to the director, but he received an adamant repetition of the request to restrain his wife. He went home, wondering what he should do.

Félice, when she was told of what had happened, was at first furious. Then, as the significance of the affair began to dawn upon her, she realized the possible consequences on Marcel's job. She quieted down and told Marcel that she was prepared to give up her involvement with the women's movement. Marcel was horrified. He bluntly refused to allow her to do this; the company had no right, he said, to interfere with his wife's activities, especially since they had no direct impact on the firm's reputation.

The next morning Marcel went to see the director. He told him in no uncertain terms that he felt that the company was overstepping its rightful boundaries of influence, that what Félice did was of no concern to management, and that no harm was being done to the company anyway.

The director listened patiently, bade Marcel a friendly goodbye, and asked his secretary to show him out. The secretary saw him to the door, looked at him askance, and shrugged her shoulders. Marcel returned to his office.

That afternoon he received a memorandum from the vice-president of marketing. As of the end of that month, Marcel's employment with ISP was at an end. The reason given was "activity contrary to the best interests of the company."

Marcel immediately went to see his lawyer, who was pessimistic. The local women's group began to organize a protest march, and Marcel found himself shunned at the local café where he habitually went to take an apéritif before dinner. He wondered where he had gone wrong. Félice was hospitalized because of a nervous breakdown.

Ethical Legislation

Some companies, in an attempt to ensure correct behavior on the part of their employees, produce elaborate documents to control the "ethical" decisions that may be required. Now it is easy to write rules of conduct for general business behavior; admonitions to refrain from bribery, immorality, and turpitude are obvious examples. It is not so easy to give managers a comprehensive guidebook for every eventuality. Furthermore, it can, on occasion, be positively dangerous to ask executives to behave in a certain way when the circumstances may not be as clearly defined as the rule book prescribes. Moral legislation is laudable in principle, but hazardous in practice.

The problem with legislated ethics is twofold. On the one hand, the values expressed in any formal code of behavior originate from some central source (in a business context, this source is usually the chief executive officer or the executive board). On the other hand, no set of rules can cover all decision situations; right and wrong can be relative only to the particular context in which a decision has to be made. The employee therefore has to interpret what the rules mean according to the circumstances in which they are to be applied; moreover, the responsibility for the interpretation can lie *only* with the employee in question. There is thus a very strong argument to be made for the view that, far from giving employees help in moral decision making, corporate rule books merely compound the difficulty by falling short of comprehensive help. In this, legislated behavior per se can be held to be thoroughly unethical.

Gulf+Western, one of the largest corporations in the United States, with interests stretching from oil to motion pictures and from construction to paper products, publishes a set of ethical guidelines for its entire labor force. On the surface, the rules are commonsensical: No bribes should be accepted or offered, no special favors considered, no compromising of universally acknowledged moral standards should occur. There is nothing that would offend the typical white Western Christian. But what happens when an American or European manager has to deal with an Egyptian or a Turk or a black African? How does the code apply when different mores come into play? Who carries the responsibility when local customs are in conflict with the stated ethics of the corporation? Is it not wrong to lay the onus of decision making in these situations on an employee who, as likely as not, could be fired if his or her verdict differs from the verdict of those at the top?

The point becomes obvious when the details of the Gulf+Western ethical policy statement of December 20, 1978, are examined:[21]

RESOLUTION OF THE G+W BOARD OF DIRECTORS

CODE OF BUSINESS ETHICS RESOLUTION

WHEREAS   it is the desire of the Board of Directors to reconfirm its policy with respect to the ethical conduct of the corporation's business in a format suitable for dissemination throughout the corporation and it subsidiaries, now, therefore, be it

RESOLVED   that the Board of Directors adopts for and on behalf of the corporation a Code of Business Ethics in the form annexed hereto as Exhibit A; and hereby directs appropriate officers of the corporation to disseminate and implement the aforesaid Code in such manner as to assure compliance with the provisions thereof.

GENERAL

Gulf+Western takes pride in a reputation of high moral and ethical standards. Our business is highly competitive, yet we have managed to build a reputation of integrity by adhering to a sound and equitable code of business ethics.

Congress has recently passed an act which (i) prohibits companies and their officers, directors, shareholders and employees from engaging in certain corrupt practices with respect to foreign officials and (ii) requires companies to maintain accurate books, records and accounts and to devise a system of internal accounting controls. This code expresses in general terms the standards of conduct which have always been and continue to be expected by the Corporation and, in some instances, which now are required by law, of all Gulf+Western employees in their relationships with those with whom the Corporation does business, foreign governments and officials, the public and their fellow employees. They constitute a body of principles for guidance in many specific situations, as well as fundamental principles applicable in every situation, whether or not foreseen or specifically provided for. Not only impropriety, but every appearance or suggestion of impropriety, must be avoided.

POLICY

1. *Compliance with Law*
It is the policy of Gulf+Western to conduct its business on the highest ethical and moral plane, and to comply strictly with all laws and regulations governing its operations. All officers and employees of the Corporation are required to comply with local laws, as well as the laws of foreign nations, in their conduct of corporate business.

Compliance with the law means not only following the letter of the law, but also conducting business so that Gulf+Western will maintain its reputation for integrity and honesty which characterizes its business activity worldwide. Even where the law is not applicable, standards of ethics and morality apply and require the same diligent attention to good conduct and citizenship.

2. *Improper or Questionable Payments*
All persons and firms with whom Gulf+Western maintains business relationships will be treated fairly and impartially. The giving or acceptance of gifts, favors, or payments of any sort, either directly or indirectly, which illegally or immorally influence (or would appear to influence) business decisions, is strictly forbidden. Specific guidelines on antitrust, boycotts and other restrictive trade practices, and improper sales aid payments are stated in separate policies and are reaffirmed here.

The use of corporate funds for payments to any government official or government entity for any purpose whatsoever (except in satisfaction of lawful obligations, for reasonable public benefit contributions or for seasonable gifts insubstantial in value) is prohibited. However, it is recognized that in some areas of the world such payments may be required, by custom or practice, to expedite or obtain governmental action to which the Corporation is entitled under applicable law. In exceptional circumstances, such payments may be made but only if first approved by the Corporate Legal Department.

The prohibitions against improper payments described in this code apply to indirect disbursements of corporate funds or property by an employee, agent or third person as well as direct disbursements of such funds or property.

3. *Act of Hospitality*
Acts of hospitality towards any employee or representative of any customer or supplier or government official shall be of such scale or nature as to avoid any impropriety or the appearance of any impropriety in connection therewith.

4. *Accounting Records* (See Account Policy & Control II–2)
The records and books of account of Gulf+Western, each Group, subsidiary and division must accurately reflect each transaction recorded therein. No false or deliberately inaccurate entries shall be made in the Corporation's books and records for any reason. No payment shall be made with the intention or understanding that all or any part of such payment is to be used for any purpose other than that described by the documents supporting the payment. The creation and maintenance of any cash fund or other asset for disposition by representatives of the Corporation is prohibited without accurately accounting for such funds and assets, and the disposition thereof, on the books and records of the Corporation. Moreover, no person shall make, or cause to be made, any false or misleading statement to an accountant in connection with any examination or audit of the Corporation's books and records.

5. *Corporate Political Contributions*
Political contributions by, or in the name of, Gulf+Western or any of its Groups, subsidiaries, divisions or operating units are strictly forbidden, as they are illegal in all Federal elections, most state elections and in many foreign countries.

Under no circumstances will a Corporate political contribution of money or anything of value, including loans, contributions or use of either goods, facilities or services, be made either directly or indirectly to individual candidates, political committees, political parties, or political organizations of any kind. The Corporation will not reimburse, directly or indirectly, anyone for his personal contribution or personal participation in political activities.

The policy is not intended to prohibit or in any way deter Gulf+Western employees from personally contributing to or participating in political activities, including contributions and participation in duly authorized employee political action committees.

RESPONSIBILITY

There is a Corporate and legal obligation as well as an individual obligation to fulfill the intent of this policy.

The Chief Operating Officer of each Group, subsidiary and division, each G+W Corporation Officer and all managers within Gulf+Western are responsible for the implementation and administration of this policy within their respective organizations. Discovery of events which are in violation of this policy must be reported directly to the Corporate Legal Department.

Furthermore, it is the responsibility of every individual in the Corporation who in any way may affect the Corporation's compliance with the laws and with standards of ethical and moral conduct to carry out the corporate policy. It is not expected that every employee will be fully versed in the law affecting his responsibilities. However, it is expected that every employee will have a working knowledge of permissible activities involved in his work and will seek guidance from a superior or the Corporate Legal Department concerning any matter on which there is any question.

We expect compliance with the Gulf+Western standard of integrity throughout the organization. Any infraction of recognized ethical business standards or of the applicable laws will subject an employee to immediate disciplinary action (including the possibility of dismissal).

The Corporate Legal Department is responsible for constant review and interpretation of the law, and should be called upon for guidance and counsel if legal questions arise regarding this policy.

It might be asked whether this corporate statement satisfactorily allows room for employees to object to it on grounds of conscience. Although it would be unfair to suggest that its injunctions are not perfectly laudable, it is stated in such a way as to leave one with the uncomfortable feeling that observance of them is mandatory on pain of dismissal.

Yet, as has already been pointed out, no statement of this kind can hope to cover all ethical problems, and employees will inevitably have to make decisions not covered by it; such decisions appear to be included under an umbrella instruction to "do the right thing," but obviously any such document cannot specify what the right thing may be in all cases.

A devil's advocate might suggest, not altogether mischievously, that the statement itself would become more ethical if it included a clause similar to the following: "It is the policy of the corporation that no employee be forced to implement any element of that policy in contradiction of his or her conscience or ethical values." The problem of legalistic models of ethics is further discussed in Chapter 6.

Incident 8: Heather Carter and Future, Inc.   Heather Carter had worked at Future, Inc., for five years.[22] She was eager to get ahead and had performed well. Future was a company specializing in the production of tools used in a wide range of construction industries, from small hand tools to very large earth-moving equipment. Heather had joined the sales department straight out of college and had slowly but surely inched her way up the promotional ladder.

She was a company person — that is, she was utterly loyal to the company and all it stood for; she believed that it was a good company producing good products and serving both its customers and its employees well. She felt that the rules by which the company operated (frequently communicated to employees in memorandums from top management) were sensible and was grateful for the guidelines they provided when she had to make a difficult decision about a sales contract. The problems she encountered in her work were frequently associated with deciding what the "right" course of action should be. The company, in turn, was thankful for her loyalty and for the efficiency with which she performed her job.

Heather eventually reached the rank of sales project supervisor, which involved visiting large construction companies and negotiating sales contracts for major construction projects. Her negotiations were always conducted according to the procedures laid down by Future, and she produced impressive sales figures. She had six assistants who were assigned to minor projects or who helped her in her negotiations with major customers; she managed these subordinates on the simple principle of telling them to follow the company's rule book.

Future, Inc., was a company that treated its employees well. As a reward for her good work, and as a means of acquiring new contracts abroad, Heather was asked to make a sales trip to the Middle East. Arab countries were developing fast; they had money to spend from their oil profits, and most of their new development projects involved considerable construction work. Future felt that the market was ripe for a sales attack.

Heather was delighted at another opportunity to prove her selling efforts. Moreover, she had never been further from the United States than Canada and was thrilled at the prospect of seeing the world.

Her itinerary took her through most of the Middle Eastern states. She picked up some profitable orders and enjoyed visiting some of the places she had often read about but had never expected to see. She shot miles of cinefilm and took hundreds of photographs; she sent letters and post-cards to all her friends and relations, describing her experiences in excited terms; she made friends through her business acquaintances and even came to like some of the strange dishes she encountered in the restaurants she visited. In short, she was having the time of her life. She constantly thanked Providence that she had found an employer like Future.

At the end of her trip, she paid a visit to an engineering consortium in one of the smaller emirates on the Persian Gulf. The country was investing large sums of money in various schemes designed to improve living standards, especially agricultural projects involving drainage and mechanized farming. Agriculture represented a rich market for Future's products, and Heather was looking forward to meeting the minister responsible for agricultural contracts since she felt that they should be able to agree on some mutually profitable deals, even though it was common knowledge that there was strong competition from European equipment companies.

She checked into her hotel late on Thursday evening, after a particularly successful meeting elsewhere that day. She had a reservation on a flight to New York the following Sunday morning, and her appointment with the minister of agriculture was at eleven o'clock on the Friday. It was her final assignment and, wanting to finish on a high note, she had a simple meal and went to bed to get a good night's sleep before her last day's work.

The next morning, she arrived at the minister's office shortly before the appointed time. After about five minutes, she was shown into a well-appointed room and was greeted by a charming man who seemed to think that no hospitality was too much for her. He had coffee served and told her that he had arranged lunch with one of his advisers so that the details of the project could be discussed at length with Heather. Until then, he adamantly refused to talk of anything except a visit he had made to Boston several years before.

By one o'clock, after a great deal of coffee followed by an assortment of sweetmeats, Heather was beginning to feel that they would never get down to business. At that point, however, the assistant arrived, and after much conversation in Arabic between the minister, his secretary, and the assistant, all of which was beyond Heather's comprehension but which seemed to concern arrangements for the rest of the day, the minister called for his car, and they departed for lunch.

At the restaurant (exclusive and expensive), the conversation finally turned to the project. The minister's assistant was certainly well informed; he explained in great detail a new drainage scheme and set out clearly and analytically the costs and benefits involved. As he unfolded the plan, Heather's pulse began to throb with excitement; at least $2 million in equipment and tools was involved, and if she could get the contract for Future, it would be a real feather in her cap.

The lunch went on and on. At half-past four, the minister announced that he had other business to attend to and suggested that Heather and his assistant return to the ministry to continue their discussion. Heather agreed readily, lured by the prospect of the biggest sale of her career. Omar (the assistant — they were now on first-name terms) took her to his office, ordered more coffee, and asked her to make some preliminary estimates to give him some idea of Future's likely bid for the contract. Heather demurred, protesting that that would take at least two hours.

"No matter," said Omar, "let us meet for dinner this evening at nine o'clock. That way you will have plenty of time for your calculations, and perhaps also by then you will be hungry again." He suggested a place for them to meet, and Heather agreed, grateful that she would have time to herself to work out the complicated estimates accurately.

Omar provided a car to take her back to her hotel. She then spent the remainder of the afternoon and much of the evening working on the estimates. She considered for a moment putting through a call to the New York office (there was still time, since at eight o'clock, it was only noon in New York), but she decided against it on the grounds of the expense and her confidence in her own estimating and selling ability.

The dinner was very enjoyable. Not only did Omar find her proposals attractive, but he also turned out to be a most charming and agreeable companion. At midnight, he offered to take her on a tour of the town and to show her some of the local sights by night. Heather felt convinced that she had won the contract, and she was also by now rather light-headed at the prospect of going home to America after a successful trip. She was further reassured and gratified by the fact that Omar's attentions were based on nothing more than gallantry. She agreed to the tour.

The contract she had proposed came to $2.2 million. Her own commission on that was .001 percent, or $2,200. That night she did something she had never done before: She stayed up until five o'clock in the morning, thoroughly enjoying Omar's tour of the city. Eventually, he took her back to her hotel. As they parted at the entrance, he expressed his enjoyment of their meeting; then he said, "By the way, I hope you included in your figures the usual percentage for government officials. The French and the Italians did. Give me a call at lunchtime. I'll be in my office."

"What percentage? You never said anything about a percentage," said Heather, horrified. "Oh, they all give a percentage," said Omar, and with a brillant smile, he bade her goodnight and walked to his car.

Heather went to her room. She flipped through the company's directives on employee behavior. She found one on "bribery." It read as follows:

All employees of Future, Inc., are required to comply with the laws of the United States. The use of funds of Future, Inc., for payments to government officials, with intent to influence those officials to give preferential treatment to Future, Inc., is strictly prohibited.

She did not know what to do. The decision on the contract was to be made the next day, and it was clear that unless she complied with local customs the decision would be made in favor of a competitive bidder. The American head office had closed for the weekend.

Personal Ethical Conflict

The conflict between organizations and individuals is as old as society itself. The basis of the conflict is that while individuals by definition seek goals that will further their personal independence, organizations look for a commonality of individual efforts to achieve corporate goals. The organization's need for conformity tends to reduce individual independence. William H. Whyte drew attention to this conflict in *The Organization Man,* in which he claimed that a "new social ethic" has been developed in recent years to reconcile individuality with the demands of the organization. In his own words, "By social ethic I mean that contemporary body of thought that makes morally legitimate the pressures of society against the individual. Its major propositions are three: a belief in the group as the source of creativity; a belief in 'belongingness' as the ultimate need of the individual; and a belief in the application of science to achieve the belongingness." [23]

This, says Whyte, is a utopian faith, an intellectual ideology. The cause of it is not the organization itself, but our "worship" of the organization. Because organizations look after us, we find it easy to conform. We are lulled into a false sense of security, but instead of meekly accepting the new ethic, we should fight it in order to retain our individuality and our freedom, though not in such a way as to destroy ourselves. This view is reinforced by Chris Argyris, who sees the basic incongruence between the self-actualization of the individual and that of the organization as a source of "conflict, frustration, and failure for the participants." [24]

These views have aroused strong feelings. The opposing argument is that people actually *need* organizations because they provide psychological support and that both sides can gain from the relationship. Furthermore, it is claimed, some differences between self and corporation are desirable in that they can "improve payouts for both the individual and the organization." [25] It is also argued that this is not a special problem of business; the same organizational and individual considerations apply also to the church, the medical profession, and the law.

Clearly, one does have responsibilities to the organization, if only because it is from that source that one derives the income to keep oneself and one's family. At the same time, the organization has responsibilities to its work force, partly defined by contracts of employment, but also partly dictated by an unwritten moral code. The relationship is thus reciprocal. Outside the organization, however, the individual is a citizen, a human being, a member of a broader society, and the line demarcating the limits of organizational influence becomes ill defined. Yet the individual, subject to the requirements of the system outside the organization, sometimes finds it hard work even outside hours of employment. Completing tax returns, insuring one's car, paying one's bills, maintaining one's house and garden, educating one's children, answering letters — all these obligations may at times make the individual feel that it is an extraordinarily difficult business just to exist. The new "social ethic," born of increasing social complexity, is certainly a reality at times like those, and it is not surprising that revolt against the demands of the system should produce such a withdrawal from society as exemplified in the Hippie culture — a nonviolent anarchy, essentially apolitical and anti-industrial, libertarian, nostalgic, and simple. In its own way, such a culture is as utopian as the new social ethic itself.

The conflict between organizational and personal values is a common enough problem, and its resolution depends very much on the relative strength of each. Albert Carr has negotiated the hurdle neatly by claiming that business, like poker, has its own rules, included in which is the rule that bluffing is allowed: "That most businessmen are not indifferent to ethics in their private lives, everyone will agree. My point is that in their office lives they cease to be private citizens; they become game players

who must be guided by a somewhat different set of ethical standards.
. . . Violations of the ethical ideals of society are common in business,
but they are not necessarily violations of business principles. . . . Decisions in this area are, in the final test, decisions of strategy, not ethics." [26]

This is a very hard-nosed attitude, and it begs a major question: Why
should executives be required to place their personal values in suspension
when they get to their offices? Business may be a game, as Carr maintains, but there can be no justifiable reason why the rules of that game
should be framed on concepts that deny a place to fairness and honesty
or that are dissonant with those that the person as a private citizen would
regard as appropriate foundations for behavior. Carr appears to forget
that actions can be viewed in two dimensions: on the basis of the act
itself and on the basis of its consequences. It may not be wrong legally
for a salesman to sell a retail customer twice that customer's inventory
requirements for a particular sales period, but if as a result the customer
finds it difficult to buy enough products from other suppliers during that
period, the act must be considered morally imperfect.

In another article, Carr seems to be trying to make amends for his
uncompromising attitude. After appearing to suggest that there are some
management peccadilloes at which we can shrug or grin, he goes on to
admit that much of business behavior is ethically reprehensible: "When
the directors and managers of a corporation enter the boardroom to
debate policy, they park their private consciences outside. If they did
not subordinate their inner scruples to considerations of profitability and
growth, they would fail in their responsibility to the company that pays
them. A kind of Gresham's Law of ethics operates here; the ethic of
corporate advantage invariably silences and drives out the ethic of individual self-restraint." [27] The main focus of the article is, what can a man
in a responsible position in the organization do without jeopardizing his
job when he thinks that certain of the company's policies are socially
irresponsible? Carr's answer, when it finally comes, is hardly the climax
we are waiting for: The executive must "show convincingly a net advantage for the corporation in accelerating expenditures or accepting other
costs in the sphere of social responsibility."

Perhaps the personal ethical conflict is nowhere more evident than in
the incompatibility of demands made by one's employer and one's family.
John Barnett, writing in the *Wall Street Journal* of May 10, 1967, drew
attention to the pressures that the requirements of employment place on
family relationships. Here ethical duality really presents problems; broken marriages, estrangement, and alcoholism are only a few of the con-

sequences of the conflict. The problems, according to Mortimer Feinberg (quoted by Barnett), "are almost epidemic in proportion." Although some companies seem to be aware of the situation and are trying (even if only in a modest way) to improve it, most are not, and little is in fact being done.

The dilemma is reiterated by J. E. Kendall, who states that the critical moment occurs when an executive stands on the threshold of promotion and has to weigh the additional success and prestige against the possible effects on the quality of family life. Faced with the choice, the individual can say no or yes: "Say no, and what happens to the forum that opens up to people in high places? . . . Say yes, and I'm not me but somebody else with a new front. I could say yes, but I have the feeling that this is my last chance to say no." [28]

Commenting on Whyte's concept of the organization man, Joseph McGuire maintains that the individual must conform to some degree: "If he does not, he ceases to belong to mankind and becomes a beast." [29] If people fail to conform, society will disintegrate; the only danger is that the pressures for conformity will be so great that people will become automatons without minds of their own. McGuire suggests that we should strike some kind of balance between conformity and individuality, conforming in some matters and being free to do as we wish in others, thus achieving the "greatest degree of individual freedom consistent with the greatest good of society." Unfortunately, McGuire does not suggest how this can be achieved or on what criteria conformity or nonconformity are to be decided.

Where McGuire seems not fully to have appreciated Whyte's point of view is in assuming that the conflict exists simply between conformity and individual autonomy in the big corporation; he says nothing of the conflict outside the organization, the pressures that the demands of employment put on the individual as a private citizen, spouse, and parent. It may well be true, as McGuire suggests, that "the major characteristics of successful executives are those which can only be displayed when men have a substantial degree of independence," but successful executives are those upon whom corporate pressures sit most heavily and whose private lives are at greatest risk.

The danger, of course, is that an executive with no clear conceptual framework of personal behavior may eventually decide to end the conflict by surrendering entirely to the values of the organization. Any person who cannot reconcile what he believes and what he is required to do is in a moral dilemma. As Clarence Walton puts it, "More likely than not, success becomes the ethic, and with success come such fringe benefits in the executive suites as carved marble toilets, swivel chairs with head-rests, company planes, and even company liquor."[30]

It might be asked, if such conflicts of loyalty are likely to occur, why does anyone pursue a business career? The answer is not simple. It is easy enough in principle to identify executive motivation (ask any class of M.B.A. students, and you will find that many of them will give money or power as their reason for having chosen a business career), but it is well-nigh impossible to do so realistically before the fruits of experience, not always sweet, have been gathered or to isolate ex post facto ration-alizations in answers given by people who have already experienced the hard facts of the personal and organizational dilemma. Money is the usual symbol of success in a modern society and is an indicator of status, prestige, and competence; however, it is also the means of supporting a family in a chosen lifestyle. Furthermore, money is not the exclusive province of business; people find equally affluent careers for themselves in the professions or in public service, and so money alone cannot be the motivation for choosing a business career. Power may be a stronger incentive. As Everett Hagen has commented, "An individual who . . . perceives each contact with other persons as involving a danger of con-flict and a threat of pain may conceive of dominating others rather than merely attacking them as a solution to the threat and an outlet for the rage which is within him. This need will express itself as a need to obtain performance from others by command, to influence or direct the behavior of others, to affect others so as to obtain desired performance from them."[31] This may be an overstatement, but it contains a great deal of truth; there can be no doubt that the popular picture of the successful tycoon encourages such an attitude.

It is important to distinguish between motivation at its different levels. Money and power are probably fundamental, but once they have been achieved, it is not uncommon for business executives to offer other, less tangible reasons for their career selection, such as affiliation, interaction, and service to others. This is perhaps a substantiation of Abraham Mas-low's theory of a hierarchy of needs;[32] however, one cannot help but wonder whether such reasons are self-delusory and compensatory, a smokescreen put up in front of reality and perhaps even a sedative for ethical personal conflict.

The study described in Chapter 7 examines the problems of identifi-cation of executive motivation in greater detail. The significant fact here, however, is that for every six executives still committed to corporate conformity, there is one who has opted out. The itch seems to make itself felt at around the age of forty, though it varies from individual to individual. The protest is not so much against the specific organization for which a person works (although it is probably that organization that brings into sharp focus the realities of conflict) as against the system as a whole. The alternative to working for one corporation is working for another, and this is merely a move to the same kind of conflict in a different environment. Frequently, therefore, the question in the forty-year-old executive's mind, when the realization that time is running out begins to surface, is not whether to move to another company, but whether to quit corporate life altogether in exchange for some different kind of activity that will preserve and stimulate personal values. Some business executives move into college and university teaching, where opportunities for self-expression are great, but this path requires qualifications that many managers do not possess; some choose social work, some government. They are industry's loss, because among them are some of the best brains in business.

The response of the corporation, for the most part, is to claim that managers expect too much. Since progression up the corporate hierarchy is perceived as the sign of success, most managers are going to be dissatisfied and frustrated because very few make it to the top. Some corporations even go so far as to blame the business schools for raising the expectations of students to such a point that "they have an exaggerated sense of their abilities and their prospects, which necessarily leads to frustration or failures."[33] For some, the alienation is a temporary problem; for others, it lasts for years and is frequently terminal. One company president, however, feels that it is a fundamental and permanent part of the scene: "Credibility in the quality of business ethics has lessened; expectations of employees, young and old, are increasing. Human costs and rewards need to be more thoughtfully balanced against economic costs and rewards in the future."[34]

The debate about the individual and his association with other individuals and groups is brought into focus by Richard Eells and Clive Walton, who distinguish between "natural" associations that are necessary for human existence (such as associations with family and state) and "historically created" associations (such as those involving modern corporations and unions). The latter are born of particular circumstances of time and place and are "man-made reactions to man-made conditions."[35] Commenting on a well-known passage from de Tocqueville's *Democracy in America,* Eells and Walton suggest that freedom of association is not an absolute right, but rather that it is dependent on the degree to which the association is necessary for survival and prosperity. By this, they presumably mean that "natural" associations involve no freedom, but that the individual is otherwise free to associate or not. This is less true today. Recent economic developments imply that in some circumstances one's existence may depend on one's association with one man-made group or another — for example, when one must take employment of a kind one dislikes because there is no other, or when one is forced to belong to a union "closed shop" in order to qualify for employment. Such situations bring questions of personal conflict into sharp focus.

One aspect of the "organization man" discussion is that although most social values have traditionally been based on the importance of the individual, particularly in America, current attitudes frequently favor larger groups and a suppression of individualism. Calls for stricter controls on behavior, greater use of the law, and increasing legislation with regard to prices and incomes are just a few examples. J. Skolwick makes the point that while Americans consider themselves a nation of individual capitalists, the actual power is held by large corporations in which only a few people make the decisions.[36]

Similarly, great importance is attached today to privacy. One reason for this phenomenon is that prospective employees are subjected to investigations that fifty years ago would have created a scandal. As a result, hidden cameras, polygraph tests, and the like are being seriously questioned as to their legitimacy. There are many examples of corporations' exerting pressure on their employees off the job, such as stipulating where they should live, the type of car they should drive, or the social organizations to which they should belong. In some cases, dismissals have resulted from contravention of such "rules."

The fundamental question is, to what extent should a corporation make allowance for an individual's values and to what extent should it insist that an individual put aside his values in the interest of the firm? The relationship, as we noted earlier, is one of reciprocal responsibility. A business cannot continue to employ indefinitely an individual who contributes nothing to its growth and well-being, especially as others may suffer as a result. On the other hand, if individuals do not act according to their own values, they run the risk not only of losing their own self-respect, but also of facing the mentally damaging prospect of dismissal.

Incident 9: Guy Mortimer and His Career. Guy Mortimer was born in a small village in the North Midlands of England.[37] He began his education at the local village school and eventually, through hard work and the encouragement of his parents and his teachers, won a scholarship to a grammar school about six miles away, to which he went at the age of ten and where he completed his school career eight years later.

At an early stage, the grammar school offered Guy the option of an education either in the arts or the sciences. On the basis of a test he took in his second year to measure his aptitude in each, Guy chose the arts. From that point, his classes concentrated on English and languages, in particular Latin, French, and German. At the age of fifteen, when it was time to take his first public examination, Guy was determined to pursue this linguistic direction. Consequently, partly through his own inclinations and partly through the enthusiasm of his headmaster (a classicist), he spent his final two school years studying Latin, Greek, ancient history, and literature. As a result, he won a place at one of the great British universities to read classics. He spent two years in military service, part of it in Asia, came back to the university, and finally graduated with an excellent degree.

During his final year at the university, Guy thought about his future. A degree in the classics fitted him for nothing very much beyond the church, the law, or teaching. He was not particularly attracted to any of these careers, and, for want of something better, he chose industry. He did at least decide to select one of the largest companies in Britain, on the supposition that if he was going to make business his career, he might as well go into that part of it that would give him the best training.

He prospered. He quickly picked up the techniques of management. By the age of thirty, having changed jobs two or three times, he was earning a salary that identified him as a successful executive. He moved to more and more responsible positions and in time came to the point where he could sit back and examine his career prospects. The results of this self-analysis were not encouraging; several of his colleagues had said to him from time to time that though he was successful, he was not at heart a businessman. He was too concerned about the affairs of the mind and not enough about the practicalities of business life. Guy protested, pointing to the material benefits enjoyed by his family — free television set, company car, generous expense allowance, and so on — but he was nevertheless bothered when people told him he should be teaching a course in classics or writing a book on Plato.

He could not see himself doing either of these things, and yet he was uncomfortable at the prospect of spending the rest of his life doing what he was doing at the time. His parents and his family (he was married with two children) supported him in his career, but he had the feeling that his wife would not be too upset at his leaving the world of business, even if it resulted in a lowering of the family's standard of living.

His preoccupation with philosophical contemplation began to affect his work. He found the pompous edicts of his chairman and managing director about what should be done and how it should be done irritating and frustrating. Guy was a board member and at monthly board meetings frequently adopted a viewpoint that was deliberately controversial. His chairman respected his intellect, but when faced with logical objections from Guy on matters of stated company policy, became visibly annoyed and told Guy that he should be more sympathetic to the needs of the company that treated him so well. Guy resented this. He worked hard, frequently devoting much of a weekend to company business, and genuinely believed that his views were in the best interests of the company; on several occasions, he had been the key figure in the acquisition of new business, and his clear and analytical presentations had been highly praised; he had also introduced new and profitable practices and procedures that were of great benefit to company operations.

At one of the board meetings, Alex McGinn, Guy's great friend and colleague, was missing. Guy and Alex often spent an hour or so at the end of the day talking about a wide range of topics, sometimes company matters and sometimes not. When Guy asked why Alex was not there, the chairman replied that the board was going to vote on a proposal for Alex's dismissal. The reason given was that both the chairman and the managing director found Alex's comments on company affairs incomprehensible and a waste of time. Guy realized that the decision had in effect already been made; he was the only person who had not been consulted before the meeting. It was obvious that Alex's dismissal was a warning to Guy.

Alex was a long-standing acquaintance of the chairman. He was the godfather of one of the chairman's children and had been very supportive during the early days of the company as it struggled to success. Guy could not believe that the company was about to rid itself of Alex after the contribution he had made; moreover, Alex was now fifty-six years of age, and his chances of finding another job were small.

Guy saw that the way he voted on the proposal would be critical to his future with the company. The managing director made the motion, and it was immediately seconded by another board member who had clearly been briefed to do so. Guy thought for a moment, made his decision, and asked for the opportunity to speak on the motion. He was deadly serious. He deplored the board's behavior, questioned the reasons for it, and emphatically declared his position: He would have no part in the affair and would strongly oppose the motion. After a brief silence, the motion was put; it was carried by six votes to one.

A week later things came to a head. The managing director came to see Guy and bluntly stated that there was not room in the company for both of them. Guy's first reaction was great relief that the conflict had at last come out into the open; his second was fear since he now had to make one of the biggest decisions of his life.

Minority Groups

On Monday, June 30, 1980, the British press reported on a meeting held the previous day by leaders of black groups in Britain at which a national exhortation had been made to all group members not to cooperate with the police. It was the culmination of years of deteriorating relationships between colored extremists, most of them second-generation immigrants, and the authorities, committed by successive governments to the promotion and development of a multiracial society in the United Kingdom. The Commission for Racial Equality, a government body set up to develop good relations and to protect minority groups against discrimination, deplored the announcement and said that the noncooperation call made its job of promoting understanding more difficult. Some Conservative politicians branded the call itself as racialist.

While this illustration may possibly paint the picture rather darker than it actually is, it serves to demonstrate the very difficult problems arising out of the existence within a traditionally homogeneous society of immigrant minorities, most of whose members originally left their own countries for a new life and the hope of employment, a higher income, and social freedom.

The problem in Britain is relatively new. Only since the dissolution of the Empire has immigration become an issue, whereas in the United States there have been substantial ethnic minorities for three hundred years or so. Nor is the question entirely one of color; some commentators prefer the term *special employment groups* to *minority groups* in the labor force, since in recent years the status of women has been added to the debate. A special employment group is "one which has, or feels that it has, its employment status relative to other workers decreased in some important way by factors which do not concern job performance."[38] This definition therefore includes any person who may experience employment discrimination on grounds of age, sex, color, race, religion, or nationality. To a lesser extent, it may also refer to people with physical or mental handicaps or criminal records.

Much has been written or spoken about minority groups, equal rights, and equal employment opportunities. For the most part, the problem has been one of acculturation; barriers of language and — to some extent — lack of skills have prevented some minorities from obtaining employment in certain jobs. Yet second and later generations, who have learned the language and have absorbed the culture, still frequently find themselves stigmatized by their heritage. This is far more true of immigrants who did not voluntarily come to a white society, such as the original black slaves of America, than of voluntary immigrants who often came with a prior knowledge of the language and skills acquired elsewhere.

A distinction must also be made between immigrant minorities and indigenous minorities. American Indians, Alaskans, Hawaiians, and Mexican Americans (apart from those recently illegally entering the United States from Mexico in large numbers) certainly did not immigrate, but they nonetheless represent historically subjugated groups who are distinguished from the dominant culture in much the same way as the black populations of South Africa and, until recently, of Zimbabwe-Rhodesia have been. Here there may in fact be resistance to acculturation and to some extent a positive desire for discrimination as an identification of cultural difference.

Whichever way the question is viewed, it is undeniable that in the past, and to some extent today, employment decisions have been and are influenced in some degree by considerations of nonconformity in one or more respects. Even in an age of so-called enlightenment and successive government acts to prevent discrimination, it would be foolish to deny that a black, female, fifty-year-old, Nigerian-born, naturalized American with a strange religion, a record of shoplifting, and a college degree would be passed over for a clerical job in favor of a twenty-year-old, white, Episcopalian, seventh-generation American male who dropped out of tenth grade. People look different from each other, and employment officers notice it.

This fact, together with the public protests that have accompanied it over the years since World War II, has prompted legislation in different countries to different extents. The riots of the 1960s in the United States, coupled with the assassination of the most articulate supporter of equal rights, Dr. Martin Luther King, resulted in several progressive moves. In 1961, even before Dr. King's death, Plans for Progress, a voluntary organization of firms committed to affirmative action, had been set up; it was amalgamated with another national program in 1969. Its only failing was that it consisted predominantly of large firms and did not really protect the interests of minorities seeking employment in smaller companies.

In 1968, a joint private-federal program, known as Job Opportunities in the Business Sector (JOBS), was started in conjunction with the

National Alliance of Business (NAB). This program not only succeeded in getting jobs for the disadvantaged, but also attracted the attention of smaller firms, which had been largely excluded from the Plans for Progress association of seven years before. The program was formed against a background of low unemployment, the war in Vietnam, a fear of public protest (the youth movement was at its height), and a feeling on the part of employers that they had a genuine moral commitment to improve the community in which they existed.

The U.S. federal government's earliest moves under the Truman and Eisenhower administrations consisted of directives that for the most part could not be implemented. They were anodyne utterances unsupported by enforceable rules. It was not until President Kennedy's Committee for Equal Employment Opportunity was established and the 1964 Civil Rights Act (Title VII) was passed that discrimination on the basis of color, race, creed, religion, sex, and national origin was outlawed. The agency to enforce the act was the Equal Employment Opportunity Commission, supported by most states and covering private employers involved in intrastate commerce.

This legislation, genuinely intended to protect minority interests, had been preceded by the Manpower Development and Training Act of 1962; it was quickly followed by the Economic Opportunity Act of 1964, heralding the subsequent Community Action Program, the Concentrated Employment Program, the Job Corps, the Neighborhood Youth Corps, the New Careers Program, Operation Mainstream, Public Service Careers, and the Special Impact programs.

Such programs are necessary and laudable, but they often contradict each other and are counterproductive. The sad truth is that although government edicts can impose legislation on citizens to ensure that equal opportunities are given to privileged and underprivileged alike, it is only through individual realization of the facts of minority deprivation that the real problem can be solved. The onus lies on each citizen to see to it that discrimination is eradicated.

In Britain, the laws are less specific and less stringently applied. Apart from the Commission for Racial Equality, there is nothing outside English common law to protect the rights of individuals against discrimination and persecution. Perhaps the reason is historical; problems of prejudice against minority groups are fairly recent. It is only in the last few years that voices have been raised in warning against possible immigrant problems. Yet the event described at the beginning of this section indicates the dangers that may lie ahead unless some coherent policy, such as the one in the United States (which, although it sometimes produces racial conflict, attempts nevertheless to be cohesive), is adopted.

The most recent demand for equal rights has come from the women's movement, evident in almost every Western democracy and articulated by numerous writers and public figures in all countries. There can be no doubt that women have traditionally been severely penalized not only in their status as citizens, but also in their candidacy for employment. The issue is at once clear and cloudy: Obviously, if a woman is capable of performing tasks as well as a man, she should be equally rewarded; yet, while the principle is indisputable in general terms, we still appear to lack some more specific definition of the types of employment that, for one reason or another, are suitable for only one of the sexes. For example, would an advertisement seeking a female attendant for a women's washroom be considered discriminatory?

The women's movement is a natural, and thoroughly commendable, outcome of modern social attitudes. It is appalling that only very recently was the female vote granted in Switzerland. In management, there are enough examples of successful females (such as Helena Rubenstein, Mary Wells, Mildred Custin of Bonwit Teller, and Geraldine Stutz of Henri Bendel) to show that business acumen is not a male prerogative; yet it is still common to assume that males have some innate superiority in running a business.

It is true that certain groups have for a very long time been neglected and denied their rightful station in the management of affairs, even the occupancy of the most menial jobs, and it is high time that black and white, man and woman, old and young should have unrestricted access to any employment. However, the issue is not so much one of color or sex as of ability, motivation, and equal opportunity, and until such time as equal opportunities are available in schools, businesses, and universities or the desire for education and training is consistent across all sections of society, the present imbalance will persist. At least two authors on women's rights have fallen into the error of focusing on the wrong problem.[39]

Incident 10: Martha Thompson and F.C. Wood, Inc.   Bruce Renken, vice-president of operations at F.C. Wood, Inc., a major U.S. tax advisory company with millions of clients in every state in the union and headquarters in New Orleans, had just read a letter circulated by the president, Hiram Wood.[40] The letter drew attention to the fact that across the country only 5 percent of all tax counselors were women and suggested that future F. C. Wood recruitment policy should take note of it. Furthermore, wrote the president, it was disturbing that there was a higher proportion of black employees in tax companies in northern states than in the South; F.C. Wood, he suggested, as a company based in Louisiana, should try to help rectify this imbalance.

Renken, in addition to his function as vice-president, was also responsible for the staffing and operation of the company's five main branches in New Orleans. He was particularly interested in the letter since he was at the time anxious to fill a recently vacated position in the legal research division, a department that investigated the finer points of tax law and that was one of F.C. Wood's strongest promotional features.

He was looking for someone with good legal qualifications who had specialized in tax law. Renken was in the habit of visiting the campuses of local universities every year to find suitable talent. The next day he was due to visit Louisiana State University, and on the spur of the moment, he resolved to recruit a suitable candidate who was not only female, but black as well. His assistant, Jim Starr, to whom he mentioned his decision, was not so sure and said so; why not, Starr asked, just hire the best person for the job? Renken answered that the company claimed on its letterhead that it was an Equal Opportunity Employer and that it should practice what it preached. Starr shook his head and walked away.

At the university the next day, Renken interviewed about a dozen candidates. He decided to offer two of them jobs as counselor trainees, which carried good starting salaries and excellent prospects. His mind was not really on these positions, however; he was far more interested in finding someone for the research position. Two candidates caught his eye: one, a white, male law student with excellent grades in his tax law courses who was presentable, articulate, and very determined to get ahead; the other (much to Renken's delight), a black, twenty-four-year-old female named Martha Thompson. Martha, an extremely attractive young woman, tried throughout the interview to turn the discussion into a debate on women's rights. Bruce resisted the challenge and was secretly pleased that he had not made it evident that he was on her side. Her academic record was as good as that of the other possible candidate, and Renken decided to offer her the job, thinking that the president would be pleased and the young woman's militant attitude perhaps modified.

Martha accepted the offer, which was $3,000 more than the one other offer she had received, and started to work for F.C. Wood on the first day of August following her graduation. She formed part of a team of ten researchers, the other nine of whom were men, who worked on projects, either singly or in groups, on the instruction of the head of research. All her new colleagues welcomed her warmly, but she was slightly disconcerted since they seemed to do so not so much because of a professional interest as because they were glad to have an attractive woman around the office.

In an attempt to overcome her unease, Martha suggested that they all meet for a drink in a local bar after the office closed that evening. Ray Brooks, one of her colleagues, said they sometimes met for a drink in someone's office before going home. At lunchtime, Martha therefore bought a bottle of liquor, some mixers, and an assortment of peanuts and potato chips, intending either to invite everybody to her office one evening or to contribute something to a party elsewhere.

At half-past five, when the office officially closed, she heard Ray calling to his colleagues by name and asking for ice, tonic, and glasses to be brought to his office. Her name was not mentioned, and she hesitated. By the time she had uncertainly gathered up a few items and gone into the corridor, Ray Brook's door was firmly closed, and sounds of laughter and animated conversation came from the other side of it. She could not decide whether to knock on the door or not; in the end, she returned to her office, packed up her things, and went home.

The next occasion was the same, as were other evenings over the next three weeks. At group meetings, nobody paid a great deal of attention to Martha, and whenever she said anything, the others did not seem to treat her comments seriously. Also, the projects to which she was assigned were either ancillary investigations on jobs that had been allocated to one of her colleagues or extremely speculative investigations that seemed to lead nowhere or were of very low priority. She began to feel frustrated, underutilized, and neglected.

One of her long-term speculative projects concerned contingency tax assessment schedules based on possible future amendments to federal tax law. Martha felt very strongly that it was a futile exercise, since on looking back through similar projects, she found none that had in any way proved to be of value in the light of IRS tax changes. She therefore came to a decision, bypassed the head of research, and marched determinedly the next morning into Bruce Renken's office. She told him that what she was doing was a waste of time and that she felt she should be given a useful project of her own that would be of some value to the company and its clients.

Renken thought for a moment and then said that he was sure Martha was doing excellent work. She left his office wondering why she had ever been offered the job.

CONCLUSION

How far any of the people described in the foregoing ten short incidents may have been assisted in their moral dilemmas by the philosophical experience outlined in Chapter 3 is difficult to say. All of them, however, faced the problem of decision against the background of their own ethical frameworks, however those frameworks were constructed, and the incidents themselves have indicated the wide range of ethical decision making that executives can face. In Chapter 6 we shall attempt to establish some structure for the manager to follow in resolving such problems, after which we shall focus on the conclusions to be drawn from our discussion. First, however, in Chapter 5 we have to examine the nature of power and authority, and to investigate the concept of corporate accountability.

NOTES

1. François, duc de la Rochefoucauld, *Les Maximes* (*Reflections; or Sentences and Moral Maxims*), 5th ed., 1678, no. 378.
2. Clarence C. Walton, *Ethos and the Executive* (Englewood Cliffs, N.J.: Prentice-Hall, 1979), p. 95.
3. Andrew Wilson, *The Concorde Fiasco* (London: Penguin, 1973), p. 31.
4. Ibid., p. 9.
5. Concorde flew commercially for the first time, British Airways to Bahrain and Air France to Rio, early in 1976.
6. This information is from a promotional leaflet issued by BAC, entitled "The Scheduled Carrier — Quo Vadis?"
7. Wilson, *Concorde Fiasco,* p. 153.
8. Hazel Henderson, "Towards an Economics of Ecology," *Columbia Journal of World Business* (May–June 1972), p. 32.
9. This case describes a fictitious situation, though similar events have taken place in actual companies.
10. This is a fictitious case. It has been developed from a case on a similar subject prepared in 1978 by the Division of Research of the University of Michigan Graduate School of Business Administration.
11. The people and situations described in this case are fictitious.
12. At the time of writing, no such event had occurred. To the best of the author's knowledge, the Conservative party is perfectly satisfied with its existing advertising agency. The example would work just as well with the Labour party.
13. Joseph W. McGuire, *Business and Society* (New York: McGraw-Hill, 1963), p. 273.
14. This case describes a real situation (names disguised).
15. F. D. Sturdivant, *Business and Society: A Managerial Approach* (Homewood, Ill.: Richard D. Irwin, 1977), p. 238.
16. This is a fictitious case.

17. J. M. Pfiffner and F. P. Sherwood, *Administrative Organization* (Englewood Cliffs, N.J.: Prentice-Hall, 1960).

18. This is a fictitious case.

19. E. H. Schein and J. S. Ott, "The Legitimacy of Organizational Influence," *American Journal of Sociology* (May 1962): 682–89.

20. This is a fictitious case.

21. This statement is not proprietary information. It was distributed by Gulf+Western executives at a public seminar.

22. This is a fictitious case.

23. William H. Whyte, *The Organization Man* (New York: Doubleday Anchor Books, 1957), p. 7.

24. Chris Argyris, *Personality and Organization: The Conflict between the System and the Individual* (New York: Harper & Brothers, 1957), p. 175.

25. K. Davis and R. L. Blomstrom, *Business and Society: Environment and Responsibility*, 3rd ed. (New York: McGraw-Hill, 1975), p. 314.

26. Albert Z. Carr, "Is Business Bluffing Ethical?" *Harvard Business Review* 46 (January–February 1968):146.

27. Albert Z. Carr, "Can an Executive Afford a Conscience?" *Harvard Business Review* 48 (July–August 1970):62.

28. J. E. Kendall, "Down the Up Staircase," *Ms. Magazine* (August 1975):32 (authorship pseudonymous).

29. McGuire, *Business and Society,* p. 172.

30. Walton, *Ethos and the Executive,* p. 75.

31. Everett E. Hagen, *On the Theory of Social Change* (Homewood, Ill.: Dorsey Press, 1962), p. 108.

32. Abraham H. Maslow, *Toward a Psychology of Being,* 2nd ed. (New York: Van Nostrand Reinhold, 1968).

33. *Dun's* (August 1972, Dun and Bradstreet Publications).

34. Ibid.

35. Richard Eells and Clive Walton, *Conceptual Foundations of Business,* 3rd ed. (Homewood, Ill.: Richard D. Irwin, 1974), p. 98.

36. J. Skolnick, "The Sociology of Law in America: Overview and Trends," *Social Problems* (supplement) 13 (1965):4–39.

37. This case describes a real situation (names are disguised).

38. Keith Davis, *Human Behavior at Work* (New York: McGraw-Hill, 1972), p. 300.

39. Charles D. Orth III and Frederic Jacobs, "Women in Management: Pattern for Change," *Harvard Business Review* 49 (July–August 1971):139–47.

40. This is a fictitious case, adapted extensively from a case prepared by Linda P. Fletcher, Louisiana State University, and Susan M. Phillips, University of Iowa.

5 POWER, AUTHORITY, AND ACCOUNTABILITY

I repeat . . . that all power is a trust — that we are accountable for its exercise — that, from the people, and for the people, all springs, and all must exist.

— Benjamin Disraeli[1]

THE SCOPE OF THE CHAPTER

One of the central themes of this book is that responsibility is a very personal affair and that, translated into the world of business, the responsibility that a particular manager is able to exercise is in direct ratio to the degree of authority that the manager can use in order to implement what he or she feels to be right.

This chapter examines the nature and structure of power and authority and the relationship that power and authority have to each other. It then goes on to study how power and authority can be guaranteed to be fair and just; this is the same dilemma faced by Hobbes and Spinoza and others throughout the history of social and political theory. The discussion involves an evaluation of the theory of social auditing and the extent to which corporate strategy can be evaluated in nonquantitative terms.

147

THE STRUCTURE OF POWER

Is power a prerequisite of responsibility in management? Machiavelli, Hobbes, and Spinoza would say yes. Yet, as we saw in Chapter 3, power in modern parlance is predicated on a separate concept called authority. The difficulties of philosophers in discussing the moral right by which rulers should rule derive from a lack of understanding of the difference between the two concepts.

In the quotation at the beginning of this chapter, Benjamin Disraeli seems to bridge the gap between traditional political theory and modern social attitudes. Abraham Lincoln expressed similar sentiments at Gettysburg. Modern democracy owes much to both men. They seem to be saying that if the will of the people decides that power should be removed from one person or group of people to another person or group, so be it. Democracy would therefore appear to be defined as the periodic opportunity given to the people to decide on these things. The difficulty, of course, lies in the determination of (1) who should vote and (2) how often. The first of these problems has now been resolved in many societies; the second is less easy.

Ideally, the will of the people should be expressed whenever the executive power of the land is perceived as acting contrary to the general will, and so an election should be available at any time. Yet this very idea conflicts, first, with consistent government and, second, with the fact that it was the people themselves in the first place who elected the government to protect their interests. Therefore, short of giving the people as a whole the total responsibility for every political decision, major or minor (which would no doubt rapidly produce chaos), some form of representative government delegating power to a few for a prescribed period of time seems to be the only answer. Neither Hobbes nor Spinoza really took the argument this far, and this vestigial element of uncertainty in what we today call democracy was clearly the obstacle against which they stumbled.

Power in a democracy, as Disraeli claimed, is a trust; the sovereign (whether an individual or a body of people) exercises power because the electorate has entrusted him to do so. In other words, this trust is the *authority* given to the sovereign by the people to use the power that is available to the highest office. The parallel between the supreme political power and the power of the corporate chief executive is plain. Maritain's distinction between power and authority, which we discussed in Chapter 3, seems to support this interpretation.

POWER AND AUTHORITY IN THE FIRM

The interpretation of the distinction between power and authority just suggested is reflected in the new imperatives of business. The term *power sharing*, a product of recent developments in labor relations, is no empty phrase. Rensis Likert maintains that power is not a set quantity; rather, like capital, it can grow as it is shared.[2] Mason Haire argues that convention has led management to stress control *over,* rather than participation *with,* workers, to the detriment of both sides.[3]

The debate over power sharing has raised questions about exactly how far management power, and the authority to exercise that power, can be maintained. In 1960, the American National Association of Manufacturers issued a statement outlining what it believed to be the rights of "management"; they included, among other rights, the right to decide product policy, operational strategy, pricing policy, job specifications, personnel policy, quality control, scheduling, and location of business activity. It is a comprehensive list, which has on occasion been called into question by decisions of the U.S. Supreme Court on the basis of the collective bargaining contract: "What management can or cannot do is made to depend . . . on agreements reached by managers with representatives of the workers and on the interpretations growing out of these agreements by those elected by the parties to review the evidence and render a decision."[4]

The Supreme Court's ruling is not really all that new a concept. Arbitration has been a principle of settlement from time immemorial. In 1968, it was made official practice by the British Parliament, and arbitrators' decisions since then have rarely been reversed by British courts. It would appear that official circles are coming to regard the rights (and therefore the power and authority) of management as shared rights. Even decisions about plant location cannot now be made without taking the opinion of the labor force into account.

In modern arguments about business, its contribution to the economy, prices, wages, and inflation, it is popular to lay much of the blame for our economic problems at the door of trade unions and their ever-growing bargaining strength. It has to be remembered, however, that union influence in Europe (and particularly in Britain) is of a quite different nature from that in the United States. Traditionally, British unions have been politically biased; the confrontation between management and labor has been one of conflict between socialist and capitalist principles. The average American trade union member has usually been just as committed to the profit motive as the management that has employed him; his British counterpart has not, and it is thus far more common for the British unions to have come in for significant criticism in the light of reduced living standards, increasing unemployment (though this is something no union wants), and soaring inflation. This criticism derives largely from the Tory party.

The final chapter of this book will comment on the wide difference in the degree of professionalism in American and British management. This is a feature of the comparison between the two countries that is not normally recognized by critics of British unionism. British management is indisputably amateurish; American management is decidedly professional. To censure workers for shortcomings that to a large extent are the fault of their managers is to be at once politically partisan and dangerously unaware of the truth.

It is true that management is closer to and much more aware of the effects of higher wages on profitability than is labor. However, a fact not frequently recognized is that, given a common goal, management and labor can effectively work together to achieve rewards for all. In America, the principle is perhaps more understood, although rarely accomplished; in Britain, the extremes of opinion are such as to produce a situation that, combined with inefficiency and ignorance, reflects to neither side's credit.

What, then, of authority and power against this background? How does such a commentary affect the premise that senior management, by the authority given to it by stockholders and investors to exercise legitimate power, is the sole bearer of responsibility for social action? The question is discussed in the following section.

AUTHORITY AND RESPONSIBILITY

"Power tends to corrupt, and absolute power corrupts absolutely. Great men are always bad men." [5] Lord Acton's celebrated aphorism might be disputed by those who knew Alfred Sloan, William Hesketh Lever, or any of the many industrialists who have recognized that their great empires would be nothing without the people who worked their machines. We live at a time that is a far cry from child labor, 100-hour weeks, and the poorhouse; the union movement grew up and showed its first teeth in protest against such conditions. Yet to suggest that all executives in positions of power, even in positions of absolute power, are corrupt and inflexible is at once unfair and uninformed.

Still, this is an opinion not uncommonly held. The authority associated with the chief executive's office is an authority immediately clouded with suspicion. A president or a prime minister, who necessarily has to protect his or her statements with the privilege of governmental privacy, can never defend official pronouncements without seeming to take refuge in protocol. Similarly, the leader of industry is suspect when in the face of questions or attacks, he or she takes refuge behind company secrecy in order to protect stockholder interests. Authority and responsibility are difficult burdens to bear.

Imagine yourself a newly elected company president. You have an authority over the affairs of the corporation. You have the power to decide on what should be done. You can fire a senior executive if you feel you should, though at some point you are going to have to answer to the board. It is not easy. You may even find yourself in total opposition to your fellow directors on some item of company policy; at times, you may encounter strong opposition to your views on how the company should be run. It is a lonely and uncomfortable situation.

Problems facing the chief executive are thus not always straightforward; they are particularly difficult if they depend for their resolution on matters of judgment rather than matters of fact. Decisions about whether or not to increase sales effort in Saudi Arabia or to run down inventories in Singapore depend on economic facts and can be determined on the basis of information that means pretty much the same to everybody. However, the choice between an extra five-cent dividend to stockholders and an expenditure of one million dollars on pollution clearance is not so clear-cut. Many company presidents have found themselves in troubled waters in such situations.

The authority of the chief executive is total, as is the responsibility that this authority carries. This is power at the pleasure of the stockholders. But what if the chief executive, in the eyes of the electorate, abuses that authority? We return, it would seem, to the problem of sovereignty posed by Hobbes and Spinoza. Who is to restrain the sovereign? The old philosophers would claim that if chief executives overstep their power — and therefore their authority — their electors can overturn them. Yet getting rid of a president is a painful affair; it requires time and patience and planning. Stockholders usually vote the way they are told to vote, and they are rarely asked to vote a president out of office.

Chief executives are as responsible as they care to be. Typically, if they have any claim to responsible management, they go through four stages after their election to the supreme office (it has to be said that an irresponsible chief executive goes through none of these stages). First, there is *social responsiveness,* in which they come to feel that there are problems to which their companies (and therefore they themselves) should respond; the specific nature of these problems may vary, but their common thread is reference to the organization's duties to the community in which it functions. Second, as a natural consequence, they have feelings of *social responsibility*; here, their initial sympathy and reaction to the problems they have perceived begin to take a more positive shape. They actually experience some guilt as a result of inaction. Their senses, already alert to the forces impinging on their consciences, begin to suggest a need for action, though they are not yet sure what form that action should take. The third stage in this ethical odyssey is one of *moral obligation,* when the need for action begins to take real shape; they realize what needs to be done, but as yet feel disinclined to commit themselves to doing it. The requirement is perceived but the will to fulfill it is absent. The final stage is *social action*; here, the executives do something. The successive stages of awareness, sympathy, and guilt culminate in a positive act; some move is made to resolve the perceived problem that activated the mental progression.

Not all chief executives behave in the manner just described. Those who feel they have some responsibility to respond actively to social problems may do so without necessarily deliberating at such length. Social action is frequently spontaneous or planned without conscious thought of justification or explanation. However, if a particularly difficult problem arises, or if there is perceptible uncertainty on the part of the executive board in coming to a decision about how to handle it, it is likely that an evaluative and deductive process similar to the one just described will be employed, either consciously or subconsciously, to cope with it. The logical progression can be identified and categorized in principle, but the speed at which it takes place sometimes makes it difficult for the different stages to be observed.

Decisions involving social responsibility often have to be made in loneliness. Supreme power, like the satisfaction of hunger, is a very personal affair; nobody else can know the problem or the means of its resolution. The thesis that ultimate authority carries with it ultimate responsibility takes on real meaning when the truth of solitary power is understood; the chief executive, while nominally sharing decisions and discussing problems with fellow directors, in the end has the onus of praise or blame. For people in middle or lower management positions, there can be no complete awareness of the weight accompanying this burden.

We are speaking, of course, of the responsible chief executive officer. To some, the problem does not apply. Questions of ethical responsibility do not arise with presidents or managing directors who have no moral scruples or who are unresponsive to the proper demands of society. It is pointless to suggest that such people should not occupy positions of power since they are to be found in countless companies; but even if pointless, the suggestion at least serves to indicate where the final moral decisions are located and why individual ethical values at lower management levels are sometimes frustratingly difficult to implement.

Power therefore can corrupt, and absolute power (which presumably means supreme authority that cannot be contradicted or gainsaid) can conceivably produce absolute corruption. Yet the foregoing discussion has shown that corruption is not necessarily the end product of power; great people are not always bad people. Acton's cynicism is not universally shared. His observation was accurate in one sense: One's natural shortcomings are magnified and accentuated when one occupies a position where one is able to display them; but so also are one's positive qualities. The result of power need not be corruption; it could equally well be enlightenment, self-enrichment, and humanization. It is no empty phrase to say that the higher they rise, the farther they fall; preeminence projects human shortcomings and capabilities onto a very large screen.

Disraeli's statement that power depends on trust contrasts strangely with Ralph Waldo Emerson's comment that "the faith that stands on authority is not faith."[6] Power, as we have seen, has to be based on trust of one kind or another, but if there can be no faith in authority, on what can faith be placed? Over the centuries, various answers have been offered: "Faith is the substance of things hoped for, the evidence of things not seen."[7] "There lives more faith in honest doubt,/Believe me, than in half the creeds."[8] "To believe only possibilities is not faith, but mere philosophy."[9] "To know not faith, nor love, nor law; to be / Omnipotent but friendless is to reign."[10] The last quotation suggests that faith does not necessarily involve affection.

"The apparent vesting of vast influence in an interlocking directorate of a few politicians, businessmen, and generals has led to a variety of denunciations of the new power élite; . . . it manipulates rather than leads, coerces rather than convinces, pressures rather than persuades."[11] This comment more or less comprehensively summarizes the current attitude toward power. The modern concept of authority (and the power dependent upon it) suggests leadership: "Honest, capable leadership involves a talent for implementing the static nature of authority with the dynamism of power. This power can be described, in a neutral way, as competence or ability."[12] Leadership is all about getting people to do things by persuasion rather than force.

Thus, the responsibility of authority is conditioned partly by power of the elected officers of the corporation and partly by the countervailing power of the corporate work force (the union, the association of employees, or whatever). When the power of either side exceeds the authority it was originally given, the result is either stalemate, and in some cases bankruptcy or business failure, or a case for external (perhaps government) intervention or independent arbitration. Whether this is a threat to freedom or authority, or both, is a nice point.

ACCOUNTABILITY AND THE SOCIAL AUDIT

Every accountant knows what an audit is. It is a mechanism by which the account of the financial performance of a company or an individual is assessed and validated. Auditors ensure that a situation is as the accountant says it is and append their signatures to their approval.

Auditing is nothing new. But what would you say, as an auditor, to the proposition that you should evaluate the social objectives of a company's activity and measure the extent to which those objectives have been met? Not easy, is it?

The theory of the social audit, an idea that developed and grew during the 1970s, is that a company's social performance, as distinct from its economic performance, can be systematically studied and assessed according to the impact that the company's activity has on the quality of life. This theory holds that human values are more important than economic and technical values and that they reduce all else to subsystems within the total system.

Much has been written about the assessment of social performance. It is without exception well intended, but unfortunately it forgets that a social audit can measure only what a company is doing, not what the social results of that activity may have been. Since, as we have seen, *good* and *bad* (and therefore *good* results and *bad* results) are relative terms, it is difficult for any social auditor to say whether or not an organization is performing ultimately in the best interests of society. In other words, social results can be measured only against social objectives; these may be desirable or undesirable according to the view of their originator. It is one thing to measure dollars and cents; it is quite another to assess an improvement of living conditions or a reduction in race discrimination.

Whether such an audit is conducted internally or (as these affairs would appear to demand) by a disinterested outsider, the question has to be raised as to whether the results should be made public. The problem is that the procedure is unofficial, unlike a public audit of accounts, and no precedent exists for the publication of the information. Some companies have attempted to accomplish public disclosure of the results of such assessments, but it would seem to be a vain effort since, in the first place, the material being measured is of doubtful validity and, in the second place, few people take it seriously. At least, in the case of an accounting audit, the law requires it.

Another question is, who is qualified to conduct such an examination? Traditional auditors are accountants, trained in the techniques and technicalities of the procedures and the rules of their profession. The people who produce company statements and annual reports know the rules that apply, and they also know what is acceptable and what is not acceptable to an auditor. Those given the responsibility of producing a "social" account have no such guidance; they can only do their best. But what happens when the "auditor" disagrees? Whose rules apply?

The criteria upon which a social audit is conducted raise some speculation. Criteria can be quantitative or qualitative. Yet how can the cultural loss involved in demolishing a fifteenth-century building be measured against a safer flow of traffic in an English village? How can the peaceful existence of two hundred citizens of a Hebridean island be counted against the profit to an oil company from building oil storage tanks, landing jetties, and a social center for its employees? How are company executives going to view these comparisons?

Social audits are defended on the grounds that (1) they supply data that enable the organization to live up to its social objectives, (2) they encourage employees to think about social affairs and the implications of what they do, (3) they can be specifically directed at a particular industry's social problems, (4) they provide some quantitative basis for social planning (a dubious claim: How are a bank's loans to disadvantaged customers costed?), and (5) they represent a defense against consumerist groups (if such defense is necessary, the corporation has something to hide).

The overall problem with the social audit is that it appears to assume that one can make management decisions that are entirely moral. Yet most managements have no machinery or apparatus that make this possible. Certainly, many organizations are unable to evaluate the company's performance in social terms, and the question has to be raised, *quis custodiet ipsos custodes*? ("Who will keep the keepers themselves?")

The uncertainty surrounding the problem of the social audit was well expressed by Daniel Gray: "Those who are afraid of mistakes are afraid of learning; they are in no position, therefore, to make any headway in the social responsibility field or in social accounting. . . . We need to invent a new kind of social accounting that will tell us how much social responsibility is enough, what the tradeoffs are between different kinds of social corporate responsibility, and what is the optimum mix amongst different responsibility activities in the social responsibility area."[13]

Easy to say, not easy to do; but the comment does raise an important point. Just as the results of consumer behavior research and experimentation can rarely be syndicated and shared because such studies are usually specific to one product or market or company, so the criteria upon which any assessment of so-called social responsibility activity is based must necessarily be relevant to the performance of a particular organization in a particular situation over a particular period. The focus of this activity will vary from industry to industry, from company to company within the same industry, at different times and in different parts of the world within the same company, and sometimes from person to person in the same firm. Thus, an organization that manufactures toys will be concerned predominantly with minimizing the physical and mental ill effects of product design, manufacture, and use; producers of chemicals may establish as a first priority the control of pollution; and banks may concentrate on affirmative action. Similarly, these same companies may set totally different social goals for their operations in Third World countries where local conditions are dissimilar.

There are several different levels of awareness of social need. Take, once again, the example of the bank that decides it is important to subscribe to the equal opportunity concept. To implement this decision, the bank begins accepting less than its usually required guarantees of repayment from minority groups. As a statement of policy, this idea is probably perceived by the bank's senior management as furthering economic development, and the degree to which such a policy succeeds will be measured on that basis. A junior loan officer, however, will regard such loans as high risk because he feels that his performance is being judged on normal banking criteria and that therefore he is not doing a good job. One of the first requirements, therefore, of any declared social responsibility program is that everybody in the organization should understand exactly what its objectives and consequences are. Otherwise, no attempt to audit results can be meaningful.

In a similar way, "gap" analysis can often show marked differences between a corporation's professed social values and what it really believes. In other words, while senior executives may make pious statements about the social responsibility objectives and policies of the organization, their actual behavior may indicate an opposite inclination. For example, although the chief executive officer of a major firm may be on record as saying that the company respects the sanctity of the family, his organization's operating policy may stress heavily the idea of a corporate lifestyle in which many family values are either subordinated to the requirements of the employer or ignored altogether. The gap between statement and reality can be very wide.

The methods employed in attempts at social auditing are almost as varied as the activity they try to evaluate. In some companies, the responsibility is delegated to the group that handles the public affairs function; in others (probably the majority), the chief executive decides the important issues to be investigated. Many companies use a social cost–social benefit approach, which measures the social benefits to be achieved from the investment of funds in one area compared with another; others merely seek to assess the improvement in the corporate image resulting from the activity itself. This very diversity suggests strongly that the social audit is a long way from universal acceptance and understanding. Before that point is reached, many of its aspects still have to be determined.

First, it would appear that some agreement should be reached on exactly what the purpose of a social audit is: What kind of things are being measured, and why? Second, an acceptable method and procedure should be established to implement the audit; this raises the thorny question of whether such a procedure should be officially standardized, as is the case with an accounting audit, and whether its results should be required to be publicly announced. Third (and possibly most difficult), consensus needs to be sought on who should be responsible for auditing. Is it to be the same person or firm as is involved in financial auditing, and, if so, what specific qualifications are necessary? Do we, for instance, institute a degree program or a corresponding professional course of studies for the purpose? These are difficult questions to answer, but before they can be answered, the problem of building ''social'' objectives into the corporate plan has to be addressed; the following section focuses on this problem.

CORPORATE STRATEGY AND BUSINESS RESPONSIBILITY

If social policy is a natural part of business activity, as it has come to be described in recent years, then, by definition, it would seem that social

strategy should be a natural part of the corporate plan. It should not —
as appears to be the case in so many organizations — be an element of
corporate strategy added, almost as an afterthought, to a comprehensive
package that has already been determined and approved. "You should
not have an add-on called social responsibility that you apologize to the
stockholders for, and brag about in full-page advertisements. What we
want is business planning infected with social awareness." [14]

So much has been written about the need for corporations to build a
social responsibility policy into their corporate strategy that at first sight
it would seem that nothing can be added. Yet, on closer scrutiny, most
of this comment falls into the trap just described; it suggests a sharp
distinction between traditional financial objectives and new and different
nonfinancial goals. Recommended elements of the corporate plan, such
as "a basic company policy for assuming social responsibilities . . .
specific corporate objectives in specific areas of social responsibilities
. . . and concrete strategies and plans to achieve them . . . policies and
plans to stimulate socially responsible actions by individuals in the company . . . goals [set] in terms of both social and economic ends . . . cost-
benefit analyses appropriate for different levels of decision making . . .
in the area of social responsibilities," [15] sound right and proper and highly
commendable, but how do they actually fit into the overall coherent
strategy of an organization as part of its natural operation? The words
seem to paper over the cracks of the problem.

"Because administration represents a major social invention, it follows
that the role cannot be disassociated from social needs." [16] The quotation
could well be the text for a sermon on corporate strategy and business
responsibility. The new communitarian ethic — whereby management
bears a responsibility not only to stockholders, but also to all other
claimants on the organization — obliges the policymakers not only to
analyze and recognize present social problems, but also to anticipate
what the future social consequences of their company's actions may be.
"Society's expectations cannot be ignored." [17]

Despite what has already been said about ethical legislation, it seems
that some new set of commandments is necessary to bring those who
formulate company policy (particularly chief executive officers) to a
realization of what is necessary if economic and social objectives are to
be combined within the same corporate plan without contradicting each
other or appearing to be discrete and unrelated:

Rule 1: A business without profit is not a business. The first requirement
is for policymakers to understand the true purpose of their business. Any

enterprise, unless it survives in the short term, can forget the long term; the immediate and overriding need is to stay in business. The only way that this can be guaranteed is through the continuous generation of profit for the satisfaction of investors and the future capital demands of the company.

Rule 2: People make a business; a business should not make people. Participants in the enterprise, from those at the top to those at the very bottom, should feel that their characters and personalities are not in any way prejudiced by the business. At the same time, they should sense that their strengths as people and their qualities as human beings are a positive advantage to the corporation; also, their enjoyment of their existence should not be diminished by their participation in the company.

Rule 3: Profit at the cost of someone else's adversity is profit undeserved. It has to be remembered that all business transactions are part of the total economy. If something is sold, something is thereby bought. The basis of commercial negotiations is fair exchange: Both buyer and seller must feel satisfied that they have achieved their objectives. If one side feels unhappy at the outcome, or if another party is adversely affected by the transaction, the exchange has not been fair.

Rule 4: Business is part of society; it owes and it is rewarded. The concession theory of business teaches us that all corporations exist at the pleasure of society and that they therefore have an obligation to do what society wants. Once they cease to do this, society has the right to call them to account. Responsible business recognizes this, performs its obligations, and draws its just rewards.

Rule 5: Part of the cost of business success is righting the wrongs that may be done. Some businesses are in the position of being able to utilize freely the facilities available to society without necessarily having to pay for them. The water from rivers, the winds of the air, even the air itself, fall into this category. In process of use, these very elements may be damaged or destroyed or the life they support endangered. It is the responsibility of business to repair this wrong.

Rule 6: No business objective can be justified by money alone. In view of the enormous profits reported in recent times by some of our large corporations, we might be forgiven for thinking on occasion that their only concern is maximum profit — that the money itself, rather than the purposes to which it may be put, is the sole objective. Although perhaps not entirely fairly, oil, insurance, and banking companies are the first organizations that spring to mind in this context.

Rule 7: Do not seek money for its own sake; seek it for what it can buy.
The seventh rule is like unto the sixth. Money is the poorest of business objectives; money can be used for good or bad; money can cloud people's minds in a way that nothing else can. The word positively peppers literature: "Business is other people's money." [18] "By right means, if you can, but by any means make money." [19] "Money is like muck, not good except it be spread." [20] "Money is the root of all evil." [21] "Money speaks sense in a language all nations understand." [22] "You pays your money and you takes your choice." [23] Although economists have written volumes on money, it is probably the least understood entity in our lives; its value is measured against gold, commodities, and international exchange rates. You pay $5 for a bottle of Scotch in the United States, £5 in the United Kingdom; you can buy cigarettes in New York for 75¢, in London for 75p; a pound of prime steak costs you $2.30 in Wisconsin, £2.40 in Winchester, England. Why? See rule seven.

Rule 8: When business seeks merely to do good, it becomes a charity.
The corollary of the mistrust of the profit motive expressed in the preceding two rules is the stark reality of commercial existence. No business can prosper if there is no money to enable it to do so. It defeats its own purpose if it deliberately sacrifices its profitability to a worthy cause. Our eighth rule has therefore stated a primary proposition of business in the context of social responsibility, which in the discussion could well be forgotten.

Rule 9: Good behavior is good business.   Many business critics and would-be reformers adopt the stance that a social conscience is something that has to be appended to all other rules of traditional business activity; in other words, considerations of social performance are not a natural element in a business plan. This is a misleading and unfortunate view. The present section has attempted to make the point that social policy is not some separate state of the realm, like the law or the church, but an inherent and very fundamental part of corporate strategy. If corporate plans are not based on laudable social objectives, they are bad corporate plans.

Rule 10: When profits cease, call it a day. The tenth and final com-
mandment carries a twist to the tail. Rules one, four, six, and eight
combine to produce one inescapable conclusion: Without a continuing
generation of funds, no enterprise can prosper. In socialist European
economies ("socialist" in the sense of a large degree of state control,
rather than communistic), it has been the fashion to prop up ailing corporations with government funds. British Leyland, Ferranti, International Computers and Tabulators, and Rolls-Royce are examples in
Britain, not to mention the state-owned mining, transportation, and communications industries. Some of this state intervention was desirable and
necessary; British coal mines were in terrible shape and in need of release
from narrow-minded and parsimonious private owners who for decades
before nationalization had spurned the need for modernization, improved
safety and hygiene standards, and increases in workers' pay. Some of
the intervention was ideological and of doubtful benefit. Yet the reason
for it was usually the same: Inadequate performance or approaching
bankruptcy offered the government a difficult choice — either to allow
the industry in question to go out of business or to support it with state
funds. It is furthermore a sad reflection upon the standards of British
management that such decisions were necessary. However, the cruel
truth is that if management is so inept or trading conditions so adverse
as to make the future profitability of a company unlikely, nothing but
harm and grief can result. In such cases, the only option is to close the
door.

Corporate planners might claim that such a set of rules is unnecessary.
Indeed, they might well take offense that they should be offered. Yet so
many businesses appear to forget these simple guidelines that it is small
wonder there should be criticism and distrust of modern corporations.
Ethical legislation has been extensively criticized in this book, but these
fundamental corporate rules of thumb are directed less at personal ethical
values than at planning technique; they are tools of the trade more than
a moral handbook. Corporate planners could usefully take to heart John
Dyer's warning: "A little rule, a little sway, / A sunbeam in a winter's
day, / Is all the proud and mighty have / Between the cradle and the
grave." [24] On the other hand, note is respectfully taken of Shaw's caustic
remark that "the golden rule is that there are no golden rules." [25] Let
Belloc have the final word: "I had an aunt in Yucatan / Who bought a
python from a man / And kept it for a pet. / She died, because she never
knew / These simple little rules and few: — / The snake is living yet." [26]

CONCLUSION

Power and authority are transient things. While they are in one's possession, one feels supreme; yet, like beauty, they exist in the eye of the beholder, or, in this case, the eye of the governed. When one dies, they die also; it is left to another to take over the reins. The power that one has wielded is power that is at once dependent upon one's own authority and the pleasure of those one has governed; after one has gone, that authority and that pleasure need to be reviewed. It is this very ephemeral character of power that makes the contemplation of it so fascinating.

To return to the opening sections of this chapter: We can see why the old philosophers found a problem in the concept of power and sovereignty. Power is a trust granted by those giving power (and therefore really possessing it) in the form of authority to govern. Those who accept such power are accountable to those who give it, and as long as they wield it with responsibility and respect, they are accepted, tolerated, and obeyed. The power dies with them, or it passes to another who is preferred; but like a bank account, it carries a statement. And like a bank account, it will allow no overdraft without permission. The day of reckoning is the moment when creditors require payment. That, in social terms, is perhaps what we mean by an audit.

NOTES

1. Benjamin Disraeli, *Vivian Grey,* bk. 6, chap. 7.
2. Rensis Likert, *New Politics of Management* (New York: McGraw-Hill, 1961), chaps. 8 and 9.
3. Mason Haire, "The Concept of Power and the Concept of Man," in *Social Science Approaches to Business Behavior,* ed. George Strother (Homewood, Ill.: Irwin-Dorsey, 1962), pp. 163–83.
4. Eli Ginzberg and Ivar Berg, *Democratic Values and the Rights of Management* (New York: Columbia University Press, 1963), p. 33.
5. Lord Acton, *Historical Essays and Studies,* ed. D. Woodruff (London: Hollis & Carter, 1953), Appendix.
6. Ralph Waldo Emerson, *Essays: "The Over-Soul"* (Boston: Houghton Mifflin, 1883), p. 276.
7. New Testament, Heb. 11:1.
8. Alfred, Lord Tennyson, *In Memoriam,* st. 96, l. 11.
9. Sir Thomas Browne, *Religio Medici,* pt. 1, sec. 47.
10. Percy B. Shelley, *Prometheus Unbound,* bk. 2, pt. 4, l. 47.
11. Richard Eells and Clive Walton, *Conceptual Foundations of Business*, 3rd ed. (Homewood, Ill.: Richard D. Irwin, 1974), p. 412.
12. Ibid., p. 428.

13. Daniel H. Gray, "The Corporate Social Audit," *Proceedings of Spring 1972 Meeting*, Atlanta, Urban Affairs Committee, National Association of Manufacturers (New York: National Association of Manufacturers, 1972), p. 26.

14. Ibid., p. 30.

15. George A. Steiner, "Social Policies for Business," *California Management Review* 15:23–24.

16. Eells and Walton, *Conceptual Foundations*, p. 576.

17. Ibid., p. 582.

18. Mme. de Girardin, *Marguerites*, vol. 2, p. 104.

19. Horace, *Epistles*, bk. 1, Epistle 1, l. 66.

20. Francis Bacon, *Essays*, no. 15, "Of Seditions and Troubles."

21. St. Paul, 1 Tim. 6:10.

22. Aphra Behn, *The Rover*, pt. 2, act 3, sc. 1.

23. *Punch* 10 (1846).

24. John Dyer, *Grongar Hill*, l. 89.

25. George Bernard Shaw, *Man and Superman*, act 4, "Maxims for Revolutionists," (London: Constable, 1906).

26. Hilaire Belloc, *More Beasts for Worse Children*, "The Python."

6 A GUIDE TO MANAGEMENT ETHICS

Good are the Ethics, I wis; good absolutely, not for me, though; Good, too, Logic, of course; in itself, but not in fine weather.

— Arthur Hugh Clough[1]

ETHICAL MODEL BUILDING

If the discussion in the foregoing chapters suggests one conclusion above all others, it is that moral attitudes are subjective. There is no single universal code to which every man and woman unequivocally subscribes. From person to person, differences in ethical orientation may frequently be minimal, but we are all subject to a variety of social, economic, and cultural influences throughout our lives, which, when combined with our individual psychological characteristics, make us the persons we are, with our unique perspectives of the world and our own ideas of right and wrong.

It is therefore surprising that scholars and commentators should attempt so earnestly to construct models of ethical values. What purpose some of these serve is difficult to understand, especially when they are applied to the practical problems of deciding on appropriate behavior in specific moral dilemmas, but no discussion of the problem of business responsibility can ignore them, even though the outcome is sometimes frustrating.

Ethical theories fall into three broad categories: *legalistic, antinomian,* and *situational.* The first two of these have produced modern formalized versions; the last will be discussed at length.

Legalistic Models

Legalistic models are those that derive from some assumed moral law, such as a religious creed. In Chapter 3, we discussed the idealistic philosophy of Plato, a perfect example of the genre. The Platonic ideal, by definition, is a dictate to reason, a regimen that demands acceptance and frowns on disapproval; it is an attitude that stems from a fundamental acceptance of a universal law — sublime, unquestionable, and inflexible. It is a philosophy that ignores personality.

The Kantian categorical imperative is similar to the Platonic ideal in that it depends on some rational command; in this case, actions derive from the maxim that one can will that they should become universal laws. This is a laudable attempt at objectivism, but an unfortunate surrender to legalism. Again, the standpoint is impersonal; it is also disturbingly confusing, although alluringly persuasive.

Utilitarian philosophy provides another instance of legalistic thinking. Bentham and Mill, its greatest protagonists, defined "good" in terms of the happiness it brings: A good act is one that results in the greatest happiness for the largest number of people.

In modern philosophical thought, there is considerable support for legalism from people who firmly believe there is something called *current ethics.* This school of thought holds that "written into the nature of things there is a whole hierarchy of rules and sub-rules, and while we do not always follow them and we do not always quite understand them, yet they are there."[2] This attitude postulates some unspecified authority, like Plato's ideal, for the definition of good or bad.

This is very hard to take; indeed, the attitude flies in the face of reason and experience. The basis of moral behavior changes, sometimes quite rapidly and frequently during the life span of one generation. Whereas usury used to be considered a sin, lending money is now perfectly acceptable behavior in our credit society; our attitudes toward sex in general — now held to be good and beautiful, whereas it was once regarded as ugly and bestial — and to birth control in particular — which more than one church in the last fifty years has first condemned and subsequently approved — show quite dramatically that moral standards change over time. The concept of current ethics is not attractive.

Another modern legalistic concept is that of *consensus ethics,* which says that the way the majority of people in a particular culture behave is the ethical norm. Unfortunately, there are too many examples of consensus leading to unpleasant behavior, such as the murder of political enemies, for such a view to command total credibility, though it does have a certain appeal.

Antinomianism

Antinomianism is quite the opposite of legalism. As the Greek origin of the word suggests, antinomianism represents the denial of moral law: "I do what I do, not what I ought to do." A world without "oughts" is difficult to contemplate.

Formal Models. Both legalism and antinomianism have given rise to formal ethical models of managerial behavior. In the case of the latter, the two most common interpretations are the *equilibrium model* and the *incremental model.* The equilibrium model stems from the view that the manager is an impartial umpire whose function is to maintain the equilibrium relationship between the welfare of the various groups affected by managerial decisions. Its basis is political rather than moral, its criteria being the principle of least dissent and lack of overt conflict.

The equilibrium model is open to some fairly serious criticism. It reflects "power" positions; also, by its nature it may unduly favor the most articulate of the groups or individuals involved. It appears to assume that managers have inadequate ethical fiber and need to be guided, and its ethical content is minimal. It is based purely on experience.

The incremental model is similar to the equilibrium model, although it does have some moral content. According to this model, the manager should try to make decisions that leave the situation slightly better than it was before. In so doing, the manager's avoidance of extremes limits the possibility of serious harm.

An example of a model based on the legalistic view, the *computer model* is a product of modern technology. It is based on deductive reasoning and represents an attempt to overcome the kind of criticism that was leveled against the Gulf+Western code of ethics in Chapter 4. The company "legislates" the values and principles to be followed by employees, but because no two situations are alike and because the legislated principles can be only very broad, the number of intermediate principles in any given situation is potentially enormous. To deal with these numbers, the computer is called into play. In principle, the process is appropriate, but in practice, it becomes artificial. It is the ultimate ethical *reductio ad mathematicum.*

The Situational Approach

Dissatisfaction with both legalism and antinomianism has been largely responsible for the growth in popularity of the modern situational approach. Situationalism is a moral philosophy that is essentially subjective but that respects cultural ethical traditions; however, because of its subjective nature, it can override these traditions if it is thought "right" to do so. As Bishop J. A. Pike points out, "You ought to recognize that a situation approach to ethics is under the umbrella of total claim, total responsibility; that everything you do affects other people, affects the creating of the world."[3] This view accords with our own conclusions; our premise was amply substantiated by Chapter 3's examination of the historical perspective. In any situation calling for an ethical judgment, we have to balance the arguments for and the consequences of behavior of one type or another. At best, we must hope for a positive ethical outcome; at worst, for "the lesser of two evils."[4] In the latter case, our decision is not just a *faute de mieux* ("for want of something better"); it is absolutely the right thing to do in those circumstances at that time.

Thus, a decision made at home about whether it is right or wrong, good or bad to buy a new washing machine to make life a little easier rather than spend the money on educational books for your children, or whether you should stop smoking because it could influence your son, or whether you should make your views on religion so obvious to your children as to influence their attitudes toward going to church, or whether to shoot your neighbor's dog if it digs up your favorite flower bed — such a decision has to be taken in the light of the situation *and* as a result of weighing the arguments for and against the action. Behind your desk at the office the next morning, you will make decisions in exactly the same way. You will not exchange one ethical rulebook for another; you will not put on another ethical hat and say to yourself and your secretary and your boss and your colleagues, "Now I am a business person; last night I had to be honest and kind and understanding. This morning I am different." Rather, you will, in exactly the same way as the night before, judge the situation on its merits, on the consequences of one path of action or another, on the effects of your decision on other people, and, perhaps above all else, in the light of your experience; for while you may in one sense be making an isolated decision on a matter that is an event in itself, that decision is part of an ethical continuum that is added to and filled out by each individual situation and your reaction to it. It is for this reason that Albert Carr's comments on the business "game" are so inimical to good sense (see Chapter 4).

The real truth of the matter is that all moral action eventually touches other people. We do not commit murder because that act, above all others, is an intruding influence on somebody else's existence. Likewise, we do not steal because it affects another's property. We do not lie because by lying we are creating false impressions in other people's minds. Similarly, we do not want such behavior from our fellow citizens because it would hurt *us*. These strictures may be part of the Ten Commandments, but they also make good, social, situational sense.

Although the ethical decisions and problems presented by business are generally not at such a fundamental level, the principles involved are the same. If we pollute rivers, we are making life unpleasant for several different social groups: fishermen, naturalists, swimmers, artists, and people who just like things to be as they were intended. If we produce unsafe or substandard merchandise, we run the risk of injuring or frustrating or antagonizing the people who buy our products. If we dismiss employees because they object to our doing these things, we cause them and their families suffering. In short, if we have a conscience, we refrain from such behavior, not because there is any universal code of ethics that tells us to refrain, but because, insofar as those actions cause distress to others, we judge the situation in terms of our responsibility to our fellow human beings. This is surely the purpose of Pike's comment: "You're on the job all the time and you carry with you the burden of others. You care what happens to people, and you are, therefore, in the end, more moral than anybody who uses just a checklist and keeps within the law."[5]

It is easy to talk in these terms; it is not so easy to put theory into practice. You may say, "That's all very well, but do decisions based on situational ethics allow for deviation from my moral code? Is it possible that faced with a choice between standing my ethical ground to the extent that I get fired because I refuse to carry out a company directive or keeping my job because I am prepared to suspend my conscience in order to provide for my family, I can choose the latter and still feel, in the context of the specific situation, that I have made the right choice?"

This question presupposes that one's conscience is the product of a code of behavior so comprehensive that it covers every eventuality. The truth is that no behavioral code can be described in such detail. The Sermon on the Mount mentions only a few categories of behavior that fail by a wide margin to allow for every ethical dilemma, and the Ten Commandments reduce ethics to an even shorter list; where does either talk about pollution or product safety or unfair dismissal? The primary characteristic of situational ethics is that all values are relative; what may be good in one context may be bad in another, or, put another way, what may be worse than the alternative in one situation may be better than the alternative in another.

Thus, the ethical decisions we reach must be the result of the values we put on the available behavioral options in a given situation at a given time. While it has already been claimed that our conceptual framework of behavior in business depends essentially on our conceptual framework of behavior in life, we must be careful not to confuse *framework* with *code*. To those of us who believe that all ethical decisions are separate from each other and that they are similar only in the sense that "I am not going to kill Mr. Smith" is similar to "I am not going to kill Mr. Jones," the fact that opposite decisions can occur in situations of the same type is part of our conceptual *framework*. Not killing and not stealing are part of a generally agreed social *code* because killing and stealing invite retaliation and that is something we do not want to have happen. Not lying falls between a social code and a conceptual framework of situational ethics because some of us may feel that occasionally we must tell a technical lie in order to keep someone else happy.

In this connection, it helps if one distinguishes between the hierarchy of one's ethical rules (for example, "I will kill under conditions of war only," "Stealing is a less serious crime," etc.) and the application of one's ethical rules to *real* situations. Most of our activities are based on intuitions, *but* our intuitions are often directed by basic principles.

All this makes the subjectivity of ethical decision making even more obvious. No one is suggesting that it is easy. As Jeffrey Barach comments:

> It is particularly hard because there is no monolithic structure to provide rules for us to follow. Moreover, there are obvious and persistent conflicts not only between evil and good but, more often, between several possible goods. This feeds the element of release that lets us pay the price of laziness. . . . The situation is hindered by the lack of clear help from the churches on practical matters of conduct. Religion is in real trouble as a helper. . . . Much of its applied ethics is permeated with sentimental oversimplifications and ignorance

of the need for prudence — for the situationally corrected administrative attempts to solve ethical problems, and this law of equity is what we need.[6]

If there were never conflict, one would become suspicious. The really easy way out is to take refuge in some high-sounding but pathetically unrealistic moral law or to surrender entirely to convenience. Either way, one avoids the issue. Nor is the objective merely compromise; the middle way is not necessarily good just because it lies between two extremes. (*Compromise,* incidentally, is a word that has unfavorable connotations in North America, while in England it suggests reasonableness and fair dealing; the latter interpretation may be appropriate to the negotiating table, but it is not the best criterion for ethical judgment.) We should be seeking something with far more balanced values than merely the *via media.* Justice may hold the scales in her hand, but they almost always tip one way or the other; they rarely weigh evenly.

Ethical decisions frequently call for great courage because they are personal decisions, unaided by advice from others and dependent solely on one's responsibility to oneself and one's self-respect. Sometimes a person may have to forget traditional axioms of divine law in order to reach a fair and just view that will result in maximum benefit to all the other people involved, within the constraints of equity. Such a decision process involves logic, not legal legerdemain, and resolution rather than romantic moralizing.

Joseph Fletcher is perhaps the most forceful advocate of situational ethics: "The situationist enters into every decision-making situation fully armed with the ethical maxims of his community and its heritage, and he treats them with respect as illuminators of his problems. Just the same he is prepared in any situation to compromise them or *set them aside in the situation* if love seems better served by doing so."[7] (The use of the word *compromise* here is the correct one, having the meaning of *adjust* rather than *taint* or *besmirch*.) This concept of love has to be understood and appreciated as the Greek *agape,* rather than in terms of its other associations of eroticism, materialism, divinity, or aestheticism; it is an unselfish subordination of personal advantage to the benefits of one's fellow human beings. This concept is the criterion for situational ethics; its observance absolves the decision maker from any blame.

Fletcher further insists that four factors underlie the concept of situational ethics: pragmatism, relativism, positivism, and personalism. *Pragmatism* is based on the idea that if something achieves a desired objective, it is good, and the objective at which it aims depends on the values of the decision maker. *Relativism* means that behavior based merely on law is not necessarily ethical; laws, both judicial and "moral," are largely abstract "in relation to the unique and totally concrete situation." *Positivism* suggests that some decisions cannot be made on the basis of logic alone and that ethical values are not absolute because they cannot be verified. In this context, we can argue, business executives have to understand that tough-talking rationality is not the only basis for a choice of action: Personal values can also prompt behavior and, through the commitment attached to them, can provide a valid justification for decision. The idea of *personalism* indicates that ethical standards are "person-centered" or, as has been maintained throughout this book, subjective. Yet this very subjectivism produces a highly objective attitude to ethical conduct, for it is only by knowing oneself that one can understand others and thus behave responsibly toward them.

This personalistic approach is central to situational ethics. The person — the individual — is all-important in the business enterprise; it is on the individual that business decision making should focus, not from the standpoint of manipulation (which has been the consequence of much organizational behavior theory), but from the standpoint that human values are paramount. Agapeic love as a basis for ethical action substitutes for, or rather replaces, the fallacy that there is a right way or a wrong way of doing things postulated by some absolute moral law; situations involve other people, and consequently if a decision helps other people, it is a good decision.

Protagonists of the legalistic argument for business conduct (i.e., that corporations are observing all their responsibilities by merely remaining within the legally prescribed limits of action) ignore or fail to recognize the role of human values. To take refuge in the statute book, to play the game of words, to score nice legal points rather than to weigh a decision in terms of its effects on people is tantamount to running a washing machine full of perfectly clean clothes, or even empty of laundry altogether, through its entire cycle just because it happens to be wash day. To be legal is not necessarily to be ethical; to follow the rules is often to take the easy escape route.

This is not to suggest that managers can throw away the rule book, that they can forget company regulations completely or can regard the laws of the land as irrelevant and unimportant. What *is* suggested is that every situation, being unique, calls for a unique decision and that individuals are responsible to themselves and other people under a code of behavior transcending mere legality. The law allows the individual much freedom of decision; if it did not, we should not need the phenomenon of a court of law, with defending and prosecuting counsel, a panel of jurors, a judge, and all the concomitant paraphernalia to interpret it.[8]

It is interesting, and somewhat ironic, that business should lay great emphasis on such characteristics as imagination, creativity, and initiative as desirable attributes in the executives they seek to recruit, for these are essentially the hallmarks of the individualist. When such people begin to display these qualities in their working life, they are as often as not frowned upon. Bureaucratic organizations do not happily accept maverick behavior; they prefer managers who conform, who follow the rules, who agree with the establishment. Nonconformist behavior, even if it is directed toward the well-being and progress of the firm, is frequently viewed as disloyalty or protest. Top-management executives are tempted to look favorably on subordinates who reflect their own attitudes, and while innovative behavior is ostensibly prized, it is privately regarded as an indulgence granted only to those at the highest level of the decision-making hierarchy. Senior executives should extend their concern for and understanding of others beyond the conformists to all members of the organization.

One of the commonest fallacies of management theory is that the organizational hierarchy involves relationships between functions, levels, or positions. Yet you cannot have a hierarchy without people; jobs do not relate to each other, but people do. If this obvious, but unappreciated notion were to become the basis of management attitudes, perhaps the conflicts, dilemmas, and problems would diminish.

Translated into the wider arena of the responsibility of business to society, situational ethics takes on a new dimension. If the human being is the center of all existence, if society is people, social institutions like business and government must hold the well-being of people to be all-important. Consequently, business decisions must be made not primarily for the economic benefit of the balance sheet (though this has to be one of the results if the organization is to survive), but above all for the improvement of human life. Business decisions based on situational ethics will therefore be directed at the optimal balance between the advantage of the firm and the rest of society. With the criteria of situational ethics, the question ceases to be one of *whether* business should clean up its own pollution and becomes one of *when* it should do so; the issue is not *whether* to build both social and economic objectives into corporate policy, but *what* those policies should be. Echoing the old dictum that what is good for General Motors is good for America, R.H. Viola expresses the new organizational ethic as, "What is good for man is good for the organization."[9]

The problem is, of course, how can the new ethic be realized? Management philosophy has followed the path to its present position over a very long time. Traditional beliefs die hard. It is one thing to suggest a radical reorientation of management attitudes; it is quite a different matter to change entrenched belief. True, the very fact that social responsibility is currently a popular topic among both practicing business managers and academic commentators indicates that the need for social action has not gone unheeded, but one cannot escape the impression that the popularity is more the result of external protest and pressure than of a positive move on the part of the business community. This impression indicates that the outlook may not be optimistic; it is also the basis of the continuing distrust and suspicion about the motives behind the "good works." One has only to examine the letterheads of a sample of fifty major organizations in America to find twenty or thirty of them carrying claims that the organizations in question are "equal opportunity" and "affirmative action" employers. Although many of these claims may well be sincere, one is tempted to be a little skeptical at times.

It might be argued that it really matters little why corporations pursue policies that result in social improvement, that the difference is a semantic one only. This avoids the issue. If business observes its responsibilities only under duress, it will cease to do so when the pressure ceases. The result will be a cyclical Toynbeean rebirth of protest and a renewal of corporate response. Ethical behavior, as was intimated in the preface to this book, is more effective in the longer term when the person who exhibits that behavior knows why he or she behaves that way.

The subjective situationist would claim that one is oneself and no one else, that one's ethics are one's alone. We all have our different frameworks of behavior. How did we formulate these frameworks? The answer is that we do not really know because we have all been influenced by different pressures and controls. If we know anything at all, it is perhaps that our *final* responsibility is to ourselves, and that if we want to find "God" — whatever that means, for it means different things to different people — we must find ourselves first. "God" in this sense is one's belief in one's own system of values.

Now one's own system of values can be an accident resulting from the concatenation of cultural, social, economic, and personal psychological influences on our lives, or it can be conscious through intellectual rationalization or even through blind faith. Whichever is the case, the system is there; it exists. You cannot change it for me, any more than you could have changed it for Adolf Hitler or Jesus Christ.

In view of this, we may well ask, is the reduction of ethics to broad models realistic, or is it a waste of time? Is not a realistic subjective approach based on the demands of the situation and the consequent effects on the people involved more appropriate? And does not this approach fit more comfortably with the complexities of modern management and the variety of problems it faces?

EDUCATION FOR BUSINESS RESPONSIBILITY

Looking at the problem realistically, all the arguments point to the need for reeducation from the top. Middle and lower managers may be totally committed to the philosophy of situational ethics; they may judge situations on their merits and come to conclusions that offer the optimal benefit to corporate interests, to their colleagues, to the labor force, to customers, and to society at large; they may minimize conflict, and they may satisfy their own criteria; but, in the final judgment, unless they convince their boss and their boss's boss, and so on right up through the management hierarchy, until the chief executive is convinced of the rightness of the action, their situational decision counts for nothing except their own ethical satisfaction.

Viola claims that management must look to the future, toward a new organizational ethic, and must not feel threatened in doing so; in striving to discover self, the individual manager is discovering reality. Furthermore, organizations should encourage "freedom to be," but at the same time they should embrace the idea of personal responsibility because human values are moving in this direction: "Work organizations will have to adapt to this new understanding of morality inasmuch as their structure, leadership, and tasks are consonant with the worker's growth and development as a person." [10] This is all very well, but it is a trifle idealistic; whether Viola is referring to the relationship between management and labor or between top and middle echelons is not clear, but either way his suggestion is unlikely to be implemented from the bottom up. Influence does not generally travel in that direction. Before anything else can happen, Viola's new ethos has to be accepted by the policy-making levels of the organization and, above all, by the chief executive.

The analysis of the structure of power in the previous chapter showed that business responsibility is a relative term; the only person in the organization who can truly be called responsible is the person at the top, because only that person has the power and the authority to implement ethical decisions. If a subordinate questions the chief executive's decisions, that subordinate is questioning not only a set of values, but also the authority whereby those values are applied to the corporate policy of the firm. It might be argued that "reason" should rule, but if it comes to a clash of wills, the odds are loaded very much in favor of the chief executive: The subordinate's strength of will inevitably leads to a refusal to accept the company's (i.e., the chief executive's) values, and consequently the subordinate is dismissed; the chief executive's strength of will, supported as it always is by dedication to the "well-being" of the firm, must not be weakened because thereby managerial authority is weakened, and that is bad for the company and the perceived quality of its management.

It is here that situational ethics assumes a further dimension. The chief executive can truly make decisions that are the product of a desire to optimize the consequent benefits to all elements in the system: consumers, shareholders, employees, and the population at large. But the chief executive can do this only if he or she is the type of manager to consider all these elements; if that is not the case, then one or more of the elements will suffer. Subordinates, especially those who feel a sense of responsibility themselves, will applaud a chief executive's decision that matches their own perceptions of right or wrong and will willingly and enthusiastically put that decision into practice. On the other hand, if they disagree with a chief executive's decision, they have only two options: They can invite dismissal by parading their consciences to a point from which there is no turning back, or they can regard the continuation of their employment as one of the required outcomes of whatever decision they adopt. If they choose the latter, they have to accept that there are some situations in which their responsibility as family breadwinners outweighs the urge to protest.

In this regard, one has to take issue with James McKie, who claims, rightly, that we have to distinguish between a business and the people who manage or control it, but who goes on to say that such people can be responsible or irresponsible without the firm's being the image of the people who manage it; a business is not "analyzable as the equivalent of a businessman. . . . The firm is a 'black box' whose conduct and purposes do not relate in any simple way to those of the people who constitute it. For this reason the task of assigning responsibility is greatly simplified whenever it can be directed to the firm as an organization, instead of to the several motives and behavior of the individual employees."[11]

McKie's view seems to be based on a desire to cut the Gordian knot, and he takes the easy way out. The task of assigning responsibility *is,* of course, very simple if it is directed to the organization and not to the individual, but we have tried to show that it cannot be so directed. Even if McKie equates the term *organization* with the collective personality of all the organization's employees (and it is by no means certain that he is doing so), his argument still makes little sense; collective responsibility, in business as well as in government, means one thing above all, and that is that the chief executive, whether chairman, president, or prime minister, ultimately has to be held accountable for the actions of those who answer to him. As President Harry Truman said, "The buck stops here."

There is more to this, however. The logical extension of this principle leads to the inescapable conclusion that even when *unaware* of subordinates' actions, the chief executive must still be responsible for them. Thus, when it came to light that General Motors' legal department had instigated an investigation of Ralph Nader's personal life in an attempt to discover evidence that would discredit Nader, the company's president was forced to issue a statement that although he had no knowledge of his legal department's activities, he was nevertheless responsible and had to accept the blame. Lack of communication between links in the management chain is no extenuating circumstance. The commander of a naval vessel is responsible for any damage or disaster to his ship even if it results from negligence on the part of one or more members of his crew; Richard Nixon would have been equally responsible even if he had no knowledge of the Watergate break-in; and you are responsible if your dog bites a neighbor, even if it is the neighbor with whom you are on the best of terms. Put another way, you are irresponsible if you are not aware of all of the dealings of your subordinates.

Viola holds the view that the centralization of power, authority, and influence at the top of the organization has resulted in a lack of involvement on the part of the large majority of employees.[12] No one individual can see his or her part in the whole, and this causes alienation. The individual has no influence on the organization's decisions, which makes it very difficult to feel responsible. Influential managers have interpreted this lack of involvement as lack of initiative, as reluctance to accept commitment, but experience suggests that whenever such initiative is displayed, it is frowned upon because it upsets the agreed course of corporate strategy and causes conflicts of interests. Consequently, subordinate protest is manifested in other ways; demands for higher pay, better working conditions, more security, health insurance, cars, and other fringe benefits become the substitutes for a real influence on the course of the organization's affairs.

One of the causes of this situation is increased specialization. Both in the structure of firms and in the management education process that supplies the firms' executive needs, there is too much emphasis on the specialized nature of business activities. People are labeled and compartmentalized into functional boxes. An accounting specialist looks after financial figures, a production specialist looks after machines and materials, a marketing specialist looks after customers, and a personnel specialist looks after the recruitment of people for all these specialist operations. Similarly, business students are encouraged to concentrate their studies in particular functional ''core'' areas that match the specific needs of business. All this severely limits the horizon of involvement and at the same time diminishes the field of responsible action. The trend has shown no signs of slowing down; indeed, we are witnessing exactly the opposite phenomenon. Within the specialist functions themselves, subfunctions are beginning to appear: Marketing executives come in an assortment of models, like new automobiles, each designed for a specific use, such as research, logistics, or communications; operations management subdivides into plant supervision, systems analysis, and operational research; organizational behavior offers a choice between personnel management, labor relations, or organizational development; and finance segments into cost accounting, management accounting, auditing, and financial control.

If management's functional terms of reference are so limited, it is hardly surprising that opportunities for the exercise of business responsibility are largely restricted to those who set the organization's overall goals. The size of the field of social decision making is in direct proportion to the scope of individual authority. Viola suggests that this restriction prompts top management to structure individual tasks even more, to assign even less responsibility, and to keep itself at a distance; and so the circle becomes more and more vicious.[13] This leads to increasing criticism of and increasing pressure on the organization from both within and without its ranks.

Thus, if in the course of their daily occupations individual employees have to face decisions that in some way involve ethical judgment, they will often be forced to choose between what top management tells them is the proper action to take and what their innermost feelings prompt them to do. It has been suggested that the most sensible approach in such a case is to decide on the basis of the situational consequences of one's action on others: on oneself, one's family, one's colleagues, and the general well-being of the firm. To take an intransigent stand on the grounds of some general moral code is not necessarily right; indeed, such an attitude could result in the well-being of nobody and would in some circumstances result in the termination of the individual's employment. This solves no problems at all, even if the top policymakers are abusing the responsibility vested in them; resignation or dismissal of a single employee will not change their outlook.

In this regard, business schools have an important responsibility. Instead of fostering in students an attitude that regards specialization as desirable and necessary and generalism as weak and superficial, they might usefully consider making a "total organization" orientation an *overriding* requirement for potential managers, even though some specific skills are undoubtedly also needed. Furthermore, they might ask themselves whether the management education process has anything to offer would-be executives in the form of encouragement of individualism and the development of values that can help to spread the opportunities for the observance of responsibility beyond the door of the chief executive's suite. If they can achieve even a modest degree of success in shifting management thinking toward the well-being of others, they will deserve congratulation. Their graduates are, after all, the chief executives of tomorrow.

SOCIAL MARKETING

Much of the discussion in this book has centered upon the difficulties facing individual managers who try to reconcile their own values with those laid down by corporate policy. This dilemma can take two forms. On the one hand, there is the problem that results from considerations of strategy on the simple level, uncomplicated by overtones of social or ethical behavior, when a manager may differ from superiors on matters of traditional business goals, such as maximization of sales potential, new product development policy, production levels, advertising, or recruitment. This is a legitimate area for objective debate between various levels of the management hierarchy, but, in the final analysis, if disagreement persists, the issue will be just as legitimately resolved through the exercise of authority by the higher level. Such is the nature of business activity, and that is why authority exists. Without such authority, the corporation would seldom reach any strategic decisions.

On the other hand, as we have seen, disagreement and conflict may result from antipathy between subordinate and superior on matters involving behavioral, ethical, or social criteria. This kind of difference is less easy to reconcile, but the onus will inevitably rest upon the subordinate; he or she will have to decide whether to accept corporate values or to press the case to the point where the issue becomes one of continuing membership in the organization. We have seen that the proper deployment of situational ethics is appropriate in such a case, for although it is questionable whether the exercise of superior authority is equally legitimate in these circumstances, there is no doubt that it will be applied if the need arises.

With this preamble, it is appropriate to look specifically at that business function that most closely impinges on society at large — namely, marketing. The marketing concept itself is nothing new, though its practice as a conscious philosophy is a relatively recent phenomenon, having surfaced within the last forty years or so as a natural consequence of the development of the capitalist system. Capitalism began in its modern form with the Industrial Revolution, which produced the three essential marketing requirements of mass production, mass distribution, and mass communication. In its early stages, the modern capitalist era was an age of production, but as competition increased and branded products became less differentiated, capitalism changed its emphasis to aggressive selling, thus acknowledging Adam Smith's principle that the only purpose of production is consumption. It was this reorientation that gave rise to the notorious excesses of hucksterism in the late nineteenth and early twentieth centuries. Gradually, however, industry came to realize that the chances of selling its production were immeasurably enhanced if it produced what the market wanted, rather than what it was easy or convenient to manufacture, and this new market-oriented attitude gradually but exponentially began to dominate manufacturing policy.

However, as obvious needs were one by one satisfied by the supply of appropriate products and services, industry discovered that its only chance of growth lay in creating new needs, or, to be more exact, in arousing latent needs that the market never knew it had and without which it had managed to exist pefectly happily. The offerings developed to meet these needs typified, and continue to typify, the "back-street abundance" (the widespread ownership of things once regarded as luxuries) that has now become a feature of modern living standards. Some products are the results of technological progress, such as has occurred in the electronics field; other products have resulted from changes in the social environment (e.g., the development of convenience foods). In all cases, competition is fierce, differentiation is less discernible, and innovation has taken on an entirely new meaning.

There are commentators who see in all this the need for a reorientation of marketing attitudes. Some believe that the increasing similarity between competing products will force industry to concentrate its promotional energies on describing benefits beyond those of simple price or performance; after-sales service, for example, is one area where differentiation will become more important. Distinctive products and services will produce a greater return on investment than those whose similarity results in marginal profit; the former will therefore be the focus of marketing efforts. Other commentators take the more extended view that marketing must now make up for its previous excesses, that "metamarketing" must attempt to imbue consumers with a new sense of values and must encourage a less competitive and materialistic attitude. Marketing, they maintain, now has a social mission to give people not what they want, but what is good for them.

Expressed this way, the philosophy is arrogant and patronizing. It seems to suggest that the public is incapable of making up its own mind. The fault lies in the advocacy, however, not in the principle. What the new attitude is in fact saying is that industry must look further than the profit potential attached to particular product ideas, that the implications of marketing activity are more important than the willingness of consumers to buy, and that the consequences of consumption are more significant than consumption itself — liquids packed in nonreturnable bottles can contribute to unsightly litter, and detergent waste destroys wildlife. Added to this, the sheer volume of products, alike in so many respects, results in aesthetic pollution in the form of excessive and unproductive advertising.

It is in this arena that the ethical battle will rage most fiercely. Since marketing management is, or should be, more closely aware of the external climate than any other functional area, it can be argued that it thus carries more than a normal share of the responsibilities facing business. One of the characteristics of marketing executives is that they frequently come from middle-class environments that do not easily square with the outlook and attitudes of the masses at which most marketing and, in particular, most promotional activity is directed.[14] Therefore, although constant monitoring of social change is essential for a proper marketing sense, it is sometimes difficult for marketing managers to accept and to understand the values and behavioral patterns of the markets at which their products are aimed. It is in this sense that objectivity needs to be maintained.

Objectivity here is a key word, for it is central to situational ethics. Behavior based on feelings for one's fellow human beings by definition puts "self" at a lower level of priority than other people. While the ethical decision is subjective in the sense that it is made by the individual, who weighs the decision in terms of its effects on others, it is objective in the sense that the individual is attempting insofar as it is possible to serve the interests of other people. One does this, not by imposing rigid rules, but by putting oneself in other people's shoes and looking at the problem from their point of view. Marketing managers are trained to do this; they are taught to analyze and to explain consumer behavior so that they can devise marketing strategies and promotional programs appropriate to the decision processes that are perceived to exist in the marketplace. They are not, however, trained to consider the social values contained in the products and services they offer. Here is where the opportunity exists.

Marketing management, at all levels, needs to be made aware of the new marketing perspective if the possibility of ethical conflict is to be minimized. Management education in its many forms and at its various stages — undergraduate, graduate, and on the job — must begin to encourage marketing executives to think in terms that involve more than an examination of profit return, market share, pricing policy, or communications strategy. The orientation of marketing planning in all its different facets must be redirected toward the optimal balance between the standard of living and the quality of life. Marketing research, for example, should be concerned not only with such questions as what consumers want, what they buy, and what they think of products, but also (and more importantly) with what the social effects of particular new product ideas may be. The problem of saturated markets and overcompetition, resulting in huge amounts of unproductive promotional expenditure, needs to be overcome. At some point, thought also needs to be given to the nature of new product offerings; do people really need all of the thousands of new brands and models launched into the market every year? Is the philosophy of economic growth, based on the traditional attitude that 50 percent of company sales revenues in ten years' time will consist of products not yet thought of, the only tenable view? A study of the Japanese experience will quickly illustrate the undesirable consequences of a mindless worship of the GNP idol: Poorer families cannot afford meat and have to rely for their existence on fish caught in Japanese coastal waters, which they know to be highly contaminated with industrial poisons and which they have been told to avoid.[15] Marketing is the means whereby such "development" programs are achieved, and as the chief weapon in the business armory, it needs critical scrutiny. Until marketing executives of all ranks are made aware of the tremendous responsibility resting on their shoulders, it is unlikely that much improvement will be realized.

This is not just pious moralizing. It is a statement of fact, derived from observation of marketing's short-run attitudes. These attitudes have been instrumental in creating the problems so heatedly debated in the literature of social responsibility — environmental pollution and despoliation, the endangering of the ecological balance, the disregard of individual rights and interests criticized so vehemently by consumerist protest groups, and the political lobbying frequently employed to protect and defend business objectives.

Marketing commentators are beginning to take the hint, and it is only to be hoped that their observations will find an echo in the classroom. Marketing textbooks are being rewritten from the new perspective; the word *social* as often as not appears in their titles. Eells and Walton have expressed the point well: "Many forces in society impede innovation. The businessman himself has often actively sought, for diverse [*sic*] reasons, to pursue interests and needs other than those of his customers. An attitude that rejects innovative practice and resists change, or an attitude that permits careless novelties to be brought to the market, are marks of irresponsible management." [16] Neither of these coauthors is primarily a marketing man, but the comment is apt. No business can with any justification whatsoever risk endangering the people who buy, use, and experience the effects of its products or services. The estimated 80 percent fail rate in new products suggests that current marketing practice is far from perfect.

William Lazer and Eugene Kelley enumerate the forces that have stimulated the evolution of social marketing — for that is what the new concept has come to be called:

1. In a society of affluence and abundance, people can afford to pay increasing attention to social goals and social needs.
2. Many younger members of society are more concerned with the social aspects of life than with the economic and business aspects.
3. Citizens and groups have accepted more responsibility for furthering activities that interfere with social marketing. Consumerism is a prime example.
4. Improved communications have increased people's educational awareness.
5. Increasing leisure, mobility, and exposure to a variety of people and lifestyles have produced consumers who are broader in perspective and more socially aware. [17]

In Lazer and Kelley's words:

The interests of consumers are not merely economic interests. The justification of the marketplace need not lie with only the lowest price or the lowest cost producer. Marketing's task lies not only in providing for expressed consumer wants and needs in a convenient manner; but also exists for providing new goods and services including housing, education, transportation, urban development, pollution abatement and manpower development. They may even require higher prices for products and services.[18]

Philip Kotler, adapting the Ansoff matrix of new product development to a social basis, suggests the following framework: *Salutary products* are those that have low immediate appeal but that are also highly beneficial to the consumer in the long run; *pleasing products* have high immediate appeal but may hurt consumer interests in the long run; *desirable products* combine high immediate satisfaction and high long-run benefit; while *deficient products* are those that have neither immediate appeal nor salutary qualities.[19] All these groups except the last, and to some extent the second, deserve the attention of manufacturers.

Many commentators agree that the consumerist movement presents both a challenge and an opportunity for marketing managers. Its terms of reference were cemented in 1962 by President Kennedy's four "rights": the right to safety, the right to be informed, the right to choose, and the right to be heard. E. B. Weiss believes that technological progress will force marketing to provide more consumer guidance, that more consumerism legislation is inevitable, that marketing will increasingly have to collaborate with government, and that the new generation of corporate executives, with an increased perception of their own individual responsibilities, will insist on new and higher levels of marketing integrity.[20] It will be none too soon.

James Patterson lists some "deliberative" questions that marketing executives might ask themselves in decision-making situations.[21] (Patterson is summarizing W.A.R. Leys;[22] the questions, derived from different systems of philosophical ethics, represent a useful checklist for the situationist.)

What are the probable consequences of alternative proposals?
Which policy will result in the greatest possible happiness for the greatest number?
Is the practice right, just, and honest?
Does the policy put first things first?
Can you will that the maxim of your actions should become the universal law?
Are you treating humanity as an end and not merely as a means?

Does the proposed solution anticipate consequences in the larger environment as well as in the immediate situation?

When discussing the social obligations of marketing, most marketing commentators take refuge in unproductive and stereotyped suggestions about organizational policies for making sure that the proper decisions are made. They do not meet the central problem head-on; for they do not acknowledge that all marketing executives, whatever their positions in the management hierarchy, have basically only two choices of action: what the company rule book tells them to do or what they think they *should* do according to the situation at that time and in those circumstances. Nor do these commentators make it sufficiently clear that everyone's values are different and that, therefore, for the organization to "legislate" for ethical behavior is at once an inherent denial of individual choice and an unnecessary complication of the problem in that it merely accentuates the possibility of conflict.

Situational ethics is, if anything, more important for marketing decisions than for those facing any other management function, since marketing as an activity is concerned with customers and consumers. What is more, marketing executives are consumers themselves; they also have families who buy and consume the products that business provides. Such individuals are ideal examples of the dual roles of citizen and employee; of all the members of the firm, they can most easily see the social effects of the firm's actions. Thus, it is through them that responsible policies and programs most obviously should originate and through them that an example is created for the rest to follow.

CONCLUSION

It is given to few of us to shape the course of history. Most of us disappear in the annals of time, dwarfed by the few whose names live on. Even among those who are remembered, an elite jumps to the forefront of our memory: statesmen and warriors like Caesar, Alexander, Napoleon, Lincoln, and Churchill; men of letters like Dante, Shakespeare, and Milton; artists like Leonardo and Picasso; composers like Bach, Mozart, and Beethoven; philosophers like Plato, Aristotle, and Descartes; men of God like Christ and Muhammad.

Yet we are important. To single out the great names for special mention is to remind ourselves that we are each a complex organism miraculous in its power. We can speak in words to each other and communicate in abstractions; we can shape tools and manufacture the necessities of life; we can overcome gravity and fly to the moon; we can feel pain and pleasure, sorrow and happiness; we can be gentle and cruel in turns; we have choice and will; we have needs and aspirations; we can succeed or we can fail. We are each, in short, a world in miniature.

Individuality is the most precious thing in the universe, and individual well-being is the most noble objective we can set ourselves. In business, people are all-important because without them there would be nothing; and to talk of corporate activity or corporate decisions or corporate responsibility is to ignore the individuals who contribute to all these things.

This chapter has tried to stress the sanctity of the individual. It has tried to give the individual a rightful place in the scheme of things. It has shown that people in the end always form their own views of the world.

In the world of business, as everywhere else, responsibility is an empty word unless it is accompanied by authority. Authority can be the power of the chief executive or it can be the collective power of the executive board. Although to be responsible, all people must be true to themselves and sympathetic to the well-being of others, the supreme authority has a special duty; only education can instill it.

NOTES

1. Arthur Hugh Clough, *The Bothie of Tober-na-Vuolich*, pt. 1, l. 20.

2. Bishop J. A. Pike, "The Claim of Situational Ethics," paper presented at American Association of Advertising Agencies Annual Meeting, 1967.

3. Ibid.

4. Ibid.

5. Ibid.

6. Jeffrey A. Barach, "Business and Personal Justice," in *The Individual, Business and Society*, ed. Jeffrey A. Barach (Englewood Cliffs, N.J.: Prentice-Hall, 1977), p. 66.

7. Joseph Fletcher, *Situation Ethics* (Philadelphia: Westminster Press, 1966), p. 26.

8. Moral philosophy is interested in the degree to which the legal code is based on a simple logic of fair play. John Rawl's *Justice and Fairness* has created a stir in philosophical circles on this matter.

9. R. H. Viola, *Organizations in a Changing Society: Administration and Human Values* (Philadelphia: W. B. Saunders, 1977), p. 45.

10. Ibid., p. 50.

11. James W. McKie, "The Issues," in *Social Responsibility and the Business Predicament*, ed. James W. McKie (Washington, D.C.: Brookings, 1974), p. 82.

12. Viola, *Organizations*, pp. 190–92.

13. Ibid.

14. J. F. Engel, R.D. Blackwell, and D. T. Kollat, *Consumer Behavior,* 3rd ed. (Hinsdale, Ill.: Dryden Press, 1978).

15. Peter Hazelhurst, "Japan's Human Sacrifices at the Altar of GNP," *The Times* (London), August 8, 1973.

16. Richard Eells and Clive Walton, *Conceptual Foundations of Business,* 3rd ed. (Homewood, Ill.: Richard D. Irwin, 1974), p. 523.

17. William Lazer and Eugene J. Kelley, *Social Marketing: Perspectives and Viewpoints* (Homewood, Ill.: Richard D. Irwin, 1973).

18. Ibid.

19. Philip Kotler, "What Consumerism Means for Marketers," *Harvard Business Review* 46 (July–August 1968).

20. E. B. Weiss, "Marketers Fiddle while Consumers Burn," *Harvard Business Review* 46 (July–August 1968).

21. James M. Patterson, "What Are the Social and Ethical Responsibilities of Marketing Executives?" *Journal of Marketing* 30 (July 1966): 12–15.

22. W. A. R. Leys, *Ethics for Policy Decision* (Englewood Cliffs, N.J.: Prentice-Hall, 1952).

7 INDIVIDUAL BEHAVIOR IN BUSINESS

It is not what you do wrong by design, but that you should never do right by mistake.

— Junius[1]

CAREER OPTIONS AND MOTIVATIONS

It is a curious fact that in Britain a career in business is usually regarded as quite different from a career in anything else. University graduates either "get a job" or they take up a profession or go into the civil service, politics, the military, or social work. Perhaps, as a last resort, they may try to earn a living by writing poems.

This distinction between "trade" and other occupations stems largely from the traditional British aristocratic objection to making money from the production and sale of merchandise, as distinct from deriving one's income from the interest on inherited wealth, such as land, investments, and tenants. In the eighteenth and early nineteenth centuries, the only occupation meriting an opprobrium equal to that of a merchant was that of a woman in the theatre.

In North America, the distinction was not so severe. The United

States, a young, vigorous country professing egalitarianism as a protest against the feudalism it perceived in Europe, was ostensibly opposed to this traditional social bias, but even here vestiges of the attitude remained, particularly in the old New England values exhibited by socially prominent families in Boston and elsewhere. It is an ironic testament to the American allegiance to the cause of trade that Harvard — with its many close links to New England's elite — was one of the first universities to offer a degree in business administration.

Nowadays, the social implications of the distinction are less obvious, but it nevertheless has to be admitted that in the eyes of the average citizen, a doctor, teacher, or lawyer is far less open to mistrust, suspicion, or criticism than a company director. This is interesting, because it suggests that there is still less respectability attached to a career in business. The explanation deserves some investigation.

Doctors have been found guilty of unethical conduct, teachers have been dismissed for incompetence, and lawyers have frequently been discovered in malpractice, but in general these professions are regarded favorably. Business executives are different; they appear to be guilty before they are proved innocent. The distinction is central to the discussion of business responsibility.

The issue would seem to crystallize into the question of whether the performance of the business function involves a different set of rules and a different morality from that attaching to the behavior of a private citizen or even of the various professional roles mentioned above. As was indicated in the first chapter, some commentators appear to think so,[2] but, as was also pointed out, the view is difficult to accept. It was to shed empirical light on this question that the research study described in the following section was conducted.

MOTIVATION: A SURVEY OF MANAGEMENT ATTITUDES

In the fall of 1978 and the spring of 1979, the author carried out an extensive investigation of the attitudes of senior executives in organizations throughout the United States, Great Britain, and Canada.[3] The same questionnaire was mailed to samples of 200 executives in America, 125 in Britain, and 100 in Canada. A copy of the questionnaire appears as an appendix to this chapter.

The three samples consisted of presidents and senior vice-presidents from a wide spectrum of business organizations representing industrial and consumer goods and services. The questionnaire was in two parts.

The first part set out to discover both personal (ego-oriented) and projected (other-oriented) reactions to specific business and nonbusiness hypothetical problem situations.[4] The second part (which is not reproduced in the appendix) probed into career motivation and attempted to examine the perceived relationship between private and corporate values.

As a complement to this study, personal in-depth interviews were conducted with senior executives (not among those questioned by mail) in the same three countries to add perspective to the data obtained through the questionnaire. Ten such interviews were held in the United States, ten in Britain, and five in Canada.

The objective of the research was to compare the ethical values of executives of different nationalities in the Western English-speaking world. The results of the survey can be segmented into contrasting categories: On the one hand, a distinction can be drawn between values pertaining to financial gain and those completely divorced from monetary considerations; on the other hand, there is an obvious separation of ethical standards in business and private behavior.

In terms of the number of replies received, the response was encouraging. However, it is difficult to interpret the differences in the response levels of the three nationalities: 64 percent of the Americans, 56 percent of the British, and only 45 percent of the Canadians replied to the mailed questionnaire. A possible clue is that 6 percent of British respondents returned the questionnaire, but refused to answer it, while no Americans or Canadians did this; this may suggest that the British regard their personal values as being more private, though this is by no means an entirely justifiable conclusion.

Replies to the first part of the questionnaire are summarized in Tables 7.1 through 7.8 under the separate headings of material gain, nonmaterial gain, business values, and private values. The questionnaire should be consulted before evaluating the results shown in the tables. Tables 7.1 through 7.4 indicate the respondents' own reactions to the ethical problem situations presented in the questionnaire (personal view), while Tables 7.5 through 7.8 indicate the reactions the respondents thought most other people would have (projective view). Each table shows the relative importance each nationality assigned to the various situations and the percentage of executives who might engage in such behavior. For example, if you refer to the entry "Would give payoffs to government officials" in Table 7.1, you will see that the Americans ranked this twenty-sixth in terms of its importance (i.e., the most important problem presented), while both the British and the Canadians ranked it twenty-fourth (or third most important). None of the Americans would engage

Table 7.1.   Material Gain (Personal View)

	U.S.		Britain		Canada	
	Rank	%	Rank	%	Rank	%
Would poach competitor's research staff	2	60	2	94	2	85
Would keep $2 (£1) picked up in post office	3	60	15	21	3	71
Would entertain supplier lavishly	4	56	8	50	6	57
Stole from store as a child	5	52	12	35	11	36
Would keep $10 (£5) dropped by man outside restaurant	7	44	11	35	4	63
Have loaded expense accounts	8	40	4	67	7	49
Would buy stock on inside knowledge	11	32	18	12	16	27
Would take things home from office for children	12	32	3	70	5	60
Would avoid paying for long-distance call	14	24	10	43	15	29
Would buy stolen TV	16	16	20	6	19	13
Would fake income tax return	17	16	19	9	21	10
Would smuggle expensive watch	19	12	7	53	13	31
Think profit sole consideration	20	12	16	21	17	18
Would cheat at penny-ante card game	21	4	22	6	20	10
Would keep $(£)5 in store	22	4	23	6	23	6
Would give kickbacks to customers	25	0	21	6	22	7
Would give payoffs to government officials	26	0	24	3	24	4

Table 7.2.   Nonmaterial Gain (Personal View)

	U.S.		Britain		Canada	
	Rank	%	Rank	%	Rank	%
Would exceed speed limit	1	72	1	96	1	88
Would not resign on conflict of conscience	6	48	13	28	9	36
Gave dishonest answers on questionnaire	9	36	9	47	10	36
Would retire salesman Harold	10	32	5	67	8	44
Have taken illegal alcohol/drugs	13	28	14	28	14	30
Think some management jobs only for men	15	20	6	56	12	35
Would take credit for another's work	18	16	17	12	18	15
Would fire executive for wife's views	23	4	25	3	26	0
Would not hire a black	24	0	26	1	25	1

Table 7.3. Business Values (Personal View)

	U.S.		Britain		Canada	
	Rank	%	Rank	%	Rank	%
Would poach competitor's research staff	2	60	2	94	2	85
Would entertain supplier lavishly	4	56	8	50	6	57
Would not resign on conflict of conscience	6	48	13	28	9	36
Have loaded expense accounts	8	40	4	67	7	49
Would retire salesman Harold	10	32	5	67	8	44
Would buy stock on inside knowledge	11	32	18	12	16	27
Would take things home from office for children	12	32	3	70	5	60
Think some management jobs only for men	15	20	6	56	12	35
Would take credit for another's work	18	16	17	12	18	15
Think profit sole consideration	20	12	16	21	17	18
Would fire executive for wife's views	23	4	25	3	26	0
Would not hire black	24	0	26	1	25	1
Would give kickbacks to customers	25	0	21	6	22	4
Would give payoffs to government officials	26	0	24	3	24	4

Table 7.4. Private Values (Personal View)

	U.S.		Britain		Canada	
	Rank	%	Rank	%	Rank	%
Would exceed speed limit	1	72	1	96	1	88
Would keep $2 (£1) picked up in post office	3	60	15	21	3	71
Stole from store as a child	5	52	12	35	11	36
Would keep $10 (£5) dropped by man outside restaurant	7	44	11	35	4	63
Gave dishonest answers on questionnaire	9	36	9	47	10	36
Have taken illegal alcohol/drugs	13	28	14	28	14	30
Would avoid paying for long-distance call	14	24	10	43	15	29
Would buy stolen TV	16	16	20	6	19	13
Would fake income tax return	17	16	19	9	21	10
Would smuggle expensive watch	19	12	7	53	13	31
Would cheat at penny-ante card game	21	4	22	6	20	10
Would keep $(£)5 in store	22	4	23	6	23	6

Table 7.5.   Material Gain (Projective View)

	U.S.		Britain		Canada	
	Rank	%	Rank	%	Rank	%
Would entertain supplier lavishly	2	72	8	67	9	67
Would poach competitor's research staff	3	64	1	99	2	90
Would keep $2 (£1) picked up in post office	4	64	14	35	4	86
Have loaded expense accounts	5	60	4	80	6	78
Would take things home from office for children	6	60	5	75	3	89
Stole from store as a child	7	52	13	35	16	40
Would smuggle expensive watch	11	48	7	67	5	80
Would keep $10 (£5) dropped by man outside restaurant	13	44	11	64	8	68
Would buy stock on inside knowledge	16	40	22	12	14	46
Would avoid paying for long-distance call	17	36	9	67	15	41
Would buy stolen TV	18	36	19	18	17	39
Would fake income tax return	19	36	20	15	22	23
Think profit sole consideration	21	24	18	21	21	28
Would keep $(£)5 in store	22	8	24	6	24	11
Would give kickbacks to customers	23	8	21	15	23	16
Would cheat at penny-ante card game	24	4	23	6	12	58
Would give payoffs to government officials	26	4	25	6	25	6

Table 7.6.   Nonmaterial Gain (Projective View)

	U.S.		Britain		Canada	
	Rank	%	Rank	%	Rank	%
Would exceed speed limit	1	80	2	96	1	95
Would retire salesman Harold	8	52	10	64	11	59
Have taken illegal alcohol/drugs	9	48	17	28	18	37
Think some management jobs only for men	10	48	3	83	7	76
Would not resign on conflict of conscience	12	44	12	43	10	61
Would not hire a black	14	44	16	33	19	35
Gave dishonest answers on questionnaire	15	40	6	70	13	57
Would take credit for another's work	20	32	15	35	20	31
Would fire executive for wife's views	25	4	26	6	26	4

Table 7.7. Business Values (Projective View)

	U.S.		Britain		Canada	
	Rank	*%*	*Rank*	*%*	*Rank*	*%*
Would entertain supplier lavishly	2	72	8	67	9	67
Would poach competitor's research staff	3	64	1	99	2	90
Have loaded expense accounts	5	60	4	80	6	78
Would take things home from office for children	6	60	5	75	3	89
Would retire salesman Harold	8	52	10	64	11	59
Think some management jobs only for men	10	48	3	83	7	76
Would not resign on conflict of conscience	12	44	12	43	10	61
Would not hire a black	14	44	16	33	19	35
Would buy stock on inside knowledge	16	40	22	12	14	46
Would take credit for another's work	20	32	15	35	20	31
Think profit sole consideration	21	24	18	21	21	28
Would give kickbacks to customers	23	8	21	15	23	16
Would fire executive for wife's views	25	4	26	6	26	4
Would give payoffs to government officials	26	4	25	6	25	6

Table 7.8. Private Values (Projective View)

	U.S.		Britain		Canada	
	Rank	*%*	*Rank*	*%*	*Rank*	*%*
Would exceed speed limit	1	80	2	96	1	95
Would keep $2 (£1) picked up in post office	4	64	14	35	4	86
Stole from store as child	7	52	13	35	16	40
Have taken illegal alcohol/drugs	9	48	17	28	18	37
Would smuggle expensive watch	11	48	7	67	5	80
Would keep $10 (£5) dropped by man outside restaurant	13	44	11	64	8	68
Gave dishonest answers on questionnaire	15	40	6	70	13	57
Would avoid paying for long-distance call	17	36	9	67	15	41
Would buy stolen TV	18	36	19	18	17	39
Would fake income tax return	19	36	20	15	22	23
Would keep $(£)5 in store	22	8	24	6	24	11
Would cheat at penny-ante card game	24	4	23	6	12	58

in such behavior, while 3 percent of the British and 4 percent of the Canadians indicated that they would. Table 7.5 shows the respondents' evaluations of the same problem in terms of other people's reactions.

By far the most important question in the survey, in view of the distinction between private and corporate values, is that concerning the degree to which respondents were prepared to contemplate a situation in which their personal values would conflict with corporate policy to such an extent that they would resign (Question 25). This is perhaps the one question where personal, as opposed to projective, answers are more valid. Indeed, on the projective measures, the answers of the three nationalities are remarkably close, with the exception of the Canadians, who could be said to imagine their fellow executives to be rather more prepared to sublimate their conscience to the values of the "corporation." However, when respondents' own views are examined, it can be seen that there are wide differences: 72 percent of British executives would consider resigning in the face of such a conflict, but only 52 Americans would do so, while Canadians fall in between the other two groups at 64 percent. This indicates either that business in North America is perceived as being more "ethical" than in Britain or that British executives place greater value on their personal freedom of thought. Whichever is the case, the difference is significant.

Answers to the remaining questions need to be viewed more from the projective than the personal view, though there are some startling variations in personal opinions. Two-thirds of North Americans, finding $2 on the post office floor, would pocket it, while only one-fifth of the British would do so. On the other hand, over four times as many British executives as Americans would smuggle an expensive watch through customs.

There are other anomalies, too, which can be interpreted only by examining the answers to the projective questions. As a result, one might conclude that honesty in money seems to go deeper in the United States than in Britain, but it seems to depend very much on the circumstances. In Britain, 64 percent of those interviewed thought that most people would keep the money dropped by the smart couple outside the restaurant when the infrequent bus arrived, as compared to only 44 percent in the United States. However, few from any of the three groups would take advantage of a mistake by a tiresome customer in a store. Also, while 40 percent of Americans and 46 percent of Canadians would indulge in insider trading, compared with only 12 percent of the British, it has to be remembered that this practice is far more strongly prohibited by law in Britain than in the United States. Generally speaking, it is difficult to identify any meaningful pattern emerging from those questions dealing with material gain.

On matters not involving financial or material benefit, the projective views of the Canadians and the British tend to correspond fairly closely with each other, but in clear contrast with American opinion, particularly in their attitudes toward women in management. This perhaps reflects the fact that the affirmative action regulations are more stringent and specific in the United States than they are in the other two countries.

All three countries are fairly well matched in their general business values, except in this matter of women in management. However, there are differences in projective views on three counts: The British and Canadians appear to have fewer qualms than Americans about poaching staff from competitors in order to gain inside knowledge of new products or processes, as they also do about loading their expense accounts and appropriating office materials for their home use.

Information derived from the projective answers to those questions dealing with executives' private values suggests that whereas British managers regard the public utilities as fair game (almost twice as many British as Americans and Canadians would avoid paying for a long-distance telephone call), they are only half as likely as their North American counterparts to break the law more overtly — for example, by buying a stolen television set or faking their income tax. Perhaps the influence of the welfare state has something to do with this, but the situation is made more confusing by the fact that 70 percent of British executives (compared with only 40 percent American and 57 percent Canadian) think that most people would give dishonest answers to some of the questions asked.

If the data emerging from the first part of the questionnaire is thought to be inconclusive, that provided by the second part more than compensates for it. As far as the selection of business as a career is concerned, there is little difference in motivation between the three nationalities: 82 percent of the Americans, 78 percent of the British, and 80 percent of the Canadians made a deliberate decision to enter business. The remainder did so because there was no alternative or (in the case of the British) by accident (15 percent). The reasons for the deliberate choice are summarized in Table 7.9. Money is clearly the greatest motivating force, which is not surprising, though it appears to be more important in Britain than elsewhere. The challenge represented by business comes a close second, especially in the United States. These differences may suggest that the Americans regard a business career as something rather more than just "a job." In the case of the 16 percent of the Americans offering some other reason for choosing a business career, most merely specified that they chose it as an alternative career.

There is a remarkable similarity between the three countries in the

Table 7.9. Reasons for Choosing a Business Career

	U.S. %	Britain %	Canada %
Money	28	39	30
Challenge	24	15	20
Specific industry	12	9	11
Competitiveness	12	—	—
Power	—	6	8
Doing something useful	—	9	—
Other	16	—	—

alternative careers considered when the choice was made. Almost identical responses were received for government work (18–20 percent), the professions (32–36 percent), and the military (Canada 16 percent, United States 20 percent, Britain 24 percent).

The differences begin to emerge when respondents express regret at their decision to enter business. Only 12 percent of the Americans did so, compared with 15 percent of the Canadians and 24 percent of the British. The Americans were not very specific about their reasons for regretting the decision or about what they would in retrospect have preferred to do, but in Canada and Britain, there was an indication that a legal career might have been preferred since it would have offered a greater degree of independence, greater mental stimulation, and more interest. Again, we are given the impression that the British, and to some extent the Canadians, regard a business career as just a means of earning a living.

Part of this attitude undoubtedly stems from the pattern of business education in the three countries. A first degree with a major in business was held by 64 percent of the American respondents and 60 percent of the Canadians, compared with none in Britain (the first degree held by 15 percent of the British included one course with peripheral business relevance). The same is true, though to a lesser extent, with second degrees: 24 percent of the Americans and 18 percent of the Canadians had a master's degree in business, compared with only 6 percent of the British. The differences in the most advanced degrees are less marked (Americans 8 percent, Canadians 6 percent, British 3 percent), as are those in business diplomas and certificates (Americans 32 percent, Canadians 35 percent, British 30 percent).

This relative lack of formal business education on the part of the

British is evidently the reason why far more of the British respondents had chosen to take advantage of short, non-degree-granting management courses offered at the postexperience level (81 percent, compared with 47 percent in Canada and 40 percent in America). In-company courses, administered both by company personnel and by visiting academics, and special external programs, such as the Harvard Advanced Management Program and other business school offerings, are very popular in Britain as a means of compensating for earlier deficiencies, whereas in the United States and Canada, they are regarded more as "refresher" activities by managers who already possess formal business qualifications. Clearly, the function of management is perceived as a far more professional activity in North America.

In view of this, it is surprising that almost identical proportions of managers in the three countries thought there were differences between the criteria governing their behavior in business and those governing their behavior in private life (36 percent of both American and British respondents and 35 percent of Canadians held this view). The reasons for this perception, however, change from country to country. While the Americans thought the difference stemmed from the fact that ethical decisions in business center largely on questions of money and fair dealing in financial affairs, the British were more concerned about the problem of ruthless and unemotional treatment of people in business (colleagues, subordinates, customers, and suppliers). The Canadians once more fell between the two extremes, supporting both views to almost equal degrees, reflecting perhaps the influences to which Canada is subjected as a member of the British Commonwealth and as a close American neighbor.

This distinction again emerged when respondents were asked whether there were any aspects of their own business with which they were ethically unhappy. The Americans were more concerned with specific financial misdemeanors, such as kickbacks to customers and suppliers, than with unfair treatment of people in a general human relations sense, which was a common concern of British managers. The Canadian complaints were divided fairly evenly between criticism of unwarranted profiteering and dishonesty and the ruthless and impersonal lack of regard for individual interests.

The in-depth interviews that were conducted with executives who had not received the questionnaire gave managers the opportunity to expand on the attitudes that the questionnaire data had described. The most significant factor that could be identified in these interviews was a strong confirmation of the professionalism (i.e., the formal education) in North

American business, compared with that in Britain. However, this professionalism appears to carry with it a much greater affiliation to, and in many cases dependence on and fear of, the employing corporation. For example, in the case of four out of the ten U.S. executives (from different companies) who were interviewed personally, the interview had to be conducted on neutral ground removed from the plant or office because the respondents were concerned that sound-detection devices would record their comments and that the company would subsequently use this evidence to their disadvantage as a possible reason for dismissal. This did not, however, appear to diminish their loyalty to their employers, nor did it in any way strike the respondents as odd or unreasonable.

It is for this reason that the personal interviews in the three countries suggested that a conflict between private and corporate values is far more likely to occur in Britain, and to a lesser degree in Canada, than it is in America. In the United States, corporate life and private life appear to be very much more closely interrelated than elsewhere, largely as a result of the extent to which a career in business seems to equate to a career in anything else.

To this has to be added the impression that materialism is of rather more concern to American business executives than it is to either the British or the Canadians, and it is upon the more materialistic aspects of business life that American concern about standards of business behavior centers.

The overall conclusion to be drawn from the study is that although there does not seem to be great variation in personal ethical standards between the three countries, there is a significant difference in attitudes to business and management action. This difference appears to stem partly from historical social norms and partly from the respective education systems of the areas studied, and it affects not only the motivation with which people approach a business career, but also the criteria upon which their subsequent patterns of business behavior are founded.

CAREER CONDUCT: ETHICAL CONFLICT AND COMPROMISE

Ethical behavior presupposes the observance of responsibility of one kind or another. As society has become more complex with the growth of organized groups that act as intermediaries between the individual, the family, and the government, the concept of responsibility has become more complex also. We now have responsibilities not only to provide for our families and to pay our taxes, but also, because the vast majority of us work for and are paid by someone else, to observe the contracts of our employment. At times, it is therefore not inconceivable that we may encounter forces pulling us in opposite and conflicting directions, creating within us dilemmas of conscience.

As Eells and Walton have noted, the fact that the individual is lost in a seemingly anonymous mass makes Lincoln's concept of government "of the people, by the people, and for the people" extremely difficult to implement.[5] By the same token, it makes it hard, and at times impossible, for individuals to preserve their individuality. Frequently, the only escape from this dilemma is to surrender entirely to Whyte's new "social ethic." [6]

Although individuals have associated themselves for divers reasons with large organized groups, it would be distressing to think that this association has destroyed individual initiative, individual values, and individual strength of will. The basis of our society is governance — that is, a situation in which people associate themselves with each other to protect all against threats to the status quo; their major desire in doing so is self-preservation. In this environment, disenchanted citizens may feel frustrated or even oppressed, and they may express this frustration in such antisocial acts as civil disobedience, overt resistence to the law, or the flagrant provocation of authority to exceed its powers. Anarchist movements for centuries have manifested such protest, sometimes through open revolution, but usually to no avail because the central driving force of social cohesion has been too strong. People do not naturally want to live in conflict with the society to which they belong. Consequently, either the protests die and are replaced by others, or society painlessly evolves to a different mode. Revolution is thus either bloody or nonexistent; there are no half measures.

Within the specific context of the organization or the firm, which is the most common form of modern association, the problem is not so easy. Eells and Walton have suggested that the private governments of large corporations have resolved the matter through a combination of patterns of cohesiveness derived jointly from the Roman Catholic church and the army; from the former, they have borrowed the notion of the minimum number of levels of command, and from the latter, the idea of line and staff positions.[7] However, as these authors have also pointed out, together the church and the army have two advantages that commercial organizations lack: The church depends for its allegiance on faith, and the army on patriotism. The private corporation therefore needs other ideals and a different motivation to bind it together.

The difficulty that attempts at organizational harmony produce is basically attributable to conflict between individuals and the associations to which they belong. Not all this conflict can be blamed on "troublemakers" (that is, those people deliberately seeking confrontation), although in certain circumstances it can be. More often than not, it stems from a dissonance between what an individual believes it is right to do and what the company says must be done.

Behavioral research has fairly conclusively proved that individuals fall into the category of either follower or leader. Thus, an authoritarian style of company management, carrying with it an overt demand for compliance, will have disruptive effects if the person from whom compliance is demanded is inclined toward leadership; such a subordinate will tend to rebel. Followers, on the other hand, will accept authoritarian direction because they naturally need it; they will frequently react to a boss as they did to their fathers. Yet when authority is temporarily absent, followers will be far more likely to display irresponsible behavior because they have no focus for their need for dependence.

The organization, in its turn, has to recognize that these different types of employees exist, and it needs to protect itself against the consequences of their behavior. In so doing, it sometimes inhibits creativity, but it must accept this as a price to be paid. Thus, the results often reduce companies to an association of mediocrity, which itself is frequently the cause of conflict. The treatment is derived from organizational theory and experiment (discussed in the following section), and its results might leave one wondering whether the individual at work is a suitable or justifiable subject for sociological observation.

ORGANIZATIONAL BEHAVIOR: SOME EXPERIMENTS

Stress

One can only speculate on the forces that drag people in one direction or another in the course of their allegiance to an employer, but one can be sure that the inevitable result of such conflict is stress. There have been more studies conducted on this aspect of employment than any other. Modern life is characterized by stress: Stress is manifested by illness, by divorce, by alcoholism, and by inefficiency. The individual displays a tendency to stress in almost every act. The relief of stress is equally obvious: The executive who leaves the city rat race to take up a more congenial and less oppressive job, the employee who trades the material benefits of a competitive position for a self-motivating and psychologically more satisfying occupation, the politician who abandons the hustings for a quiet life — all are escaping, even if they do not know it, from the stress of a prescribed and organized existence. Stress is meat and drink to the sociologists.

The basic cause of stress is the conflict between a person's innate inclinations or abilities and the demands placed upon that person by authority. That such situations should arise indicates that the management of people has not yet reached the state of a perfect science. It follows that the nearer it comes to such a state, the lower the incidence of stress will be. Since the turn of the century, many theories, largely derived from laboratory experiments, have been put forward to suggest methods of behavioral control to narrow the gap between management expectation and actual events. In the course of these experiments, some strange aspects of human behavior have emerged, most of which have been the subject of exaggerated interpretation; the examples that immediately come to mind are the electric shock experiment in which subjects were driven to the point of agreeing to bizarre and barbaric treatment of colleagues in order to avoid further pain and the Stanford jailer/prisoner role-playing exercise in which participants displayed similar disturbing characteristics. These glimpses of the animalistic aspects of human nature might remind us of our evolutionary development, but whether they really help us to determine an appropriate and effective management style is open to much doubt.

Behavioral Science

In recent years, behavioral science has become the recognized basis of the approach to management. It has taken two forms, one being the *internal approach,* which explains behavior in terms of mental processes, and the other being the *external approach,* which concentrates more on environmental results and operates on the belief that "behavior is a function of its consequences."[8]

Perhaps the two most popular versions of the internal approach have been those of Maslow and Herzberg here. Both are too well known to deserve more than the briefest description. Abraham Maslow, postulating his celebrated theory of the hierarchy of needs, advanced the view that human behavior is stimulated by a succession of personal needs that follow a predictable order of required satisfaction, beginning with the physiological needs for food, warmth, sex, and protection, progressing through the needs for safety or security, love and belonging, and esteem, and culminating finally in the need for self-actualization.[9] The theory has instinct, but not empirical research, to commend it. What Maslow did not appreciate was that while needs can certainly be categorized in this way, they do not necessarily form a hierarchy. A person may, for instance, choose to buy cheaper food in order to pay for a more expensive car or may sacrifice love in order to achieve self-actualization.

Frederick Herzberg developed the notion of "hygiene factors."[10] These are not like Maslow's needs (which are held to motivate), but rather things or events that prevent dissatisfaction, such as closing a window on a cold day. In this, they are negative rather than positive, a distinction in behavioral modification to which we shall return. Satisfaction of needs thus defined does not necessarily advance the status quo; rather, it corrects a situation that has deteriorated. Both Maslow and Herzberg have been criticized because their theories explain satisfaction, but not motivation.

The shortcomings of the internal approach led to the development of external theories. (Whether *any* theory satisfactorily explains ethical conflict is open to question, but we shall nevertheless offer a brief overview.) Clark Hull's drive-reduction theory, according to which the strength of a particular habit is the result of the number of previously satisfied drives, holds up well when a man is thirsty, but not so well in difficult management decisions.[11] L.W. Porter and E.E. Lawler, as well as V.H. Vroom, look more to the future with their expectancy models: Future outcomes govern motivation, though these can be wrongly estimated and thus performance may still be poor; reward is more influential than satisfaction.[12] These theories, commonly called process theories, begin to move away from the internal to the external.

One of the most important contributors to organizational behavior theory is B.F. Skinner, who has written voluminously on the control of human behavior in organizations. He is responsible for the critical distinction between *respondent* (unlearned) and *operant* (learned) behavior. Skinner, whose theory is based on experimental research, claims that we learn how to behave through the consequences that our behavior produces.[13] Skinner's view, in contrast with Maslow's, offers an understanding of human behavior in practical terms, and, in many ways, it is closely akin to the ethical standpoint of Fletcher and situationalism. Because behavior is learned, it is controlled by the environment, and while it may be possible to identify through experimentation some of the atavistic root causes of behavior, it is only through the study of environmental impact that useful guides for management can be found.

The question is, of course, how? Mention was made earlier of the distinction between negative and positive controls. Much modern management theory polarizes into these two extremes. Theory X and Theory Y, achievement motivation, and so on, illustrate the point. Should controls on employees be such that in the event of noncompliance, the situational environment will be more hostile or, in the event of compliance, it will be more friendly? Both can be said to strengthen immediate behavior, but over time the effectiveness of negative control tends to diminish.

To illustrate the difference between positive and negative control, consider a production first-line supervisor who is encouraged by the prospect of extra fringe benefits for the achievement of a particular production target; that constitutes *positive* control. If, on the other hand, the supervisor is threatened with reductions in remuneration for nonachievement, management is through *negative* control. Either method can be found in industry, though the latter is becoming less common.

Positive control and reinforcement should not, however, be confused with rewards. Rewards are subjective, but positive controls and reinforcements are in the eye of the manager. Money is a reward, but it is not always the most appropriate reinforcement; for example, the employee may perceive improved status or prestige as more desirable than money. Money is what is known as a *generalized* reinforcer, as indeed are status and prestige, as distinct from *primary* reinforcers, such as free education for children, trips to Florida, or turkeys at Christmas. The important point is that what represents a reward for some is totally unattractive to others; I hate cigars, other people love them. It is thus vital for a manager deciding on an appropriate reinforcement program to be sure that the reinforcement held out is perceived as such by those whom the manager is attempting to motivate.

M.R. Blood experimented with a test that attempted to rate the rewards an individual might expect to receive on the job.[14] Ten reward categories were identified in the following order, with the first item representing the top reward:

1. Achievement or sense of accomplishment;
2. Responsibility or control;
3. Opportunity for personal growth;
4. Recognition from the community and from friends;
5. Job or company status;
6. Interpersonal relationships or friendships;
7. Pay or monetary reward;

8. Job security;
9. Provision for family;
10. Support for hobbies or avocational activities.

This experiment was conducted in 1973. It would be interesting to see how the priorities would have come out in 1981. In view of recent economic problems, one might wonder whether "job security" and "provision for family," or even "pay or monetary reward," would not have appeared higher on the list than they did at the time of Blood's research. Economic stress is a sobering influence on social and ethical standards. One has to ask whether this is true of all cultures: Have the social ideals of Saudi Arabian or Japanese business managers been in any way compromised by inflation and depression? If so, is the economic climate the only conditioner of business ethics? A British business manager reading the leading article of the *Observer* of July 27, 1980 might well be persuaded to feel so. In an unprecedentedly scathing attack on the British government (and in particular on Prime Minister Thatcher), the newpaper stated: "Mrs. Thatcher leaves the impression that rising unemployment is a deliberate arm of policy. . . . Mrs. Thatcher appeared both heartless and unrealistic last week when she urged people to move to find new jobs. . . . Either the Prime Minister shows a willingness to respond to the real world, or she clings to the obsessively dogmatic attitude she has recently displayed, apparently oblivious of the possibility that she might be wrong." The introductory sentence of the article went straight to the point: "Mrs. Thatcher has three choices: to make major changes in her economic policy; to be driven from office by revolt in her own party; or to suffer the same fate at the next General Election . . . she is at this moment laying the foundations of defeat." With unemployment in the United Kingdom at its highest level since the 1930s, what price can be put on social responsibility?

Negative Control

The previous paragraph is as good an introduction as any to the subject of negative control. Negative control is characterized by punishment and lack of reinforcement. The executive who wants to do well, or who wants to do the "right" thing, can be discouraged by criticism or penalty or threat of dismissal, as well as by management's failure to recognize performance. Yet negative control can still be an enforcer in the sense that its withdrawal strengthens behavior. It is much used and much abused. A great deal of behavior in business involves escaping punishment; this escape behavior does not improve job performance. Managers who habitually employ punishment as a means of encouraging or stimulating job performance on the part of their subordinates can frequently achieve the same ends by their very presence. Their authority is therefore negative, and when they are absent, their subordinates will often rebel. Negative reinforcement is a dangerous and unproductive management style.

Punishment is not an unusual aspect of modern life. It is used in schools, in family life, and by the law. We are all used to punishment, and to a very large degree, we accept and expect it. Yet its nature is misunderstood, and its effects are clouded in ignorance. Sometimes it is carefully and deliberately administered in the hope that it will have a specific effect; at other times, it is fickle, hasty, and arbitrary, sometimes applied in blind anger. Whatever its nature, we all live our lives in fear of it: We try to keep within speed limits when we drive, we pay our telephone and electricity bills because we want to avoid disconnection, and we make some attempt to stay within the tax regulations to escape being audited. Life, in this sense, is based on negative reinforcement.

The connection with legislated ethics is obvious: "Do what I say, or else." There can be no greater indictment of legislated business behavior than that lack of observance should carry a penalty. Behavioral scientists stand guilty of accepting that punishment in any form should be a legitimate form of management. Advocates of negative control fail to realize that punishment will eventually fly back in the face of the person who uses it; punishment has to be continuous to be successful — once it stops, the punished will not conform.

Translated into the area of personal ethics, this philosophy carries disturbing overtones. If one is dissuaded from doing what one wants to do because somebody else's values are different, or because one will suffer on grounds of principle, or if one offends some official code of behavior, or if one performs an act contrary to what one's immediate boss says should be done, or if one offends one's religion or some other such regimen and is uncomfortable at the thought that one might in some way be punished for this behavior, one faces negative control and negative reinforcement. Not to conform might well mean the loss of one's job. An example of this collision of values can be seen in the case of Sikh motorcyclists in Britain objecting to a law enforcing the wearing of crash helmets because to obey it meant they could not wear the turbans required by their religion. Similarly, Sikh bus conductors eventually won the right not to wear the peaked caps of London Transport.

Experimentation

Experiments on the reaction to negative control suggest that our management theorists are in danger of reducing a very personal matter to an impersonal art. In the eyes of the behavioral scientists, people seem to be developing into laboratory animals, guinea pigs that are subjected to one experiment after another; the human consequences are documented and discussed in learned journals as if people do not matter. What the members of the labor force think of this (if they perchance read the journals), one can only conjecture. The literature is depressing: "Applied behavior analysis experts . . . point out that whenever punishment is used, there must be a corresponding presentation of an opportunity to emit one or more incompatible responses which are then positively reinforced." [15] What on earth does this mean?

Whatever one's perspective, the notion of negative reinforcement and control holds little appeal. It is all very well to claim that a "desirable alternative behavior should be made available and positively reinforced," [16] but the very fact that negative management methods exist suggests that employee enrichment and personal self-satisfaction are difficult goals to achieve.

Whether research into work behavior of this kind is legitimate is another matter. It has been claimed that such experimentation offends ethical standards. Even the term *O.B.Mod.* (meaning organizational behavior modification) has been the subject of opprobrium; it suggests, it is said, an Orwellian doublethink or newspeak — as well it might, for such is the language of modern commentators — though that is no doubt unintentional.

Rat-centered is the term offered by critics to describe experiments conducted with animals for the purpose of investigating human behavior, but since animals are not humans, there can be no evidence for us as human beings. The comparison is both uncomfortable and uncertain. Much research has been applied to animal behavior, and behavioral scientists have established certain similarities with human behavior. Both animals and humans have pecking orders; they also have their own territories. Yet there are many differences. To assume that the very simple and primitive impulses of animals are a clear guide to human behavior (and especially behavior in the complex and sophisticated environment of an organization) is to suppose that the uppermost behavioral evidence in human beings is at the very basic animal level. If this is so, then the experiments have some validity; if it is not, then the psychologists, sociologists, and anthropologists need to look for something else.

Fred Luthans and R. Kreitner quote the example of Winston Smith in Orwell's *Nineteen Eighty-Four*: "Loving Big Brother was an avoidance response — verbal allegiance to Big Brother enabled Smith to avoid further cruel physical torture."[17] Yet experiments involving physical punishment exist in behavioral research (though not on such an inhuman scale), and we have to question their validity.

The control factor is another element. Are experiments on the control of human behavior ethical? Luthans and Kreitner apparently think so: "The question of ethics should not be a problem for anyone choosing to live in a society where managerial effectiveness is a desirable goal."[18] Again, the question is begged; why should ethics not be a problem in such circumstances? Why are ethics less relevant in a managerially oriented society? Even if we choose — and it is debatable whether we actually have a choice — to live in a society where management is all-important, why should this make us set ethics aside?

Behavioral experiments have been viewed as a threat to freedom in that they attempt to test resistance to authority and control. Modification of behavior has likewise been condemned as brainwashing or manipulation. It is true that when under pressure, people may deny what they fundamentally hold to be right. It is also true that they may do this repeatedly even though they know they are betraying themselves or others; the reason they do so is pain or the avoidance of it. Torture is effective, but conscience is ultimately indestructible, even after betrayal of some fundamental belief. To resist torture is therefore senseless because ethical values apparently destroyed or damaged in such circumstances are not damaged at all; one is not one's normal self when under torture, and what one says at that time is not a true reflection of one's real thoughts. Why any country should demand patriotism of its citizens to the extent of personal physical pain is difficult to comprehend.

The same is true of experiments in management behavior that involve pain. Organizational behavior textbooks protest inordinately at the opposition to behavioral experimentation: H. Wiard claims that although there are practical difficulties and an expense in applying behavioral technology to large groups of employees in a modern organization, the effort is worthwhile.[19] Whether such technology works is a matter of opinion; labor strikes and industrial downtime might suggest otherwise. Edward Feeney has commented that "we do what works . . . what gets a payoff. For us, this behavioral approach got results." He was describing the success of Emery Air Freight's program of feedback on performance.

Are behavioral modification and control manipulative, and if so, are they unethical? Behavioralists would claim that the manipulation is more of the environment than the individual; Machiavelli's "ends and means" seems to come into play here. But when the behavioralists criticize Machiavelli on the grounds of "selfish control," they seem to condemn themselves with their own words. Indeed, they confess that the issue is not so much that of manipulation versus management, but rather precision versus imprecision. Machiavelli would have been appalled.

The subject in behavioral experiments is often unaware that research is taking place. The justification of this omission is that awareness colors performance and that results obtained under conditions of awareness are therefore invalid. In any case, it is claimed, workers have become so accustomed to having their job performance measured and evaluated that the question of awareness no longer matters. Another justification seems to be that nonawareness is "a necessary evil:" "Subjective observation of nonperformance behavior will be replaced by objective observation and measurement of behavior that is critical to performance improvement." [20]

Governments are very interested in intrusions into individual privacy, but one has to wonder if businesses are equally sensitive to this issue. In the research study described earlier, the comments of American managers about sound-detection devices in their offices were odd in that they indicated no surprise. How far such clandestine methods resemble more common observation and measurement techniques is not easy to say. Some behavioral scientists would claim that employee ignorance of performance measurement is frequently justifiable because the final beneficiaries are the employees themselves; yet this is an arrogant attitude, for if employees do not know that their performance is being assessed, colds or hangovers, worries about spouses, or nasty letters from bank managers can distort the results.

Whether research into the behavior of people in organizations can be compared to the therapeutic efforts of psychiatrists, we cannot yet say. An even more difficult question is whether it is right for such research to be conducted at all, whether its contribution to the well-being of the enterprise is in any way a tenable justification. A man, claimed Robert Burns, is "a man for a' that";[21] human dignity needs to be respected. No matter how much an individual may shirk and avoid work duty and responsibilities, we have to ask to what extent, if any, can individual privacy be ethically invaded. The behavioral scientists have been very active; as a result of their efforts, we know a great deal more about people at work, but we are really no nearer to making them happier human beings. Perhaps the reason is that only they have the final answer.

MIND AND MATTER: INCLINATION AND REALITY

The poet Keats once wrote a letter in which he claimed that "the only means of strengthening one's intellect is make up one's mind about nothing — to let the mind be a thoroughfare for all thoughts." [22] There is nothing more frustrating than the gap between what is and what one would like it to be. "Between the idea / And the reality / Between the notion / And the act / Falls the Shadow." [23]

All of us have ideals. We would like to be, we even imagine ourselves to be, people we are not, people with whom in our dreams we identify, even though in reality, we may fall a long way short of them. "Dreams are true while they last, and do we not live in dreams?" [24]

It is hard to believe that there is anything more terrible than that one should do something of which one is subsequently ashamed. Indeed, there is probably nothing more cruel than conscience. Man is his own jailer; he can be harsher to himself than any judge or jury; he can cause himself far more suffering than any critic or accuser. In this, he appears in his own court, and he needs no counsel. The reason is that only he knows his guilt or his innocence; only he knows whether he is right or wrong. The distance between his aspirations and his achievement is the measure of his failure. Few people have been able to match the two; Christ, Muhammad, and Buddha, perhaps, but even they recognized their own frailities.

When we talk of the responsibility of executives in organizations, we really refer to their senses of justice and their own consciences. They are conditioned to believe that their jobs carry requirements that they, as occupants of the job, need to observe, irrespective of what they, as individuals, think should be done. They may not think as individuals, and they may therefore tend to forget that their institutionalized consciences are different from their personal inclinations. This is at the center of the social responsibility debate; mind and matter, inclination and reality diverge in positions of power. Some senior executives are incapable of separating their roles as individuals from their roles as managers.

As two cats survey each other, look for signs of hostility, and then wash themselves, so managers may comfort their egos in the business game. Behavioral research may brand them as one kind of manager or another, but the essential manager is the manager's own self-image. Inclination and reality are very present in management situations.

We need to return to our picture of the executive in front of the television in the evening and the same person behind a desk in the morning. At home, he or she is the perfect parent; as the manager, impossible, thinking and doing things that as a private individual, he or she would never dream of doing, an ogre to subordinates, a saint to the children. Why? Inclination and reality, ethical duality, or just schizophrenia? Business seems to do things to people that friends or the morning's mail cannot.

Let us close this section with an instructive tale. A senior executive (we will call him John Jones) gets up in the morning to find that his daughter has burnt his toast and boiled his coffee; he laughs it off, gives her a pat on the head, and goes to work. One of his subordinates, Dan Smith, misses a delivery schedule, gets an accusing letter from a customer, and confesses it all to Jones. Jones gets angry, gives Smith a warning, and snaps his secretary's head off. Nobody will go near John for the rest of the day. Reality? Inclination? Management? Or just human nature?

CULTURE, HISTORY, AND MODERN BEHAVIOR

"Culture being a pursuit of our total perfection by means of getting to know, on all the matters which most concern us, the best which has been thought and said in the world."[25] To ignore what has gone before, to forget what others have apprehended, to throw aside the learning of the past, to assume some new testament or modern law is to escape into a world unknown and a life uncharted. History has given us our heritage and has shaped our existence. The thinkers and writers of the past have conditioned the things of today.

Against this background, nothing that one does can be divorced from one's history and one's ancestors. Every new event, every new acquaintance, and every conversation are links in the learning chain, and although few of us have any really significant effect on the grand plan of the world, we each contribute just a little. In our small groups and our limited circles of friends and acquaintances, we form an aggregate of social behavior.

In our modern world, differences in our cultural and historical heritages are becoming blurred and bridged. Some might feel that this is a pity. The United States, a vast country, has probably smoothed out the distinction between its regions more than any other, largely because it is young and its culture has developed rapidly; yet similar phenomena are visible in geographically smaller and culturally more homogeneous nations, such as Great Britain. No longer are the socially historical gaps between north and south, urban and rural communities, rich and poor, so evident. Population mobility and twentieth-century communications are the fundamental cause; television "personalities" (to use an unfortunate term) are family friends, equally accepted in London and Liverpool, Boston and Baton Rouge, Charlottetown and Calgary.

Yet there is some hope to be derived from this narrowing of social and cultural differences, which has occurred not only within nations, but also between them. Any development that reduces the possibility of another world war has to be welcomed; the question of whether such a war is inevitable must be ignored if we are to avoid it. Dangers to world peace, such as events in Iran, Afghanistan, and Vietnam, must be subordinated to a bigger theme and a larger scenario, as must petty violence among different factions of indigenous groups. In the end, the problem becomes one of the confrontation of human and human, not Jew and Muslim or capitalist and Communist.

The ethical conduct of managers in an increasingly global context is thus a subject that is not only of paramount importance in itself; it is also a necessary accompaniment to a central theme. Just as the bickering and arguments between governments will in the end be settled only between people (and not necessarily the politicians who seem to make such a hash of it), so the international business scene will come right only when people — the people on the spot, the people who have to do the talking, the people who carry the ultimate burden of responsibility — can meet each other in friendship and an understanding of each other's culture, history, and values.

To do this, they need to realize that ethics is not a game. They need to acknowledge that they each have different ethical legacies and that no fair or happy resolution of their differences can be achieved unless some kind of give-and-take position is adopted. The suggestion made in the previous chapter — that ethical decisions can be judged only against the results that they prompt for all other interested parties — would seem to be the only sensible and realistic approach. Everything in the end comes down to personal conscience, even though that conscience may be set against the heritage of a different culture and a different modus vivendi. People are people, wherever they live, and their pressures and conflicts vary little on a personal level.

CONCLUSION

Journeying through ethical jungles is not a trip one would recommend for a vacation, though in the end it might be more rewarding. While other forms of recreation may produce a suntan, an excursion into the basis of proper behavior could hone our minds at a fraction of the cost. Whether the present exercise has been useful, it is for readers to say. In Bunyan's words: "Some said, 'John, print it'; others said, 'Not so.' Some said, 'It might do good'; others said, 'No.'" [26] Well, it has been printed.

APPENDIX

In the first part of the questionnaire (the second part is not reproduced here), respondents were asked to indicate their reactions to the following situations and statements, as well as the reactions they thought most other people would have. No attempt was made, when the questionnaire was designed, to attach any relative importance to the questions themselves. It was imperative that respondents be given no indication of what answers were expected.

1. John accelerated down the street and cursed the traffic jam that had delayed him for twenty minutes. He might miss his meeting, the most important presentation of his life. The speed limit was 30. He was doing 55. He could just make it, only five minutes late, if he stepped on it.
2. If I knew it was safe, I would buy a new color TV worth $800 (£400) from a friend for $80 (£40), even if I knew it was stolen.
3. Waiting at customs, Sam pushed his watch further up his wrist. He had bought it in Switzerland, and the duty payable, if he declared it, was $300 (£150). He decided to say nothing about it, because nobody could prove that he hadn't been wearing it when he left the country.
4. I have at some time illegally taken alcohol or drugs.
5. As a child, I took something without paying for it from at least one store.
6. I would be quite happy taking things like pens and note pads home from the office for my children.
7. Fred was completing his income tax return. He saw that he could save another $200 (£100) by claiming donations to charity. He put down $150 (£75) under "church donations," even though he hadn't been inside a church for twenty years.
8. Cheating at cards in a penny-ante game is excusable.
9. Pete turned away from the post office counter and saw the $2 bill (£1 note) on the floor. He picked it up and put it in his pocket, saying to himself that if he hadn't, somebody else would have,

and that, anyway, if he handed it in, the teller would only pocket it himself.

10. If I could get away with it, I'd avoid paying for a long-distance telephone call.

11. Dick watched the well-dressed couple leave their expensive car and enter the smart restaurant. His bus was due, but he saw something drop from the man's pocket as he put away his car keys. Dick walked over and picked up a $10 bill (£5 note). At that moment, his bus arrived. He climbed aboard, wondering whether he should have followed the couple into the restaurant and returned the money. The next bus was two hours later.

12. After a hard time with a fussy and difficult customer in the crowded department store, George accepted the money for a $(£)3.95 purchase and rang up the total. He discovered that the customer had given him two $5 bills (£5 notes) instead of one, since they were both new. He handed the customer $(£)1.05 change and said nothing.

13. Ken walked out of his boss's office glowing with pleasure. He had just been highly praised for a report he had submitted, and his boss had told him that it meant promotion. There was one small worry, however; the report had been written by Ken's assistant and published over Ken's name as head of the department. He wondered for just a moment whether he should go back to his boss and tell him, but then decided that he could have written the report himself in any case.

14. Jane sat in her usual place at the board meeting, thinking of the proposed takeover of a smaller competitor that her company chairman had just announced to the directors. The competitor's stock price was low at the moment, but it would rise significantly when news of the bid was made public. If Jane bought shares now, she could make a killing.

15. One of your competitors has just made a major technological breakthrough that has given him at least a year's lead over your own product development program. The only way of cutting his lead is by trying to hire one of his research staff who would have inside knowledge of the new process. Would you do it?

16. I have loaded my expense account on at least one occasion.

17. I think that lavish entertainment of a supplier to get preferential treatment is perfectly legitimate.

18. I think that kickbacks to purchasing executives to obtain orders are perfectly legitimate.

19. I think that payoffs to government officials to avoid government interference are perfectly legitimate.

20. Whatever the qualifications of individual women, there are some executive positions for which only a man should be considered.

21. Dave said good-bye to the last applicant for the job of personnel officer and returned to his desk. The man was clearly the best qualified of all the applicants he had interviewed, and his experience was impeccable. Furthermore, Dave had liked him from the moment he had walked into his office. The question was, how would the union take to a black?

22. Don, sales manager of a successful company, was uncertain about what to do with Harold Stevens, who had been with the firm for thirty-five years and had always served it conscientiously. Harold had worked hard, but he was now fifty-eight, and Don knew that a younger person would almost certainly achieve better results on Harold's territory. Unfortunately, the sales director felt the same and was pressing Don to replace Harold. This would mean that it would be almost impossible for Harold to get another job, and he could not afford to live on a company pension seven years before his official retirement age. Don knew that the sales director would not consider for a minute bringing Harold's pension policy up to the official retirement level, since this would cost the company $20,000 (£10,000). On the other hand, they were losing sales. Should he retire Harold or take the loss? There was no other job for Harold in the organization.

23. A company has every right to dismiss an executive if it believes that an organization to which the executive's wife belongs holds views with which the company disagrees.

24. A company's responsibilities go no further than returning maximum profit and capital gain to its stockholders, creating the necessary funds for investment, and obeying the law.

25. It is quite inconceivable that my own personal values would conflict with company policy to such an extent that I would resign.

26. Some of the decisions that I have indicated I would make about these situations differ from what I think is really right.

NOTES

1. Junius, *Letters,* Dedication, 1. 12.
2. Albert Z. Carr, "Is Business Bluffing Ethical?" *Harvard Business Review* 46 (January–February 1968): 150–53.

3. The author is indebted to the University of Wisconsin-Eau Claire for the financial support of this project.

4. The projective aspects of the study owe much to the questionnaire designed by Frank S. Leonard and published as an addendum to Albert Z. Carr's article referred to in n. 2.

5. Richard Eells and Clive Walton, *Conceptual Foundations of Business,* 3rd ed. (Homewood, Ill.: Richard D. Irwin, 1974), pp. 378–79.

6. William H. Whyte, *The Organization Man* (New York: Simon & Schuster, 1956).

7. Eells and Walton, *Conceptual Foundations,* p. 380.

8. Fred Luthans and R. Kreitner, *Organizational Behavior Modification* (Glenview, Ill.: Scott, Foresman, 1975), p. 3.

9. Abraham H. Maslow, "A Theory of Human Motivation," *Psychological Review* 50 (July 1943): 370–96.

10. Frederick Herzberg, B. Mausner, and B. Snyderman, *The Motivation to Work,* 2nd ed. (New York: John Wiley, 1959).

11. Clark Hull, *Principles of Behavior* (New York: Appleton-Century, 1943).

12. L.W. Porter and E.E. Lawler, *Managerial Attitudes and Performance* (Homewood, Ill.: Richard D. Irwin, 1968); V.H. Vroom, *Work and Motivation* (New York: John Wiley, 1964).

13. B.F. Skinner, *Science and Human Behavior* (New York: Macmillan, 1953).

14. M.R. Blood, "Intergroup Comparisons of Intraperson Differences: Rewards from the Job," *Personnel Psychology* 26 (1973): 1–9.

15. Luthans and Kreitner, *Organizational Behavior Modification,* p. 126.

16. Ibid., p. 129.

17. Ibid., p. 177, quoting Orwell.

18. Ibid., p. 179.

19. H. Wiard, "Why Manage Behavior? A case for Positive Reinforcement," *Human Resource Management* 11 (Summer 1972):15–20.

20. Luthans and Kreitner, *Organizational Behavior Modification,* p. 185.

21. Robert Burns, "For A' That and A' That."

22. John Keats, letter to G. and G. Keats, September 17–27, 1819, from *The Letters of John Keats,* ed. M.B. Forman (London: Oxford University Press, 1952).

23. T.S. Eliot, *The Hollow Men,* st. 5.

24. Alfred, Lord Tennyson, *The Higher Pantheism,* l. 4.

25. Matthew Arnold, *Culture and Anarchy,* Preface.

26. John Bunyan, *Pilgrim's Progress,* "Apology for His Book," ed. James Wharey (London: Oxford University Press, 1960), p. 2.

CITATION INDEX

Ackerman, R., 14
Acton, Lord, 150
Anshen, M., 15
Argyris, Chris, 131
Aristotle, 59, 65
Arnold, Matthew, 210

Bacon, Francis, 160
Barach, Jeffrey A., 169
Barnard, C. I., 30
Bauer, R., 14
Behn, Aphra, 160
Belloc, Hilaire, 161
Berg, Ivar, 149
Blackwell, R. D., 180
Blomstrom, R. L., 16, 131
Blood, M. R., 203–04
Brooks, G., 18
Bunyan, John, 212
Burns, Robert, 208

Carr, Albert Z., 4, 132, 168, 188, 189
Clough, Arthur H., 164
Colton, Charles C., 60
Conford, F. M., 62

Davis, K., 16, 131, 139

de Girardin, Mme., 160
de Jouvenel, Bertrand, 74
Dickens, Charles, 61
Disraeli, Benjamin, 147
Dyer, John, 161

Eells, Richard, 9, 19, 37, 85, 135, 153, 154, 158, 182, 199
Eliot, T. S., 209
Emerson, Ralph Waldo, 153
Engel, J. F., 180
Engels, Friedrich, 50
Evans, C. E., 27
Evans, W. A., 188–98

Fletcher, Joseph, 170
Friedman, Milton, 14, 17, 31

Gibbon, Edward, 69
Ginzberg, Eli, 149
Gray, Daniel H., 156, 158

Hagen, Everett E., 134
Haire, Mason, 149
Hamilton, W. H., 9
Hampshire, Stuart, 75
Hazelhurst, Peter, 181

Numbers refer to pages on which authors are cited; complete references are given in notes at ends of chapters.

217

SUBJECT INDEX